MEANDER

Meander

East to West, Indirectly,
Along a Turkish River

Jeremy Seal

B L O O M S B U R Y

NEW YORK · LONDON · NEW DELHI · SYDNEY

Published by Bloomsbury USA, New York

All papers used by Bloomsbury USA are natural, recyclable products made
from wood grown in well-managed forests. The manufacturing processes
conform to the environmental regulations of the country of origin.

LIBRARY OF CONGRESS CATALOGING-IN-PUBLICATION DATA HAS BEEN APPLIED FOR.

ISBN: 978-1-59691-652-4 (hardback)

First published in Great Britain by Chatto & Windus in 2012
First published by Bloomsbury USA in 2012
This paperback edition published in 2013

Paperback ISBN: 978-1-60819-435-3
1 3 5 7 9 10 8 6 4 2

Printed and bound in the U.S.A. by Thomson-Shore Inc., Dexter, Michigan

To Nick Morris

CONTENTS

*

MAPS

AUTHOR'S NOTE

The Turkish script, introduced by Mustafa Kemal Atatürk, is based on the Latin model but uses a range of diacritics, including the cedilla and umlaut, to establish phonetic rules for the pronunciation of characters. It also assigns unfamiliar pronunciations to some characters; those that native English speakers tend to find most confusing are given below.

- The Turkish c is pronounced j as in journalism
- ç as ch as in church
- ş as sh as in shower
- ğ is silent but denotes a lengthening of the preceding vowel
- ı is the flat 'schwa' sound, as in shower, whereas the dotted i is pronounced as in ink
- ö and ü are both hard to render but indicate characteristically Turkish modifications of the vowel sound; they are more commonly used in Turkish than the plain forms of these vowels

The Meander River is often given in Turkish as the Büyük Menderes, or the Great Meander, to distinguish it from at least two lesser Turkish rivers of the same name.

Readers may wish to consult the Chronology and Cast in the course of their reading, which they will find on pp359-365.

BULGARIA

Istanbul/
Constantinople/
Byzantium

SEA OF MARMARA

Salonika
Kuçkar Kavala
Iznik

Gallipoli Bursa

GREECE AEGEAN SEA BITHYNIA
Pergamum Eskişehir/
Dorylaeum

Mitylene *Cyme*
Chios Izmir/*Smyrna* Uşak

ITALY Athens Çivri
Salamis Deniz

IONIAN SEA *Sparta*

Bodrum
Marmaris
Kos Fethiye

Crete Rhodes
Antalya/
Adalia

MEDITERRANEAN SEA

For a large scale map of the Meander Valley, please see overleaf

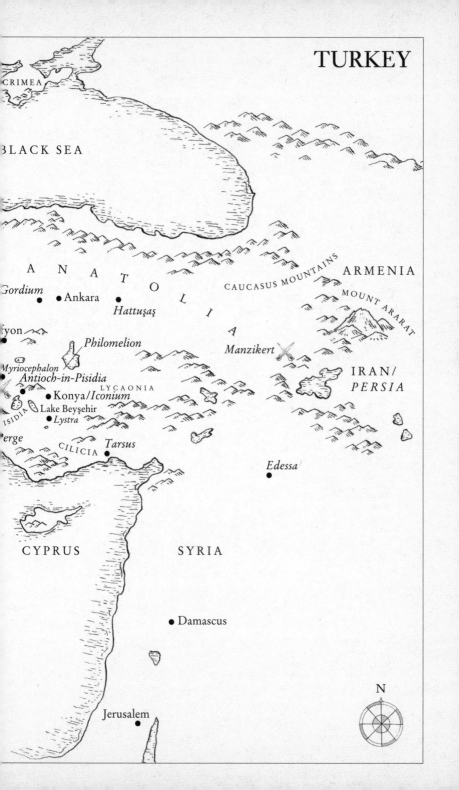

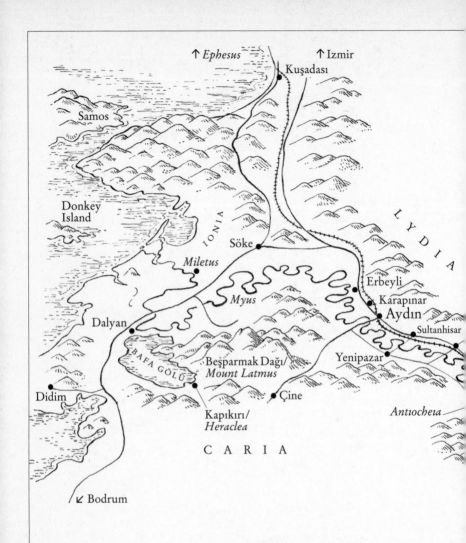

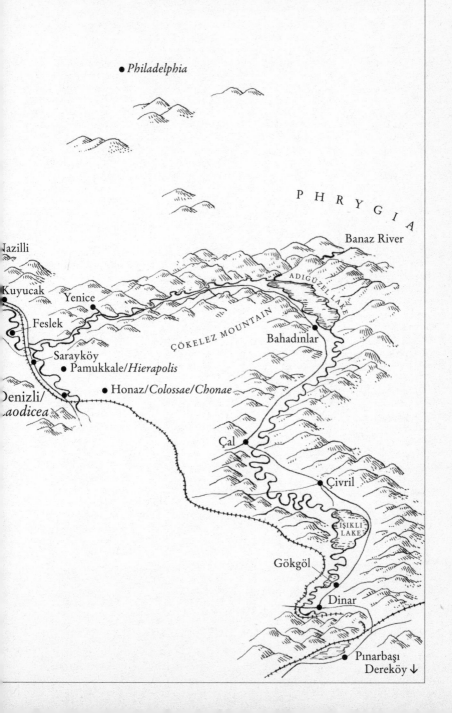

THE MEANDER VALLEY

Philadelphia

P H R Y G I A

Banaz River

Nazilli

Kuyucak

Yenice

ADIGÜZEL LAKE

Feslek

ÇÖKELEZ MOUNTAIN

Bahadınlar

Sarayköy

Pamukkale/*Hierapolis*

Denizli/*Laodicea*

Honaz/*Colossae/Chonae*

Çal

Çivril

IŞIKLI LAKE

Gökgöl

Dinar

Pınarbaşı
Dereköy ↓

PROLOGUE

I would have gone down the Meander years ago if I'd known it existed.

All through my travels in the country I described for a living, however, I had never dared to imagine that this alluring proposition might lie within conventional reach; the original winding river appeared so entwined in the remote past of Anatolia, or Asiatic Turkey, as to have forfeited any geographical place in the present. The Meander was no more accessible than the mythical Styx or the mislaid Rubicon, or so I supposed until the day I came across it.

A few years ago I was travelling in a *dolmuş*, one of the public minibuses that serve Turkey's thousands of villages, when a series of slowing jolts roused me from my back-seat reverie. Glancing beyond the window to the iron parapet of a reed-fringed bridge, I happened to spy a blue sign bearing the name of the river – *Menderes* – that we were crossing. In that instant, and no doubt thanks to some random connection triggered by my wandering thoughts, I saw at last through the Turkish rendering, and wondered that a disguise so thin could have held for so long; the Meander still ran, as it had always done, and now ran directly beneath me. It was then I realised how much more there was to know about Turkey, and what I would do about it; by the time the *dolmuş* cleared the bridge I had resolved to follow this singular river's every last winding to the sea.

Windings being, of course, what I was to expect from the Meander. The river's course from Anatolia's plateau interior to the Aegean – it showed on the map as a longitudinal squiggle, which roughly bisected the westernmost reaches of this vast and roughly rectangular land – was so sinuous that the Meander had established its byword reputation even before the first historians went to work; the earliest of them all, Herodotus, chose as his default simile the river that reached the sea just forty miles north of his home city, now Turkey's foremost tourist mecca of Bodrum, to describe a particularly mazy stretch of the Nile.

The river compelled me, of course, not only because it ran through the land whose holiday attractions had long been my subject, but because its very name embodied such resonant associations. Those associations had been actively evolving since the time of Christ when the great geographer Strabo, another Anatolian writer, was to describe the Meander as 'running in a direction

excessively tortuous, so that from the course of this river all windings are called meanders'. The river's name had already embarked,
in other words, on its etymological odyssey towards all manner of
often conflicting meanings and resonances. It was even then
acquiring a figurative currency in both Greek and Latin, one which
would duly flourish among their offspring European tongues. By
the seventeenth century English writers had come to use the word
in a prodigious range of contexts, variously deploying that distant
river's name to describe everything from the intricacies of legal
process to those of the serpentine gut, from delirium or the mental
effects of strong drink to the devious nature of 'oily eloquence'.
By the nineteenth century its innate lack of direction especially
commended the word to writers of, for example, reports on shift-
less Victorian schoolboys.

In all the word's current associations it was this pejorative
sense that predominated. To judge by *meanderthal*, a modern
colloquialism that busy individuals favoured to describe dozy
types given to wandering around, getting in the way in shops,
or to dithering behind the wheel in streams of traffic, there
was something contemptible about meandering. The
dismissive coinage spoke of a sensibility, of nineteenth-
century schoolmasters and metropolitan yuppies alike, which
despised deviation, believing that progress was properly
measured in straight lines.

Others had sensed something far more appealing, however,
in the river's name. It was evidence of the word's innate elasticity
that Ovid, a near contemporary of Strabo, should instead have
been so patently in thrall to what he described as the loose
straying of 'soft Meander's wanton current'. On this one I was
firmly with the Roman lyric poet; to me, the word encapsulated
the freewheeling, romantic spirit that was the essence of true
travelling.

The fitting thing, then, would have been to go to the river
and go aimless when I got there – aimlessness being a productive virtue I had mislaid and thought to rediscover on the
Meander. Except that I knew enough about rivers, and Turkey,
to know that simply turning up, directionless as the river I meant
to follow, was not wise; I had a family, after all, and was not
about to cast myself adrift and unaccompanied upon a river
before learning all I could about the hazards and challenges I
might be letting myself in for. At the computer and in the library
I therefore set about familiarising myself with the Meander.

The basic geography was relatively simple. The regional
maps, though they were poor, at least revealed that the river
rose somewhere near a hinterland town called Dinar and drained
into the Aegean between the resort towns of Kuşadası and
Didim. Along the way it looped and strayed for some 500 kilometres, in the process losing 1,000 metres, or a single kilometre,
of elevation, which is to say that the river's average gradient at
least appeared reassuringly gentle.

Not that my researches threw up much else, however, in the
way of bringing me to expeditionary readiness. They instead
confirmed such colourful details as that the Meander Valley was
famously fertile from the substantial silts carried down by the
river, and quite as rich in historical figures as it was in fruit and
vegetables; an epic cast of gods and mythical heroes, conquerors,
kings, traders and travellers had trodden the ancient road that
ran along much of its broad valley to connect the Aegean with
the vast Asian hinterland. This was all of interest, of course,
though at this stage I was more concerned by failures to progress
along the more practical avenues of my research – like not
turning up anybody, ever, who had attempted an actual descent
of the Meander.

For what I urgently needed was the advice of boatmen with

hands-on experience of the river: its up-close character, that is, from the height of the banks to the caprice of its currents. It soon became apparent, however, that such men had never thought to steer cargoes down the Meander, no doubt because those in the freight trade, counting themselves with the school-masters and the thrusting yuppies, were deterred by the river's famously errant course. The only certainty about the one possible exception, the marble consignments rumoured to have been shipped from the Roman-era quarries at the river's midway point around Hierapolis, was that no marble man's rafting memoir had survived to throw light on the ways of the river.

My other hope was to track down modern accounts of expe-riences on the Meander. I soon learned, however, that expedi-tionary adventurers had shown no more interest in the river than the cargo men of the centuries long before them, and for reasons I readily guessed; they thought they knew enough about names, that is, to assume that the adrenaline they craved was unlikely to course through their veins on a river called the Meander.

So the Meander Valley, though it might have served as historic thoroughfare between worlds, bore a river that nobody for various reasons had ever thought to travel; a river known, then, almost entirely by the associations conjured by its name. I could there-fore suppose no more than that my descent, apparently a first, was sure to be indirect, and likely to entail a feeble seaward incline; sufficiently feeble, at any rate, to have passed beneath the notice of other expeditionary parties. I hoped, being a party of one, that these intrepid types were right about the river; I was banking on the fact that the Meander might live down to its name. What I wanted was not white-water thrills but the freedom to drift gently downstream, freely attentive to the rich past of this valley on the historic borders of Asia and Europe, East and West, as well as to its present at a time when Turks especially questioned their place between these two worlds.

Against all this uncertainty I could at least claim to know my way around Turkey and speak the language reasonably well. I had also come to have a deep regard for the locals, if not for their formidable dogs, and was sufficiently confident in the sincerity of Turkish hospitality to reckon I had a good chance of finding lodgings in the many valley villages along the way; all I could otherwise do was pack as properly as possible. Before leaving home, I had therefore drawn up a priority list of every last item of gear that I might struggle to find in the Turkish hinterland. This list included maps, iodine tablets, a first aid kit and a lightweight sleeping bag. It also featured walking boots, various creams and tablets, and dry bags. It ran to a reducible walking pole sufficiently stout to fend off the dogs, and even a collapsible boat.

What it did not include was a trowel.

CHAPTER ONE

Trowel was a Turkish word I didn't know, so I improvised. Hardly had I requested a pocket-sized spade, however, before the ironmonger's eyes were narrowing to wary slits.

It had not crossed my mind that laying my hands on a trowel might present a problem in a place like Dinar. How but with trowels had the chillies, peppers and aubergines that ran amok in the scruffy little town's kitchen gardens been planted? What of the geraniums that bloomed in rusty cooking oil tins at the foot of whitewashed walls? The potted pine saplings that stood in long rows at the state railway's nursery opposite the station? And the apple and cherry orchards that blossomed across the springtime plains west of the town? Dinar was where Turkey's fertile western lowlands, liberally watered by the Meander's springs, ran up against the plateau interior to breed a last-ditch growing fervour among the locals – but one that their iron-monger did not appear to share.

He stocked, that said, every other item that the practical man might need; his shop was a monument to all the manual work that even now was done in rural Anatolia. Every corner, half-lit and dusty, brimmed with those brunt-bearing objects – axe handles, mattock heads, scythe blades – that interminable usage was apt to blunt or break. There were also whetstones, washers, lengths of plastic piping, buckets of nails, screws and bolts, reels of rope and chain, jubilee clips, bridles and heavy-duty sheepdog collars, their blades ferociously skewed to keep the wolves off. Wolves being something, it now struck me, that I hadn't planned for.

The closest things to trowels, however, were the spade heads. They were royal green, with tapered blades, and so like the shape of medieval shields as to put me in mind of heraldic devices. For a moment I expected to spot adjacent piles of escutcheons, chevrons and bends sinister, as if some alternative history had turned out an altogether more prosperous land; one in which Dinar's ironmonger instead ran a profitable sideline in knocking up kitsch coats of arms to order, no doubt to adorn the entrance gates that fronted the extensive spreads of the town's proliferating nouveau class, along with the same fake-grained plastic plaques bearing the carved swirls of manorial addresses standard in the affluent West. It was a fragile fancy, however, which lasted no longer than the time it took to glance through the shop door to the make-do concrete structures that in fact lined Dinar's gridded streets, the bare block walls with their hanging tongues of hardened cement, and the plots strewn with spoil. I thought of the wider town, with its shattered pavements and the tile-strewn roofscapes of rusting air-conditioning units beneath skeins of sooty cables and wires, and the scruffy villages that lay beyond Dinar, all crumbling walls of baked mud, and I had no more thoughts of entrance gates, heraldry or of prosperity in the Anatolian backcountry.

'Like them.' I pointed at the spade heads. 'Only smaller. With a handle.' The ironmonger folded his arms. He threw his head back and batted languid eyelids, which eventually reopened to reveal an elsewhere gaze, all interest drained, almost to the point of insult. It was the graphic Turkish negative, but sufficiently aggravated to express something more spirited than a shortage of stock; that the ironmonger was not minded, in fact, to sell me a trowel. On principle. He took me for a treasure hunter.

I had not anticipated such an obstruction quite so early in my journey. I nevertheless supposed it could do the lone traveller no harm to be reminded that Turks resent some things about foreigners. Not least when it comes to digging. I might have pleaded my case (that it was not, after all, a bulldozer, or even a spade, that I was attempting to buy) but for the fact that foreigners in Turkey have the sort of digging form as to discredit even the most plausible excuse. Anatolia has haemorrhaged treasures throughout its history, to conquering occupiers from both East and West. By the nineteenth century, however, such artefacts were not the spoils of victory but articles of purchase, albeit of questionable process, as the European powers set about filling the Grecian-style halls of their newly endowed museums.

From the 1700s collectors descended upon Turkey to haggle with ruin-weary Ottoman beys and provincial governors for all manner of dirt-caked antiquities. Crated marbles were carted to the decks of waiting brigs all along the ruin-strewn littorals of south-west Anatolia; the spades, crowbars and squealing pulley blocks sounded especially loud, however, across the ancient city sites thickly clustered around the delta of the Meander River. At Miletus, the great port that had once commanded the river's mouth, the excavators found beneath the accumulated depth of silt such treasures as the monumental entrance gate that had once served the city's south agora; the gate was removed to Berlin, along with columns, capitals, pedestals and inscriptions from the Temple to Athena at nearby Priene. The temple friezes from Magnesia on the Meander, a city a few miles inland, were dispatched to Paris; and the statues that lined the Sacred Way between Miletus and the oracular temple at Didyma, the seated figures worn to an oddly modern amorphousness, went to London.

It is a national grievance that the museums of the West, to say nothing of its clandestine art collections, are often rich in finds purchased, purloined or plundered from Turkey. The soil of Anatolia even today conceals perhaps as many carved sarcophaguses, statues and inscriptions, coins, pottery and jewellery as anywhere else on earth. The Turkish state assumes that among the Western arrivals are those intent on persisting, only more covertly, in the ways of their filching forebears. The airports provide stern reminders that the unlicensed removal of antiquities from the country is punishable by a lengthy stay in prison. It's a message that clearly bears repetition, though it can often manifest more gently, as an appeal to the visitor's moral and aesthetic conscience by reminding him, typically, how 'Every flower is beautiful in its own garden. Every antique is beautiful in its own country.'

Which was not the approach they favoured at Dinar. The locals' view was that their inland region had in turn become victim to the same process of plunder that had befallen the Meander Delta in earlier centuries; that grasping foreigners, having exhausted all such coastal opportunities, had now worked their way upstream to eye the unexcavated and unguarded archaeological sites located at the top of the same river. The locals judged that the only legitimate business these same foreigners could have with the Meander was back at the river's mouth, at the beach resorts that had sprung up at nearby Kuşadası and Didim; those who found their way as far inland as Dinar must have come not as tourists but as clandestine trowellers. That same morning a man in a brimless woollen cap, the favoured headgear among senior males in the Turkish interior, had expressed precisely these common suspicions by meeting my request for directions to the Roman theatre with a vigorous query of his own; was I, he asked, an 'accredited archaeologist'? It was only once I had strenuously argued my

innocence that he pointed me up a hillside track, but with the
parting discouragement that a dog – 'large, often unchained'
– lived there. I had barely checked in, besides, before Turgay,
the Dinar hotelier, was mentioning the old coins I might wish
to view, as if my apparent interest in the local river masked my
real intent, which was the illicit acquisition of local antiquities.

The locals were right in one respect: Dinar had certainly enjoyed
a past worth guarding. Celaenae, as the city was first known,
not only stood by the source of the storied river but occupied
what was once the most strategically significant site in all
Anatolia; it commanded the pass through the Samsun Dağı
range, a modest set of mountains by regional standards, but one
that finally saw off the Aegean littoral as the contours stepped
up to the plateau. The climb from the coastlands to the high
interior, a prime communications consideration, was more easily
managed at Celaenae, in the ancient region of Phrygia, than at
anywhere else in Anatolia.

   All through its early history, from perhaps two millennia
before the birth of Christ until some four hundred years after
his crucifixion, Celaenae remained a place of exceptional
geographical consequence; the great longitudinal land routes
across the ancient world's Mediterranean heartlands – anywhere,
that is, between the sandy shores of North Africa and the black
steppe of Ukraine – necessarily funnelled through Anatolia
before converging on the pass at Celaenae. The route had first
connected the foremost Aegean port of Miletus, the silt-sunk
city that awaited me at the end of my journey, with the early
Mesopotamian civilisations of the Assyrians and Hittites. This
great highway to the East – 'the public frequented road by which
all travellers pass' – set out from the shores of the Aegean along
the lower Meander Valley before returning to the river's

headwaters at Celaenae and continuing via the pass, 'on, in a straight line, as far as India'. Vast caravans of wool, wheat and spices, marble and ivory, trundled through the pass, establishing Celaenae as the commercial and administrative hub of the western Anatolian hinterland. It was no surprise that the keepers of Celaenae's pass made immense fortunes. In the year 481 BC, for example, a resident of the city called Pythius had occasion to calculate his personal worth. His two thousand talents of silver, 3,393,000 gold pieces, plus unspecified slaves and estates, made him the world's second richest man.

For all this, however, inland Celaenae could be dismissed as a glorified toll house in comparison with Miletus, the city at the seaward end of the Meander. For in the course of the sixth and fifth centuries BC Miletus had spawned a unique crop of what Strabo called 'illustrious persons'. The great port city, which Greeks from their homelands across the Aegean had settled some centuries earlier, was home to musicians, poets and sculptors. Miletus also boasted planners, engineers and the earliest map makers, and philosophers such as Anaximander and Anaximenes, to say nothing of the great Thales, who would duly be credited with nothing less than the founding of the Western rational tradition. The neighbouring cities of Ionia, as the settler Greeks called the coastal region that encompassed the Meander Delta, were barely less impressive; Priene was a haunt of artists and home to Bias, one of the Seven Sages of Antiquity, while Magnesia on the Meander a short distance upstream swarmed with orators and singers.

This atmosphere of inquisitive and civilised enlightenment appeared coastal by instinct; in the fifth century BC it certainly did not appear to extend to Celaenae. The hinterland city, popu-lated by its Persian ruling class and by Anatolian locals such as Phrygians, Lydians and Pisidians, failed to measure up to

Miletus when it came to the production of famous sons. Easy affluence bred little, it seemed, by way of local accomplishment. The residents of Celaenae apparently felt no need to distinguish themselves beyond the breadth of their wallets. The city appeared mired in a provincialism from which even its extraordinary wealth could not drag it. If the coastal Ionians knew anything of 'the pasture lands of Celaenae', it was merely that these uncultured wastes were home to the long-haired and uncouth Anatolian barbarians who were to serve as fodder at the Roman-era gladiatorial shows.

Yet Celaenae was to rise above this dearth of home-grown talent by achieving a reputation of its own, even if it was a borrowed one. The city found it in the one resource it could count upon: passing traffic. Celaenae was to make its name largely by association with the epic deeds – however far-flung their actual execution – of those who passed through the place. In this respect Celaenae recalled a small-town restaurant, the walls pinned with promotional photos, complete with scribbled wishes, of the generously disposed stars that happened to halt there. Back in an age, that is, when the stand-out stars were marchers. If Miletus was renowned for its revered philosophers, then Celaenae came to be known for the marching columns, or at least for the men in command of those columns, who took their rest there; as it was for the achievements of the head that the city at the river's foot was known, so it was for the exertions of the foot that the one at its head was to be remembered.

For in the course of the fifth and fourth centuries BC it happened that the three most celebrated ancient marches of all passed through Celaenae. These had much in common, not least in terms of the infinite ambition of their leaders, but given how quickly the dust obscures the facts of ancient history it may not be facile to suggest that the most glaring similarity, however superficial, was the incidence of the letter X in their names. The first one to enter the city, exceptionally enough, had two; the arrival in 481 BC of Xerxes, King of Persia, was the very event that prompted the same Pythius to reckon his fortune, the local tycoon thinking to commend himself by offering up his wealth to serve the war chest of the new arrival, the only man in existence richer than himself. Xerxes was scion of the Persian imperial line that had ruled Anatolia – even unto its Hellenised western littoral – since 546 BC. After leading his army hordes out of Persia and along the great Anatolian road, Xerxes had arrived at the eastern gates of Celaenae. At this centre of provincial Persian rule, the King ordered his armies to rest while he took himself off to the palace that he kept by the banks of the Meander. In the company of advisers he fine-tuned his plans for the invasion of Europe. Greece, for too long defiant of Persian dominion, was now to be brought to heel.

Or so Xerxes thought. To this end the so-called Great King had assembled a force that matched the scale of his ambition; his armies, stuffed with the levies of countless subject people, were so vast that it was feared their combined thirst must drain Anatolia's rivers, if the dust the columns put up did not first turn the waters to slurry. In time, of course, the rested armies were to continue out of Celaenae, and on towards the epic events for which posterity was to remember them: the gigantic pontoon bridge, an engineering marvel, which bore the invaders across the Hellespont into Europe; the Persians' frustration before the heroic stand of Leonidas' 300 Spartans at Thermopylae; and the subsequent destruction by Greek forces of Xerxes' huge trireme fleet in the shallows around the island of Salamis.

Back to the comparative backwaters of Celaenae, however, to await the arrival eighty years later of another oft-remembered army at the city gates. Among this lot of mercenary marchers the man that history was destined to single out was one Xenophon, who would not only gain an entry adjacent to Xerxes in encyclopaedias but was also, it happened, in the pay of the same Great King's great-grandson, a Persian prince called Cyrus the Younger. Cyrus, who had been appointed the ruling satrap or governor of Phrygia, installed himself in his palatial hunting lodge by the headwaters of the Meander, just as Xerxes had done before him, where he too considered the audacious scale of his plans. The vital difference was that Cyrus and his armies arrived in 401 BC not at the eastern but the western gates of the city. Cyrus, having largely gathered his forces from among the Greek cities of the Aegean shore, was resting his armies at Celaenae for a month before leading them east to make Persia his own; the Persians, that is, were now fighting among themselves.

Like the hordes of Xerxes before them, Xenophon and the rest of the 'Ten Thousand' Greeks under Cyrus's command would advance out of Celaenae to a momentous future. The temptation might once more be to follow, accompanying these adventurers on their legendary up-country expedition, or anabasis, if the focus of this narrative did not require us to remain at Celaenae, through the levying of the tolls, the counting of fortunes and the finding of new ways to dent them, perhaps commissioning personal insignia to adorn the gates of villas, in anticipation of the arrival of the next lot of marchers at the city sixty-five years later: the armies of Alexander the Great, a Macedonian Greek intent on subduing all the world, who in 334 BC halted his men at Celaenae where they were to stay for ten days before he led them east to conquer Persia.

It is now that our loyalty to Celaenae pays off, the perspective of the city's gate men revealing the historical significance of the 150 years spanning the arrivals there of Xerxes and of Alexander in the simplest terms; where Persians had once headed west, that is, Greeks were now marching east. So the pattern of the marchers' passing through the city first told of the Easterners who meant to incorporate the West, still-born, into the vast territories of the Persian Empire, and of those who resisted, then reversed, a process of global significance.

We only know of these marches, of course, because of the writers who saw fit to describe them: Herodotus, who immortalised Xerxes' invasion march by placing it centre-stage in his magisterial *Histories*; Xenophon, whose own account of the great expedition in which he himself took part, the *Anabasis*, would soon be recognised as worthy of the great achievement it celebrated; and the Roman historian Arrian whose own *Anabasis* was just one of many accounts to commemorate Alexander's great campaign. By these literary works, mainstays of the classical canon, the place in history of the marches was assured. They have since been sanctified as key moments in the West's founding myth, and repeatedly treated by artists, poets, writers and film-makers, raised on separate pedestals to develop distinct, if overlapping, mythologies. The effect might have been to cast these epic trudges adrift, united only by a vaguely comprehended notion of a shared Near Eastern setting, if it were not that they had had Celaenae in common.

For the fact that all three marches made lengthy stops in the city and over a comparatively brief period – roughly a lifetime in each case dividing their arrivals – invited me rather to think of the marches collectively; as different stages, even, in one unfolding, archetypal event. The composition of the three expeditions – the men and the direction in which they were headed – demonstrated a classic reversal. For the process that began when Xerxes' Persians headed in one direction to conquer Greeks – and reached a turning point when Cyrus, a Persian,

marched against his own land – was to end 150 years later with
Macedonian Greeks heading east to conquer Persians. History's
tide had turned.

All Anatolia, and the valley of the Meander especially, has
been perpetually subject to this pattern. The fall of the East
and the rise of the West was to be repeated, of course, but the
process was also to be reversed. The Eastern invaders who took
their lead from Xerxes included the Selçuk Turks in the eleventh
century, with the Mongols, Tamburlaine's Tartars and the
Ottoman Turks advancing in their wake, while those who
opposed their progress, in turn invoking the glorious example
of Alexander, included the armies of the Byzantine emperors
and of the Western crusaders. It was a process repeated even in
the twentieth century when Greece's invading divisions pushed
up the Meander Valley in 1919 before running into the resistance offered by the Turks – the ensuing war leading to the birth
of modern Turkey. The one lesson East and West learned, though
they might take turns to encroach, the East now claiming the
Balkans, the West now the steppes of Asia, was where they ended
and began: in Anatolia, and most especially in the plains and
defiles of the Meander Valley. The river might have come to
signify digression, but I was not about to forget that my subject,
and my route through westernmost Turkey, also wound through
the historic marches, the marching lands, between two worlds.

And now I was in Dinar, where the men with the Xs in their
names and their marching columns had left no impression.
Along dusty streets lined with soup shops, the flat roofs topped
with corrugated iron, nothing of Celaenae's glorious heritage
remained. There were no reminders that the world's two richest
men had once met here. In fact, at the original keystone of the
Anatolian land bridge – the birthplace, that is, of the metaphor

that even today defines Turkey – they were now having trouble finding me a trowel.

The city's decline had not been immediate. In fact, it was lavishly rebuilt in the third century BC with funds plundered from Persia's sacked treasures; the city was renamed in honour of Apama, mother of one of Alexander's successor kings. Apamea admittedly suffered a series of earthquakes so acute that even the Romans, those inveterate tax collectors, temporarily exempted the city from their levies. Even so, it continued to flourish down to the time of Christ when Strabo called it 'the common staple for merchandise brought from Italy and from Greece'.

It was not until the fourth century, when the rise of Constantinople to the north reconfigured Anatolia's roads, that Apamea's decline gathered irreversible momentum. Increasing volumes of traffic ignored the pass for more northerly routes and so the wealth of Apamea began to erode. Of the great palace that Xerxes had had built by the banks of the Meander, perhaps by way of consolation for the irreversible loss of his fleet and his aura of invincibility at Salamis, nothing was known; the same was true of his great-grandson Cyrus the Younger's hunting lodge. These Persian vanity projects perhaps fell victim to earthquake or plain neglect if, that is, their stones and marbles had not been pointedly earmarked for deliberate dismantling to serve in the triumphant redevelopment of Hellenistic Apamea. Time, meanwhile, eroded the citadel which Alexander had considered so strongly positioned that he preferred to negotiate with its garrison; nothing but the foundations of the walls remained. The city dwindled and died, and the names that recalled its imperial past went with it. By the nineteenth century some locals knew the place as Geyikler, or Deer, for the wild animals that roamed the ruined parklands of Celaenae-Apamea.

Dinar, the name finally settled upon the modern town,

continued to suffer from earthquakes into modern times. The most recent one struck in October 1995 when half of the town's buildings, about 5,000 in number, collapsed. Much of Dinar was not even teenage, with almost nothing of those many pasts that we have barely begun to explore – Phrygian and Persian, Greek and Roman, Byzantine and Ottoman among them – poking above the foundations when I arrived in the spring of 2008. No wonder, then, that locals like the ironmonger should have wondered what had brought me to the place.

The truth is I wanted nothing from Dinar. Not its coins nor the prospect of discreet excavations in the remains of the Roman theatre. I had no wish to dig for the potsherds liberally scattered across the hilltop site of Celaenae's once-impregnable citadel. I only hoped that Dinar would provide me with a beginning. That and a trowel.

The trowel; this was nothing more, if its purpose must be known, than a routine expeditionary necessity. With only the vaguest idea of the progress I might make along the river, and of where I would end up sleeping, I was hardly in any position to guess at the toilet facilities I might find there. The trowel was not for the secretive unearthing of treasures, then, but for the disposal of my bodily waste; all proper and responsible, of course, though I was not about to clear my name if it meant spelling out the plain facts to a Turkish ironmonger. I left the shop empty-handed, newly mindful of the unforeseen challenges that might arise before I was to experience the carefree progress I had so readily anticipated.

CHAPTER TWO

I had arrived in Dinar the previous evening.

The bus did not bother to call at the town's little *otogar*, or bus station, but dropped me by the roadside before it continued east towards the city of Konya. I watched the rear lights shrink through a stain of brown exhaust as it made for the high steppe. Beneath a wide sky stuck with stars and a black minaret I dragged my luggage into the town. The streets smelt of coal and I heard their footfalls before I saw them – the solitary men in brimless caps and the women in headscarves who stooped beneath half-lowered shutters, their worn faces flaring in the spills of buttery light, to make late purchases of bread, vegetables and cigarettes.

The little hotel stood within a scruffy garden. It had been built after the 1995 earthquake, its concrete walls swagged in telephone wires, electricity and TV cables, which had been customised as washing lines where they festooned the balconies. The open-plan ground floor was sparsely furnished; a calendar and a portrait of Mustafa Kemal Atatürk, the man currently on the coins, a lifetime dead, decorated the walls. A reception desk, with a diary and hooks for room keys, overlooked the lounge area, where chairs and a sofa corralled a flickering television. At the other end of the room two metal-topped tables indicated the eating area where I found the hotelier the following morning. I was just back from a walk to the town's Roman theatre, where the views over the westerly plain had allowed me my first glimpse of the Meander's down-stream seam.

Turgay Darkeye, as the hotelier's surname translated, was working his way through a bunch of parsley. 'Diabetes,' he muttered. 'Only just diagnosed.' Turgay's pronounced features confirmed the Turkic, even Mongol, origins that his surname appeared to acknowledge. He had motioned for me to join him when the shawled Mrs Darkeye, a newspaper folded under her arm, arrived to take charge. Anxious to spare her husband the least dietary temptation, Mrs Darkeye redirected me to the unoccupied table, which she set about covering with pages from her newspaper. I noticed that the paper was recent; I had not been in Turkey for long and was keen for the latest news. To a tablecloth largely composed of small ads, I therefore got the obliging Mrs Darkeye to add the front pages. By the time she returned with my breakfast – a tight-waisted glass of black tea, bread, crumbly white cheese, ship-lapped slices of tomato and cucumber, honey and a boiled egg – and with more parsley for her husband, I was deep in the lead stories.

Turkey had lately run into a political swell considerable even by its own turbulent standards. The country's secular establish-ment, backed by the military, was confronting the ruling admin-istration of moderate Islamists. Dates had been set, the newspaper reported, for the case that was to be heard against the governing party. *Ak*, as the party was called, had for some weeks been facing closure for what the chief prosecutor described as promoting an Islamic, and therefore unconstitutional, programme; the govern-ment had recently sought to overturn a time-honoured ban on the wearing of headscarves in universities, ministries and public offices. The secularists, prominent in the army and the state bureaucracy, did not like Islamic headgear. Invoking the example of Atatürk, the arch-secularist Father of the Nation, who had taken a tough line of his own against the superstitious fezes and turbans of the Ottomans, they meant to close down the government for supposing that its female citizens should be free to decide what they wore on their heads in the workplace.

For almost five hundred years Turkey had been run as an Islamic theocracy. With the end of Ottoman rule in 1923, however, Atatürk's secularists gained firm control; religion's place in the public sphere was radically reduced, and many of the mosques and religious schools were closed. At the end of the twentieth century, however, the balance of power had begun to shift. *Ak*, having gained an impressive popular mandate in the previous year's elections, now found itself in a position to demonstrate rather more muscle than was usual from the traditionally cowed Islamic lobby. In fact, *Ak* and its supporters had got their shot in first; months before the secularists had brought their closure case the Islamists had charged these opponents with unconstitutional activities of their own. The secularists, they claimed, counted among their number members of a clandestine organisation responsible for numerous kidnappings, executions, bombings, extortions, protection rackets, fixing of contracts and narcotics' trafficking. This illicit organisation took its supposed name, *Ergenekon*, from the legendary valley in central Asia's Altai Mountains where the Turkish national story had popularly begun; from this valley the Turks, guided by a talismanic wolf, were said to have emerged to make their destined migration westwards from the sixth century.

Ak had it that *Ergenekon*'s dyed-in-the-wool secularists were behind a terror campaign whose sole design was to bring down the elected government. The objective, they claimed, was to spread such disorder that the army must intervene, as it had done in the past, and so wrest control of the country from

the Islamists and return it to Atatürk's secularists. The
discovery the previous summer of incriminating documents
and a half-empty crate of grenades in an Istanbul flat had
spurred the authorities to pick up scores of disgruntled secularists – military men, journalists, academics, nationalists and
assorted mavericks – in a series of dawn raids. Some Islamic
sections of the media subsequently presented these supposed
Ergenekon operatives as members of a vast organisation, which
had been responsible for almost every instance of Turkish
political violence over the past decade. These unlikely claims
they substantiated by linking the grenades' serial numbers
with those of grenades apparently known to have been used
in other incidents, as if *Ergenekon*'s entire terror campaign
could be traced to the one crate of meticulously documented
munitions.

The secularists contended, in turn, that *Ergenekon* did not
exist; *Ak* Party schemers, they claimed, had fabricated the
organisation to exaggerate the extent of the secular establishment's secret hand. These Islamists presented the rounded-up
secularists as agents of the so-called 'deep state', as tools of
the military-backed bureaucratic elite whose undying fealty
was to Atatürk's secular vision, whatever the expressed wishes
of the electorate. The actual truth, according to the secularists, was that *Ak* and its supporters nursed a secret agenda of
their own, and one quite as destabilising as the secularists'
was alleged to be; the *Ergenekon* investigations, designed to
discredit and disarm the secularist opposition, were by way
of preparation for an increasingly Islamicised, even Islamic,
state.

Turgay had finished his parsley.

'So, what are you doing in Dinar?' he asked. I was here, I
replied, to spend some time on the Meander. In that word I

heard the romantic character of a venture the locals would surely
recognise; but what Turgay understood from my interest in the
river was that I must be in irrigation.

'No, no, not irrigation,' I hastily replied.

'Fish farming, then? Hydroelectricity?' I did not much care
for our parlour-game exchange. Turgay's alarming assumptions,
a local's view of the Meander, conjured a different river from
the one I had imagined. Anxious to head off his next best guess,
in case it was that I must work in sewage treatment, which might
fatally undermine my own enthusiasm for the project, I told
Turgay what had brought me to Dinar. The hotelier appeared
puzzled.

'History?' he echoed. 'So you'd be interested in old coins?'
he asked, brightening visibly. It was then that three policemen
entered the hotel.

They were from the *Zabıta*, the paperwork police, and they
wore pressed blue uniforms, with holsters. At their gesture the
hotelier wiped the parsley from his mouth and followed them
into the front garden. I watched through the open door as they
gathered by a tree. They had slipped beyond my hearing.
Deliberately, I supposed. I guessed I was witnessing one of those
whispered visits that small businesses were commonly presumed
to suffer east of the Balkans; an irregularity detected in the
hotelier's tax affairs that the *Zabıta*, as servants of the state,
were duty bound to refer unless a discreet cash consideration,
one the officers were happy to disburse, could be found to resolve
matters.

'Trouble?' I asked knowingly once the police had left.

'The chief's after a new tree for his garden,' Turgay explained.
'He wondered if he could take a cutting from my linden. Now,
for the *Menderes*. The man you want is Truehero.'

Mehmet Truehero, author of a local history, made his living

as a defence lawyer. I was directed to his office opposite Dinar's judiciary building. It did not resemble any legal practice that I knew; the lawyer ran his business from a single room, workshop-style, which gave directly onto a bustling lane along with the clouds of cigarette smoke that billowed through the open door. There were no security buzzers, lobbies, reception desks, appointment books or obstructive assistants. One apparently sought Truehero's services much as one might pop in to the key cutters, or drop off a frayed shirt at the tailor's. This refreshingly open approach had attracted a crowd of chatting smokers and tea drinkers, which was already larger than Truehero's premises had been designed to accommodate. The office, though it aspired to legal gravitas, with shelves of Turkish law digests and a prominent desk topped by a brass-effect name plaque, more convincingly functioned as a favoured tea salon. I had barely peered through the window when the man at the desk was beckoning me to join the gathering.

The men assembled at Truehero's turned out to be farmers and small-time business types; their interests included cherry orchards, machine workshops and kebab houses. They discussed the drought, the price of diesel, tractor parts, impending marriages and irrigation systems. The noise they generated was impressive, even overpowering, though it did not appear to disturb the meeting even then taking place between the man at the desk, whom the plaque identified as Truehero himself, and the large client in a suit with a shimmering grey weave who sat opposite him. It might be said that the congenial and good-humoured hubbub in fact sustained the two men in their toil across the arid wastes of legal discourse; even that their friends and acquaintances had assembled precisely to supply the wayside wells of conversational distraction that might refresh the pair and so provide them with the necessary strength to continue.

Truehero, I sensed, had bigger interests than the law. As for the client, he especially appeared to welcome those interruptions that acknowledged his authority on subjects such as diesel, then as expensive as anywhere in the world, or the price of cherries, or big business. Big business, the client declared, breaking off from the meeting, was all this government cared about. The farmers, as far as the politicians were concerned, could all go hang.

'Yes,' came a voice from the crowd. 'But you've got to credit what they're doing for the poor.'

'Poor or rich, yes,' the client conceded, warming to his theme. 'It's the ones in the middle they're squeezing.' The cigarette smoke parted to reveal a boy bearing a shiny tin tray of glasses of fresh tea.

'Poor or rich but definitely religious,' someone added. 'That's what you need to be in this country.' As the client raised a forefinger to signal his further intervention, Mehmet Truehero took the opportunity to lean across and shake my hand. The lawyer had an angular frame, with thinning hair and sallow skin, and his eyes brimmed with curiosity.

'And how can I help you?' he asked. Not, admittedly, with anything for which he could readily charge me; but then I had already reached the welcome conclusion that Mehmet Truehero was not the sort solely interested in those he was paid to represent. It was instead his historical knowledge I sought, hoping it might lead me to what must be my beginning, the Meander's true source, which neither my researches nor the maps in my possession had quite confirmed. The topography of the Meander's headwaters had always been contentious; some of the doubts that Richard Pococke, a pioneer traveller, had expressed in the 1740s – the 'many difficulties in relation to the account, which different authors give to the rise of these rivers'

– even now remained unresolved. So I told Mehmet Truehero that I meant to trace the Meander's route all the way to the sea, and must therefore begin at the very top, if I could only find my way there.

Mehmet rose promptly from his desk, grabbing a set of keys. 'Something's come up,' he informed his client. 'We'll pick up again later on.' As the relieved client threw himself into the general conversation, Mehmet led me outside to a little brown car.

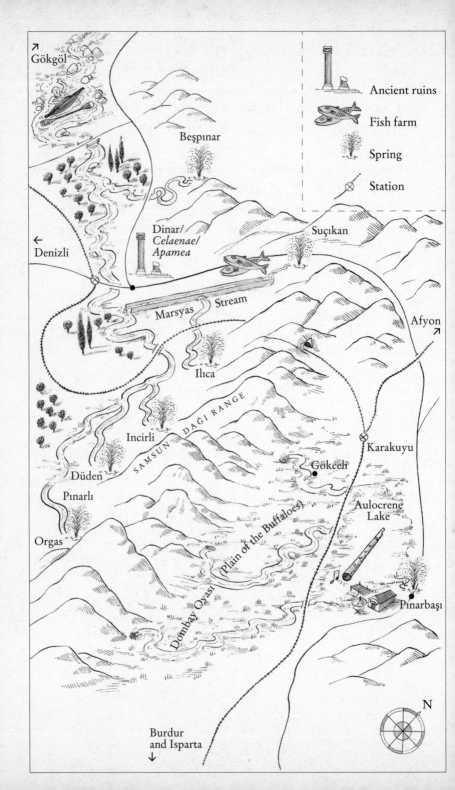

CHAPTER THREE

It was almost as if I had done Mehmet the favour. For having turned up, out of the blue, to rescue him from another day of legal tedium, he actually made me feel generous – if not, from the moment he shoved the car into gear, safe. Mehmet drove with one hand. With the other he sifted the back seat for papers, articles and books, and flung flapping law tomes aside, smoking the while. We made unsteady progress out of Dinar.

'We'll start with the Orgas,' Mehmet declared, tossing me a copy of the local history book he had written. We turned south, following the foot of the Samsun Dağı range where it edged the unfurling plain. The fields were fringed with a pink blur of distant cherry blossom.

I was busy with Truehero's account of the Orgas, one of the Meander's celebrated tributary streams, which had featured on the coins of Roman Apamea, when with a lunge a set of spittle-strewn teeth briefly loomed at the passenger window. It was a roadside *kangal*, or Anatolian sheepdog, a creature I so little cared for that I was convinced something must give; the collar, the straining leash, the ring bolt or even the scruffy farmstead to which the creature was secured, the entire edifice ripping free of modest footings to strew a cascade of roof tiles in the road, the fearsome hound surging from the whitewashed wreckage of worm-eaten timbers to chase us down. I focused on the road ahead. A sign indicated Pınarlı village.

'Pınarlı, pah!' exclaimed Mehmet, suddenly cantankerous.

The name translates, prosaically, as 'With a Spring', and some decades earlier had replaced the ancient name, Norgas, as Mehmet had known the village in his childhood.

The twentieth century, its early decades especially, had witnessed the remaking of Turkey and Turks alike. Atatürk's social revolution turned people and place towards a modern, Western future. A Latin-style alphabet was drafted. The people were urged to dress in modern clothes and a new law code came into use. Surnames lifted, it could sometimes seem, from comic books were introduced.

The new Turkey, though Western in its adopted modes, was also to be Turkish in its avowed origins. A programme was therefore devised to rid the nation's villages of foreign-sounding names. Norgas, in which the local stream's ancient name was clearly preserved, had the taint of Greek; a replacement was found for it, as for many village names where other foreign influences, chiefly Armenian, Kurdish, Arabic or Persian, had been detected.

The other target was religion. Names that made reference to superstitions or to religious figures – local shrines, one-time resident dervishes – also fell foul of the authorities. One such Dinar village, the supposed site of King Xerxes' pleasure palace, had in more recent centuries been named after a Muslim holy man called Sheikh Arab Sultan. The village was duly renamed Bülüçalanı; Mehmet had no idea why 'Place of Small Chickens', as the replacement translated, should have been chosen. Less imaginative alternatives, often topographical, were more commonly employed to rename villages; the likes not only of Pınarlı but also Çamlıyayla (Pine Pasture) were repeatedly deployed to remake some 25,000 villages across Turkey.

'It means we lose our history,' Mehmet growled. The echo of the brook's classical name, undistorted beyond a snagged 'N', could no longer be heard. Its erasure by bureaucratic intervention had done for a tenacious fragment, one that time alone had failed to erode, from Anatolia's distant past.

That same brook, Turkish now, closed on the road as we drove into low hills. A dwindling dirt track halted at a scruffy picnic site where concrete tables stood among pine trees and rising red rocks. The stream twisted among the rocks, the banks climbing to form a modest defile. Mehmet and I set out on foot, tracing its course upstream. We had not gone far when the stream pooled beneath an overhanging rock, briefly bubbled, and disappeared into the hillside.

'The Orgas spring,' said Mehmet. He flipped a fresh cigarette between his lips. If one thing was clear, it was that Mehmet had not led me to the head of the Meander; nor was the source-seeker's standard prescription – continue upstream, keeping to the main fork, to the end – about to bring me there. The Orgas went where I could not follow; the pioneering Richard Pococke had a point. A consequence of the especially permeable local limestone was that the water courses tended to plunge beneath obstructions rather than circumvent them by the usual surface route. It was a trait that the epic poet Nonnos confirmed when he described the Meander 'lurking in the secret places with his water in the lap of the earth – who rolls deep through the earth and drags his crooked stream towards the light, crawling unseen and travelling slantwise underground, until he leaps up quickly and lifts his neck above the underground'.

The Meander's tributaries, Mehmet explained, did reappear above ground along their upper reaches beyond the mountain; there they crossed a high plain before running into the eastern flanks of Samsun Dağı. It was at those rising slopes that they went underground, and in the dark, like ropes pushed and twisted, the gathered channels unbraided before emerging as the Orgas and as the other springs, which rose all along the western base of Samsun Dağı. But the water courses above the mountain were for another day; Mehmet clearly meant me to visit these secondary or lower springs before introducing me to the one where my journey was truly to begin. I felt a twinge of impatience before admonishing myself; it was not in the spirit of things to fight indirection on the Meander.

So we returned to Dinar to draw up below the theatre hill – the heights of Roman Apamea – which I had visited earlier that morning. Before an arcade of crumbling arches, where a raised road had once run, was a pool roughly finished in a combination of crazy paving and off-white, institutional tiles. The water was clear. A few bubbles rose. Small fish shoaled in the pool. There were also floating patches of scum. Plastic bags and tins were strewn across the weedy bottom. The spring the pool housed pushed a bead of water over the tiled ledge to disappear down a culvert. 'I swam here as a child,' offered Mehmet, suddenly subdued, and I could not tell whether it was his childhood or the pool, long since neglected, or even the ancient glories of his home town that he mourned. The spring, Mehmet explained, was known as Ilıca, or hot spring. In fact, the water was barely tepid to the touch. Any thermal activity had dwindled broadly in keeping with the fortunes of the town. A muezzin announced the midday prayers but a stray dog, a safely small one, was all that stirred, and only to crap beneath one of the arches. At that moment it was harder than ever to credit that Celaenae had ever been home to pleasure parks and palaces, or had played host to armies whose leaders meant to conquer the world.

The truth was that the city, call it Celaenae or Apamea, had been captivating readers in the cloisters of European academe from the seventeenth century. In their Anatolian studies the early accounts of Celaenae's illustrious past, and the magnificent ambitions of those who had led their forces there, had lent the city a particular prominence. Not so much among the treasure hunters, who tended to favour the coastal sites precisely because they were accessible and their antiquities readily extracted, but among the less nakedly acquisitive antiquaries who made their way to Turkey. For though these scholarly travellers were quite as zealous in their pursuit of ancient objects, coins and inscriptions especially, they tended to see their finds not as lucrative collectables they might flog to museums so much as clues in an exploratory process, one that paralleled the momentous geographical discoveries taking place elsewhere. Just as James Cook and Alexander von Humboldt, Henry Morton Stanley and John Franklin sought glory in the New World, in Africa and in the polar regions, so these erudite men, often ex-soldiers and one-time diplomats, serving clerics or leisured nobles, were quietly bent on retrieving Anatolia's classical past; a past that the Turks even in our own times, to judge by the village brook now known as Pınarlı, sought to wipe clean.

From their reading these scholarly men knew Asia Minor – they favoured the Latin designation over the Greek-derived Anatolia – as the cradle of Western civilisation; it was the birthplace of history and philosophy, of Homer, Heraclitus and Herodotus, of coinage and town planning, and defining advances in medicine, mathematics and architecture, and was latterly the seedbed of a Christianity newly alive to its missionary reach. The more adventurous, beginning with the likes of Richard Pococke, now began travelling to this unimaginably rich historical repository to see for themselves. What they found was abandonment beyond all their expectations. The last millennium had done for the place.

For Anatolia, weakened by centuries of relentless raiding, had from roughly the time of the Crusades suffered a protracted decline. By 1300 the Byzantines were in headlong retreat towards Constantinople, abandoning the Anatolian provinces to the Selçuk Turks, and then to the devastating ravages of the Tartars and Mongols. The Turkish clan that finally eclipsed the Byzantines, the Ottomans, put expansion, primarily west-wards into the Balkans, above any social or economic consoli-dation of the imperial backyard. The land that the travelling scholars subsequently discovered was not only unmapped but subject to the sometime law of local chieftains, where brigands and raiding Turkish nomads ruled the roost well into the nine-teenth century. One such scholar, Richard Chandler, evoked a Wild West atmosphere, where bodyguards and tooled-up desperadoes came as standard, when he described his travels through western Anatolia in the 1760s. 'We now perceived four men riding briskly toward us, abreast, well mounted and armed,' he wrote. 'Our janizary and Armenians halted, as they passed, and faced about until they were gone beyond our baggage.' Such security concerns only increased as the party ventured inland. They eventually forced Chandler to abandon his cher-ished plan, which was to explore the lands around the head-waters of the Meander.

Many problems – a shortage of supplies and lodgings, the dreadful roads, constant ill health, ferocious *kangals* – confronted these travelling classicists. Perhaps the greatest challenge, however, was the one they had set themselves; relocating ancient history in the contemporary landscape. Nowhere had the constit-uents of the classical and early Christian canon – places, events, individuals, myths – lost touch with the original settings more comprehensively than in Anatolia. The route described, for example, in Xenophon's *Anabasis*, among the most widely read of the classical texts, remained largely unlocated. Equally elusive were the Anatolian cities of St Paul's evangelising mission and what might be found there; so profoundly mislaid was Colossae, the city Paul had addressed in one of his epistles, that its citizens were mistakenly associated with Memnon's Colossus of Rhodes, a monumental wonder of the ancient world, and therefore assumed to hail from that island. Other Anatolian places visited by Paul – Antioch in Pisidia, Lystra, Derbe – might have been prominent in Christian history; geography, however, had not touched them. It was no surprise, then, that the classical map of the Anatolian hinterland should have largely struck the Reverend Francis Arundell, scholarly-minded chaplain to the English factory at Smyrna in the 1820s, as a sorry blank. 'What spaces yet remain unappropriated, and to how many cities of importance is the modest and hesitating mark of interrogation affixed!' he wrote despairingly.

Classical topography taught those who presumed to master it all manner of tough lessons, chiefly that time never stopped; the problem in the case of Anatolia – the name derived from the Greek for 'east' or the 'sunrise land' – was the degree to which place had also moved on. Earthquakes had not so much reduced the sites as reconfigured them, at once turning them into quarries of conveniently dressed stone. The stones were often carted away to be reused, and the telling inscriptions they bore were concealed, often lost for ever, in the rude construc- tions of later ages. Even the language, in a rare example of the conqueror's tongue prevailing, had changed. Original Anatolian or Greek place names had progressively lost out to Turkish replacements. 'The reader can now form a very good idea of the extreme difficulty,' Reverend Arundell concluded, 'of fixing with positive certainty the sites of ancient cities.'

Such sites as had been positively identified, Ephesus, Miletus

and Xanthos among them, mostly lay close to the coast and
served only to peg the ancient past at the region's geographical
edges; Anatolia's classical topography therefore resembled a
loosely secured tent, but one that these redoubtable scholars
were bent on making fast. As they set about extending the
identification of Anatolia's lost classical sites, so the available
sources of information, often slight or unreliable, soon taught
them the comparative value of classical literature in their search.
The ancients, for all the inconsistencies in their texts, had had
much to say about Celaenae, a place Colonel William Leake,
another explorer-antiquary, considered 'a point of great
importance to the ancient geography of the western part of Asia
Minor'.

We have previously glimpsed something of Celaenae's abundant ancient detailing: in his chronicle of Xerxes' great march
Herodotus had occasion to emphasise the city's conspicuous
rivers and springs; Xenophon described how the Meander ran
through the grounds of Cyrus's hunting lodge, near the palace
of Xerxes, before winding past the city; and Arrian detailed a
citadel so impressive that even the all-conquering Alexander
was minded to negotiate a settlement with its defenders. Strabo's
Geography also noted the city's springs; they were fed, he added,
by a lake that lay beyond a mountain. The likes of Pliny and
Livy weighed in with further contributions.

These sources evoked a place rich with association, then, but
their chief value to the antiquaries was in the abundant topographical clues they provided. No lost city of the Anatolian interior occupied such a setting; one so distinctive, besides, that no
amount of earthquakes could have recontoured it beyond all
recognition. It was surely possible to locate the city, and so provide
a crucial fixed point for the identification of further sites deep in
Phrygia and across neighbouring regions. Celaenae-Apamea, as

some scholars termed the site, consequently acquired a particular significance for the region's early topographers, Leake among them, who expressed frustration that the place remained undiscovered as late as 1824. 'There cannot be a stronger proof of the little progress yet made in geographical discovery in Asia Minor,' he wrote, 'than the fact, that the site of Apameia still remains unexplored.'

The truth was that Richard Pococke had come tantalisingly close to finding this Anatolian El Dorado as early as 1740. Not that the pioneer traveller had known it. He reached modern Işıklı some forty miles north-west of Dinar, only to lack there the 'opportunity of an onward caravan'. He did subsequently include, however, in his published journal a second-hand description of 'a high hill . . . and a village called "Dinglar", where the Meander rises, and, as they say, falls down a hill from a lake at the top of it'.

That very sentence, if attentively read in the context of the classical sources, should have sufficed to reveal the modern location of the lost city. Pococke had been proved so awry in his identification of other ancient sites, however, hopelessly confusing many of their locations, that those travellers who followed in his footsteps paid little notice to his notoriously unreliable journal. The clues contained therein were to remain overlooked for more than eighty years. Only then did Leake recognise Pococke's account as containing nothing less than an X-marked map; in his own book he was to concede that the 'Dinglar' details chiefly provided by Pococke accorded 'precisely with that of Celaenae as given by several ancient authors'.

It was Francis Arundell, conveniently based at Smyrna, who was first to act on Leake's observations. Reaching Dinar in 1826, the chaplain soon convinced himself that 'the ruins could be no

other than those of Apameia'. Classical topography had its
Anatolian breakthrough; here was the fabled city. Credit for the
discovery went to Arundell, even if it was Pococke's observations
and Leake's deductions that had largely led him there. The discovery's significance was accounted such that other travelling scholars
were soon to weigh in with competing claims; they buoyed their
nineteenth-century Anatolian travelogues, a remarkably crowded
literary sub-genre, with their own reiterations of the Apamea find,
as if it were only the subsequent support they lent the discovery
that finally confirmed it. One pronounced that he had 'little doubt
that Apamea and Celaenae stood at the present town of Deenare'.
'After examining the whole of the country in the vicinity of
Deenair, the course of the various rivers, and its distance from
those places, the situations of which are ascertained,' another
loftily declared after a visit in 1835, 'I have no doubt that it stands
upon the site of Apamea . . .'

These wandering scholars therefore found the past they
sought, though the price they paid was the extent to which they
seemed unaware of the present. Perhaps it was their intense
focus that blinded them to so much of their surroundings, not
least to the inhabitants. William Leake typified the European
attitude, writing off contemporary Anatolia as 'modern barbarism
and desolation'. Another antiquary, travelling in Anatolia in the
1830s, concurred. 'As the most interesting period of the history
of this country was the time of its accommodation by the
Greeks,' he wrote, 'so the remains of their cities form now the
chief attraction to the traveller.' The locals, in terms of what
foreigners tended to make of them, were left to choose between
the treasure hunters, who stole from under their noses, or the
antiquaries, so caught up in the remote past as to see clean
through them. Which was the greater offence, I wondered; being
fleeced on one's own patch, or being ignored there? I rather

suspected, whatever the answer, that vestiges of these attitudes must cling to modern travellers. I therefore made a point of reminding myself that Mehmet Truehero, though he appeared grateful for my company, had put himself at a stranger's disposal, despite the fact that I had given no notice whatsoever, in a way unimaginable in the West.

Our time among the lower springs, that said, was beginning to drag. Once Mehmet's tour had taken in Beşpınar (Five Springs) and the lake-like Düden, I was done with these hydrographic curiosities. So much so that the stand-out feature of the fifth spring, Incirli, or Place of Figs, was that it stood in the grounds of an outdoor restaurant.

We passed beyond flaking concrete and exposed chicken-wire walls into a pseudo-grotto, the Incirli Family Park, where an obelisk of rough concrete stones surrounded by a low slab wall marked the spring. The waters spilled into a network of concrete channels, some spanned by miniature willow-pattern bridges, to low tanks where farmed trout swirled. Our table was topped by a white paper cloth and surrounded by a sort of moat. The waiter, in shiny shoes and pressed white shirt, arrived to indulge our pretence, expressed with vague pointing gestures, of selecting particular fish from the tanks. Mehmet lit a cigarette. A plume of smoke rose through the still air into the fig trees. He was sixty, he told me, and a native of Dinar. His people, Bosnian Muslims, had settled in Turkey during the upheavals of the 1920s. Mehmet had lived an eventful life, having been arrested as a political activist at the time of the 1980 coup, so it was in keeping with the tenor of his story that he should have lost his home, and narrowly escaped with his life, in the 1995 earthquake; that he should have spent much of the following year in an aid agency tent writing his book; and that *rakı* drinking – Mehmet had since forsworn the aniseed-based national spirit – had done for his first marriage.

He had since remarried, to a woman called Pınar; that word again. Springs are revered in most cultures but in Turkey, where the word is a common girl's name, the veneration seems particularly heartfelt. The Trueheroes had gone a stage further, calling their daughter, now nine, Nehir; a River issuing, then, from a Spring, in the local fashion, but with an obstetric literalism that bordered on the graphic. I asked Mehmet about his feeling for the Meander.

'It's our history,' he replied. 'It used to be a beautiful river. But with all the irrigation schemes, the factory effluent and the fish farms, they are destroying it. The flow is nothing like it used to be. I have still to show you Suçıkan, the best-known of the lower springs, but I remember the many watermills it drove when I was a child.' It had initially struck me as wondrous that a classical river should have endured into the modern age, but by their words both Turgay and now Mehmet warned me that a price had been exacted.

The trout arrived, slack-jawed and strewn with sprigs of rocket. Mehmet lifted a laden fork to his mouth, laying his cigarette aside at the last moment. 'And it's not only the river they are destroying,' he added. 'They are closing schools. All they're building are mosques.'

Mehmet venerated Atatürk; the lawyer was a staunch secularist. I asked him about the court case against the *Ak* Party – the fortuitous acronym, which stood for Justice and Development, formed a word meaning white or pure.

'They are talking about closing it down for unconstitutional activities, and banning the party leaders from politics for five years.' Mehmet spoke approvingly. I suggested that Europe would regard such actions as undemocratic.

'Europe?' he replied. 'I can't see Europe admitting us under any circumstances.' We were continuing in this gloomy vein when Mehmet's phone rang. It was the client wondering when his meeting was to be resumed.

'I should get back to the office,' said Mehmet, beating me to the bill. At my objections Mehmet's throat rose through a series of tuts as if it were that of a seabird opening its gullet to an intake of sprats.

'You are my guest,' he said, peeling off some banknotes. On the way back to his car he offered to lead me to the true source of the Meander the following day.

'Can I drop you at the hotel?' he asked. I asked if he could instead point me to an ironmonger's.

That evening a crowd of men gathered around Turgay's television to watch the weekly episode of *Wolves' Valley*. This Turkish drama featured black-suited mobsters who carried black mobile phones. They travelled in black cars, chasing each other along empty roads before simultaneously slewing to halts, without apparent reason, but separated by such distances that they were required to take careful aim at each other over the rolled-down windows of their opened car doors. There were summonses to the homes of gangland bosses where shaven-headed security men ushered the visitors into interiors, spare except for elegant women and white but for the yellow frames of abstract art pieces, there to receive whispered instructions, which they acknowledged by patting their bulging holsters.

Wolves' Valley told the story of a Turkish agent who had gone undercover to infiltrate the country's shadowy underworld. The series had been transfixing Turkey's TV and cinema audiences for five years. In the very name, of course, it was hard not to hear a reference to that valley, *Ergenekon*, whence a wolf had once led the Turkish people on their national journey.

It was a connection I might have further pondered if it had not been for the distraction caused by the advertising banner, which repeatedly flashed across the bottom of the screen; the message touted, with a startling lack of euphemism, 'genital hygiene wipes'. *Wolves' Valley* must have what marketing people knew as a female demographic, though there was no sign of one at Turgay's hotel that evening. The guns were still going off, the tyres squealing, as I made for bed.

CHAPTER FOUR

Mehmet turned up at the hotel, as promised, the following morning. He skidded to a halt, *Wolves' Valley* style, and fixed a suspicious eye on my walking pole as I climbed into his car. 'The stick?'

'The dogs.' I aimed an explanatory stab at the glove compartment before feigning the whine of a chastened *kangal*.

'No dogs in my car,' announced Mehmet. It did not impress him, apparently, that I should have felt the need to arrange my own security. He spun the wheel and we made our way through Dinar.

The road had barely cleared the town before we entered the historic pass to the east. An observation post topped the heights to our left where the national flag – red, with a white star poised in the jaws of a crescent – hung within a thicket of barbed wire. To the right a giant figure in boots and khaki plus-fours, a *kalpak* or high astrakhan hat on his head, rose from rusted supports; it was a stooped, defiant Atatürk in the garb of the Independence War, which had raged through much of western Turkey, the Meander Valley especially, before the Turks finally drove back the invading Greek armies in September 1922.

Far below those elevated symbols of nationhood, however, the nation itself appeared in a more ruinous state; the series of watermills that Mehmet had mentioned stood derelict, their neoclassical façades and rust-stained balcony balustrades visibly crumbling. Of the spring that had once turned the mill wheels – Suçıkan, or Rising Water – there was no sign.

'It rises among the trees directly below Atatürk,' explained Mehmet. 'These days, it runs down that roadside ditch. But when I was a boy the water that used to flow through here! I remember it flooding our house.' What with those floods and the earthquake, Mehmet's various homes had clearly suffered their share of natural setbacks. It struck me as odd, even so, that he should have mentioned the house without thinking to indicate its whereabouts.

'We're driving over it just about now. They flattened it to widen the highway about twenty years ago.' Mehmet spoke without sentiment, and with a pothole jolt we had left the site of Mehmet's sometime-submerged childhood behind us.

The road climbed out of the town into clouds of exhaust. The car closed on the labouring trucks, their green tailgates overpainted with the red petals of tulips and lines of yellow Arabic script, and it raced erratically towards an eroded grey skyline. Cresting the pass, Dombay Ovası, the Plain of the Buffaloes, stretched ahead. The transition was immediate and impressive. The lush orchards were gone; a treeless expanse of spring pastures patterned by the odd rectangular plot of turned earth now ran to snow-lit uplands. William Ramsay, prominent among Anatolia's scholarly wanderers, might have been describing this very plain when he wrote how the 'bright and varied' scenery of the Aegean land gave way to this 'continuation of central Asia, vast, immobile, monotonous'; for the first time the Asiatic steppe stretched before us.

The road made south-east across the plain towards hills where an indistinct azure spill gradually resolved into a lake. In the shallows dazzling egrets appeared freshly laundered, and there were yellow buntings among the reed beds. At a sign to Pınarbaşı,

Springhead, Mehmet turned down a rough track to draw up by a waterside restaurant.

'The true source of the Meander,' he announced theatrically. Mehmet had delivered me to my proper point of departure, the bonus being that I could now expect to have travelled in his car for the last time. It was an unworthy thought, of course, given the debt I owed the lawyer. The only thing for it was lunch, and on me this time. Mehmet accepted, but with a resigned dip of the shoulders as if my gesture had devalued his hospitality, and him in the process.

He led the way into a crumbling concrete foyer, empty except for a fridge. The fridge shuddered alarmingly, having somehow succumbed, it seemed, to the cold it itself had generated. The appliance had now begun to work its agued way across the floor, shuffling towards the sunlight – it and David Beckham who gazed from the poster taped to the fridge's door. An awning covered a terrace of immaculately laid tables, which protruded into the lake. We were the only guests. Brown nets hung from floating platforms: fisheries, which spared us requesting the menu.

'Trout,' proposed Mehmet, lighting up a cigarette. I looked out, like Beckham, past the reed beds and the buntings to the lake, and remembered the myth that had once taken root along its shores.

This lake the Ancients knew as Aulocrene, or Flute Spring. The reeds harvested there had historically served as mouthpieces of flutes or pipes, a usage supposedly preserved from that uncertain time when men, gods and lesser immortals were forever consorting and colliding with each other across these lands. It was said that the vain Athena, playing by the lake, caught her own reflection there and at the sight of her puffed-up cheeks threw down the pipe in self-disgust. The discarded pipe was found, inevitably, and by one who could not begin to appreciate

the instrument's fatal significance: Marsyas. This satyr, whom
some dismissed as a hirsute, cloven rustic but others revered as
a close consort of Cybele, the Anatolian mother goddess, soon
demonstrated a particular talent for the pipe. In time Marsyas
came to reckon himself a musical match for anybody, even for
the god of music himself. It was a challenge that Apollo, whose
writ ran strong through the Meander Valley, was eager to accept;
and an affront, besides, that the lyre-playing Olympian was not
prepared to tolerate.

So the two went head to head, but not before the stakes had
been signally raised; rather than the celebrity that passes as
reward in our age, the winner in this case was to enjoy the
ultimate freedom, which was to do with the loser as he wished.
To the assembled panel of Muses, mythology's on-call sages,
the contest's special significance was all too apparent. Each
participant played not merely to prove his own musical
supremacy, nor even to establish the inherent pre-eminence of
the tradition – strings or wind – at which he excelled. The
judges' decision would ultimately find between the cultures that
laid claim to this land: the indigenous Anatolian civilisation
represented by Marsyas or the encroaching Hellenism of the
Olympian Apollo.

It was an age-old, even defining, opposition, one that preceded
any Persian interest in the land by centuries. In key elements it
constituted a ritualised retelling of another scrap that had once
taken place on Anatolian soil, albeit on an altogether grander
scale: the Trojan War, with historical footings that were to serve
as the setting for Homer's epic *Iliad*, had first pitched Anatolians
against invading Greeks, an Eastern people against a Western
one, around the twelfth century BC.

From roughly that same time the victorious Greeks had been
extending their influence into Anatolia, securing preferential

advisory appointments in the courts of Eastern potentates, working as physicians or establishing trading interests in ports all along the peninsula's coasts. From the tenth century BC migrants from southern Greece began to colonise the coastlands around the mouth of the Meander – the region they called Ionia. Hellenic colonies were duly established around the coasts – the Black Sea, the Aegean and the Mediterranean – of Anatolia. By the sixth century BC the cities of the Meander Delta, Miletus chief among them, had emerged as the undisputed cradle of Western art and philosophy; the pressing question was how far the West might extend its influence inland into Asia before running into the torpid oriental headwind that traditionally blew there. At the source of the same river a face-off, the original talent contest, was staged to settle the matter.

So beautiful god and bibulous satyr bent to their respective instruments. Their performances proved so impressive that the Muses were unable to reach a verdict; the siege of Troy, it will be remembered, had similarly been heading towards stalemate. The deadlock was broken in this instance when Apollo proposed a deciding round in which each should play his instrument reversed. Marsyas, despite an exceptional ear for music, clearly had no kind of nose for guile; just as the Trojans fell for the Greeks' gift, the wooden horse and its bellyful of concealed warriors, so Marsyas rashly accepted his rival's challenge. He proved unable, of course, to coax notes from the wrong end of his flute; Apollo, all back-handed dexterity, was left to sweep the field. And so to a settling of accounts; the god, not content with bringing his vanquished opponent down a proportionate peg or two, perhaps by condemning the despised piper to a season working the mythical equivalent of the pub circuit, instead had the satyr flayed.

Talent show rejection no doubt hurt; the world had had a

considered look at what was on offer, after all, before it passed. But it was not like flaying; even crucifixion was a written warning by comparison. A preliminary flogging was administered not so much punitively, though it can have been no less painful, but by way of preparatory process, for it was in a tenderised state that the skin was most easily worked. With a forensic clarity Ovid detailed Marsyas's torment:

'As he screams, his skin is stripped off the surface of his body, and he is all one wound: blood flows down on every side, the sinews lie bare, his veins throb and quiver with no skin to cover them; you could count the entrails as they palpitate, and the vitals showing clearly in his breast.'

Flaying was commonly practised across the ancient world. One Persian king had a judge flayed for accepting a bribe from a party in a lawsuit; the king then ordered that his victim's chair should be reupholstered with the skin of the very man who had lately sat in judgement there. The Scythians, a feared race of warlike barbarians, were said to flay the bodies of their defeated enemies. The deities were equally partial to flaying; Athena herself had sanctioned its use on her own father, for attempting to ravish her, and on the monstrous Medusa, for being a gorgon. Corruption, defeat, incestuous violation, hydra-headedness: while the case might be made that all these crimes justified such punishment, the ultimate sanction may seem excessive in such a case of mere musical presumption.

Except that Apollo saw his Dionysian rival's transgression in less forgivable terms; any challenge to the supremacy of the Apollonian lyre, whose seven strings were said to represent the planets over which Apollo ruled, was a threat to the very harmony of the spheres. The ancient writers broadly sympathised with the occupying Olympian's view; to them, Marsyas's grisly fate appeared as a deserving instance of hubris. Certainly, the god meant to make an example of the uppity satyr, suspending his tanned hide from a plane tree by the shores of the lake where the native nymphs, spirits and deities of the land gathered to mourn him. The hide remained on display as late as the fifth century BC, according to Herodotus, though it had by then been rehung more prominently in the centre of Celaenae. Herodotus, of a time in which men and gods, events actual and mythical, were forever slipping between the permeable membrane that divided them, felt no compulsion to question the true provenance of Marsyas's skin. Our rational age, relic wary, would assume it must in fact have been some conspicuous animal pelt, opportunistically press-ganged into serving a myth that had achieved a durable resonance: the triumph of the West.

For Apollo displayed his gory trophy as a raised finger; it was like a hawk hung from a fence post, a deterrent used even today by sheep farmers in rural Turkey, or a highwayman's tarred corpse strung from a roadside gibbet in eighteenth-century France. Marsyas had transgressed, not by thinking too much of his musical abilities but by rating himself with his superiors. His fate warned against Anatolian presumption; it served to remind the people that they should accept subjugation as their natural state; as they had once been subjects of the Persians, they must now bow to their Western overlords. The place of Marsyas's punishment marked the edge of a cultural claim, a hammered stake asserting that Anatolia, at least as far as the Aulocrene Lake, had historically belonged to the West; and even had been Westernised, some would claim, to a degree that no subsequent occupation could quite erase.

So my journey was to begin precisely where the seam between worlds had once run. According to the ancients the West and the East met not along the shoreline of the Aegean and the Bosphorus, as modern geopolitics had it, but where the coastal lands visibly gave way to the steppe. The Meander's source had once marked the end of the West, as our surroundings indicated. For while the floating fisheries to our left told us only what we could expect for lunch, the foundation stones clearly visible in the lake shallows to the right confirmed an ancient frontier.

These footings marked the floor plan of a Roman garrison fort. The fort, known by the lake's corrupted name Aulutrene, guarded the eastern border of the Roman province of Asia; the so-called region, that is, within Asia Minor, as the Romans knew Anatolia, which in turn was contained, like etymological wooden dolls, by the vague but vast continent of Asia. This border the Roman authorities, making good their point, had further confirmed in the first century by raising a monumental column dedicated to the frontier gods in the hills just above the lake. Time was that Roman territories had extended far beyond the column, of course, to Persia, Syria and to Bactria, just as Greek possessions had done under Alexander. Passing the column into wild Pisidia, however, a region renowned for its brigand resistance to outside rule, was to leave the sphere that the Greco-Romans had truly made their own. It was to venture beyond the homelands.

William Ramsay was among the last of those to have witnessed the frontier marker intact, and among those whose conspicuous interest had condemned the 'large inscribed column thrown from its base' by convincing the locals that it must contain concealed treasures, which a few well-aimed blows were sure to expose. The shattered column, with not a hidden cache to show for it, was long gone, like the fort before it, and by what had become a thoroughly Turkish lake the Marsyas myth had also faded.

What continued was the perpetual argument over the identity of Anatolia; a struggle that seemed to derive, even now, from oppositions as fundamental as those that had once consumed Greece and Troy, Greece and Persia, Apollo and Marsyas. European antiquaries once combed the landscape for a classical past; local bureaucrats duly pasted Turkish names across the least such evidence of a classical heritage. The rusting image of Atatürk, the great moderniser, loomed over Dinar, but across that *Ak* stronghold mosques were being newly built and most women wore the headscarves that the leader's supporters desired them to remove. Across the country Islamists and secularists indicted each other. Some Turks dreamed of being enfolded within Europe; others instead cherished hopes for a greater Turkey that might extend its influence across the Muslim world.

We finished our meal, thanked the waiter, who was busy levering the errant fridge back into position, and strolled down to the shore. The water, strewn with lily pads, was still except where it rose a few yards from the fort footings to a restless, braided camber no larger than a manhole. From this underwater spring the Meander slipped into being. Meaning to honour the moment of departure, however makeshift my arrangements, I took from my rucksack the small jar I had emptied only that morning; it still smelled of the evicted garlic tablets. I thrust the jar among the blooming bubbles. The water was cold and pure. I screwed down the lid and returned the jar to a rucksack pocket, theatrically patting down the flap to seal the ritual of departure.

With an expressive twist of his open palm, however, Mehmet indicated in the Turkish way that he had not understood.

'I'm carrying the water to the sea,' I explained, ready to leave, and offered Mehmet a grateful hand, which his own, twisting to signal his continued confusion, was not ready to receive. 'Where are you going?' he asked.

'To Dinar.' Mehmet gestured patiently at his car. It had not occurred to him that I meant to walk; I now understood the remark with which he had greeted me that morning, that I was to encounter no dogs in his car, had been literally meant.

'I'm going to follow the river,' I explained.

'To the sea?'

'To the sea. Today, though, just to Dinar.' Mehmet stared at me.

'You're going to Dinar on foot?' he eventually asked. The man had survived flood and arrest, divorce, alcoholism and earthquake, but the prospect of a four-hour walk apparently floored him. Many Turks proudly claim descent from Anatolia's nomads, the Yörüks, a tribal designation said to derive from the Turkish word for walking; the odd thing was how little they thought of the activity for which their descendants were named. They could argue, I supposed, that their calloused forebears had done quite enough walking to count for all their descendants, for ever. Or that Allah had clearly signalled the walking should cease by providing people with cars. Or that the ambivalence was the damaging consequence of an extreme overexposure to walking, much as miners' descendants might not feel the homely warmth of a coal fire without bitterly recalling the racking coughs of their emphysemic grandfathers.

I was heir to no such feelings; rather, the discomfiting obligation to sit – through a long education, then the daily regime of the writer – had left me fidgeting to leave precisely the same seat that Mehmet cared only to occupy. I could wait no longer. So when my companion again offered a lift, casting a palm in the car's direction, I raised the walking pole to signal that my intention was fixed, though I did fish out my phone and promised to use it in case of the least trouble. Then I set off along the shore of the lake.

Alone, I looked out across the lake where the infant Meander's diluted drift lay lost among the reeds. Kingfishers flitted among the seed heads; the little blue flashes they trailed lingered against the retina, and I felt my spirits lift. The sun was high, and from the lake's marshy fringe a gravel embankment rose into the sky. It carried a railway line, a single track,

which made off in the direction I meant to go. At the outset
of my journey, yet to gain my bearings, I wished only that my
progress be certain; as certain, for instance, as where the Dinar
Railway must lead me. So I climbed the slope and set out
along the tracks, my stride hobbled by the sleepers, as I covered
a first few kilometres to the north-west.

  After some time a raised farm track cut across the line,
heading across the high plain for the boulder-strewn slopes of
Samsun Dağı. I followed it, thinking to pick up the river's progress
beyond the lake. The shoreline proved indistinct; beyond the
open water was a thick ruff of reeds, which gave way, like a
broken hairline, to a few scattered stalks at the fringe of the
grazing land. All along the lake's western edge furrowed streams

seeped from its punctured rim and nudged curling routes across the little that remained of the plain. Where they reached the foot of the hills these streams had formed dark pools. I stood beside one, ten feet across, and I watched the catkins turning in its lazy gyre grow sodden before they followed the flow into the sinkhole, burrowing downwards by unknown channels to emerge at Orgas, Ilıca or one of the other lower springs. The river had gone where I could not follow. So I retraced my steps to the railway line and walked north, past a series of raised concrete irrigation canalettes, past the empty dirt lanes and rough-tiled roofs of Gökceli village, until I came to the station at Karakuyu.

The junction halt stood isolated and incongruously neat. Baskets of flowers hung from the pitched platform roof, and the Victorian-style lanterns were freshly coated in black paint. A moped, aged but cared-for, was parked outside the station-master's office. A harmless dog lay across the doormat. A little way along the line a work gang had broken for tea. They had gathered by a track-side tent, a cone of faded white canvas, where a kettle wheezed on a coal brazier. The men beckoned me to join them. They were dressed in flat caps and stout boots, and wore their sleeves rolled up. They seemed, with their native courtesy and sweat-stained evidence of honest industry, like people from another age. Their foreman, the spit of James Mason, spoke for them, fielding their whispered questions to quiz me on exchange rates, on the retirement age in my country, and on the availability there of procedures to fit prosthetic knees. I was still pondering the knees when Mason spoke again.

'A practical people, the British,' he ventured approvingly. 'They built this railway.' The line, the very first in Turkey, had from the 1850s linked the Aegean port of Smyrna with the city of Aydın along the lower Meander Valley. By shadowing the once-great road to the east, the Meander Valley Railway had wrested from the Turkish camel drivers the lucrative carriage of grapes, figs, opium and all manner of other agricultural goods. The railway's success encouraged its owners to extend the line eastwards, by stages, until in 1889 it followed the lead of the ancient road through the pass at Dinar, to Karakuyu, and on past the source of the Meander. I guessed I would be seeing more of this neat, compact railway, then, in the course of my journey. I commended the workers on their repairs.

'They needed doing,' Mason replied. Not that they reflected, he was quick to assure me, the least discredit on the original British contractors. 'After all,' he conceded, 'the work they did was a long time ago.'

We drank our tea in companionable silence. When I rose to leave, Mason rose with me. He took me by the wrist and raised my hand in the direction of the railway line, touchingly oblivious to the possibility that he might achieve the same effect by pointing there himself. I was to follow the line onwards to Dinar. I thanked Mason and his men, gently freed my hand and set off. The men were returning to work when I looked back, and I noticed now that one walked with a pronounced limp, and I understood the enquiry about artificial knees had not been baseless.

The railway line began a gradual climb towards the smoke-grey limestone heights. Then it suddenly veered straight for the hills, destined to collide, until a tunnel swung into view. At the entrance I knelt and put a precautionary ear to the rail before I passed beneath the mountain. The light faded with every step. The entrance at my back, suspended like a diminishing lamp, was eclipsed and finally extinguished by the tunnel's curvature. The dark was total; what light this place had ever known – from the lanterns of the tunnel's one-time diggers or from the

windows of passing trains – was either old or occasional. It was
a darkness to set the mind adrift. I thought of the river's own
progress, spilling blind down the passages it had itself made,
immeasurably gradual digger of its own tunnels. I surfaced,
dislocated, from the darkness. I blinked in the sunlight and
scanned the landscape to establish my path, finally recognising
a distinctive shape on the skyline; it was the rusted reverse of
the Atatürk outline. I descended through orchards to the one
lower spring I had not yet visited, which Mehmet had pointed
out that same morning: Suçıkan, which the Ancients had known
as Marsyas.

For it was from the tears of the flayed satyr's mourners that
the same waters that had overrun the boyhood home of my
lunch partner were said to have sprung. The spring was set in
a wooded park where ancient inscribed marbles had been
displayed; here I came across a young couple dissolving their
relationship in a hail of insults. I backed away, taking refuge in
the pleasant tea garden where a sign above the entrance quoted
Arif Nihat Asya. 'Friends,' the Turkish poet declaimed, 'it would
be remiss not to tell that I saw at Dinar the very birthplace of
the Meander.'

I knew otherwise, of course, but Asya's twentieth-century
rhetoric echoed an assumption local people had long shared; it
was from this watered grotto at the foot of a romantic crag,
according to popular belief, that the Meander issued into being.
The setting of Suçıkan was more persuasively attractive than
that of upstream Pınarbaşı; another certainty was that it had
always been more accessible, given that here had stood 'the very
market-place of Celaenae'. The lower spring's urban location,
all things considered, constituted a more suitable setting for the
display of that talismanic hide – and its relocation appeared to
have caused the entire myth to up sticks and move to Suçıkan,

even to the point of the Meander's primary source being repositioned there.

In reality, of course, rivers rarely rose in such suggestively attractive spots; they rather more typically seeped from nondescript bogs high in the watershed. Rivers were born plain, without fanfare, which did nothing for the claims, however widely held, of pointedly good-looking locations like Suçıkan – and for that matter Pınarbaşı. For if the tale of a local peasant was to be believed, a third source for the Meander merited consideration.

The tale in question was told in 1929. It supposedly related to events that had taken place some twenty years earlier (but had no doubt related to twenty-year-old events, that safely remote time lapse, all through the history of its telling). Once, let's say, a shepherd was digging at Dereköy village some fifteen kilometres east of Pınarbaşı when he came upon an underground spring. The shepherd was curious to learn where the freshly revealed spring emerged. Into the water he dropped the object that happened to be at hand, which was his music pipe. An encampment of Yörüks duly chanced upon the pipe in the lake shallows at Pınarbaşı. If the tale's narrative purpose was to confirm the lake's ancient association with flutes, then it was not without interesting incidental implications: that modern Anatolians seemed as ready to discard their flutes as Marsyas had been eager to pick his up, certainly, but also that the Meander might have its true beginnings on some drear upland known only to a local shepherd.

Not that Dinar's townfolk were about to acknowledge these prosaic geographical realities; what was there, besides, in the way of tea rooms that could possibly merit the slog out to rustic Dereköy? And how could the views there compare with those at Suçıkan, especially given the topographical improvements the

locals had carried out? For barely had the waters bubbled out
of the grotto when a rusted pump diverted them to the top of
the crag to create a cascade. The effect was picturesque even if
the artificially assisted flow did happen to fall directly beneath
Atatürk so that the great leader appeared to be doing nothing
so much as taking a torrential leak. The waters, having apparently passed through the Father of Turkey, then collected in an
ornamental pond where tethered rowing boats bobbed. Fishermen
dangled home-made rods from a wooden footbridge. This
harmonious scene was disturbed by the appearance of the girl
who had evidently failed to resolve her argument with the young
man; tearfully wresting the ring off her finger, she flung it into
the water and ran out of the park. Two men in freshly pressed
shirts, arms linked, lowered their heads at her passing. I recognised the men from the hotel; we had watched *Wolves' Valley*
together the previous evening. We traded distressed winces and
the handful of freshly picked green almonds that they placed
on my table seemed like a gesture of universal conciliation. I
drank the tea and ate the almonds, soft furry shells and all, then
I began my descent down the Marsyas.

It was a stream which had enjoyed a long reputation, quite
unlike the river it was soon to join, for energy and spirit.
Herodotus knew the Marsyas as the 'Cataract'; it was,
according to Ovid, 'the clearest river in all Phrygia'. An
antiquary on a visit in 1887 described the stream emerging
'at the foot of a precipitous cliff, from a dark hole . . . and
flowing through a narrow wooded glen, to presently dash
down a steep slope through the modern town of Dineir'. By
the spring of 2008, however, it resembled no such thing.

Beyond the boating pond, where a portrait of Donald Duck
adorned a sun-bleached slide in an abandoned playground, the
stream disappeared without ceremony down a metal sluice. On

the far side of an empty municipal swimming pool it resurfaced but briefly, like a gasping gangland victim invited to talk, before a gully dragged it through a hole in the block-built shed wall of an adjacent fish farm. The Marsyas emerged, fouled with fish shit, to drain into a steep-sided concrete ditch, which ran beside the road. At a shop selling canned drinks, cigarettes and disposable razor blades, approximately where Mehmet's childhood home must once have stood, it ducked beneath the road. On the far side it resurfaced to run beneath the concrete span of a miniature Italianate bridge in the gardens of the Pines Pavilion Café. An open culvert frogmarched the stream along the rear of some empty shops before forcing it underground opposite the petrol station. It reappeared as an open ditch, which ran across a patch of waste ground until another ditch, concrete-lined, arrived from the left. There the combined waters of four other springs, the Orgas, Incirli, Düden and Ilıca, joined with the Marsyas. So these united tributaries were lost in the river, which here bore the name it would carry to the sea; I found myself by the banks of the true Meander. So I might have expected more of the moment than the green beer bottles, tins and discarded CDs that were strewn across the shallow river bed. Nothing remained of the Persian palaces and the hunting parks. Modern times meant a tough infancy for the Meander.

Mehmet appeared relieved to learn that I had survived the walk to Dinar. He insisted on buying me dinner. Over another plate of fish the conversation ranged across the long history of Mehmet's home town before settling upon a single event that had occurred here in the second century BC. About 160 years, that is, after Alexander the Great had passed through on his way to subduing all Asia, another arrival had taken place at the city gates, though this time it was not a passing army but a column of carts and footsore civilians, some 2,000 Jews, who had been relocated to Apamea from their homes in distant Babylon. The reigning Seleucids, dynastic successors to Alexander the Great, rated the Jews for their civic reliability; at this time of particular instability their presence in Apamea was intended to have a moderating effect on the regional tendency, especially among the neighbouring Pisidians, to rebellion.

This ancient displacement interested me. It instanced, for one thing, a theme of Anatolian history that recurred with an institutionalised regularity: all through their history the inhabitants had been subjected to forcible resettlement. Those who controlled and administered the contested peninsula – the kings and satraps, emperors and governors, sultans and emirs – habitually shifted and shuffled the population packs under their control. With no regard for the regional attachments of their subjects, but with a close eye on their own security and prosperity, they regularly transplanted communities so as to dilute insurrectionist instincts, to bolster depopulated frontier regions, or to improve thin soils by reassigning industrious agricultural communities there.

In the Meander Valley especially, where new arrivals originated from elsewhere in Anatolia but also from further afield, ragged communities had been raising walls among new ways, among unfamiliar languages, dialects and soils since Herodotus recorded how the Paeonians, a people of Macedonia, had some 2,500 years ago been forcibly settled 'in a Phrygian territory and village by themselves'. Some settlers received attractive inducements; the veteran soldiers of successful campaigns were encouraged to make comfortable lives in the lands they had helped to subdue. The authorities in Apamea sweetened the exile of the 2,000 Babylonian Jews by offering them prime housing plots and productive land for their crops and vines.

Others came, however, as prisoners of war; in the fourth century gangs of captive Goths were dispatched to Phrygia and compelled to toil until their Byzantine masters required them for military service. There were mass transportations of captured Slavs to the region during the seventh century. In the twelfth century, as the Byzantine authorities settled Serbians, Hungarians and Petchenegs in imperial lands, newly established Turkish emirs busily abducted Christian families from the protection of rival warlords and dispatched them to areas under their own command. It was a practice that continued in recent centuries; eighteenth-century travellers to Anatolia regularly stumbled across picturesque communities of Cossacks and 'Old Believers', ultra-orthodox religious sects, whom the Ottomans had taken prisoner in the course of successive wars with neighbouring Russia. Mehmet, himself the grandson of refugees from Bosnia, was living evidence that the same process that had brought all manner of formerly scattered peoples to the headwaters of the Meander continued to shape the population across this land.

As for the 2,000 Jews, the new community settled well in Apamea. It helped that they were able to furnish their new home with the old myths they had transported there; a chief claim emerged that the Ark of Noah had come to rest not on distant Mount Ararat but in the very hills that rose above the Jews' adopted city. Perhaps the frequency of the floods, the same floods Mehmet was to experience during his childhood, helped to establish the story. It certainly flourished; Apamea came to be known by the common epithet Cibotus – Apamea of the Ark – and several coins issued during the third century commemorated the association.

It must be admitted, however, that my particular interest in this ancient story was hardly historical. The truth was that an ark, even a mythical one, constituted a big improvement on the dinghies I had seen on the Suçıkan pond; as a grander precedent, that is, for my own boating ambitions.

'Your own what?' asked Mehmet, twisting his palm. He did not speak until I had finished.

'You've a boat in a bag?' Mehmet eventually asked. 'Which you're going to paddle down the river?'

CHAPTER FIVE

T he bag was at the hotel. It was heavy, but not for what it contained. From the moment I had first stumbled upon the Meander I knew that the only way to tackle the river was by being *on* it; there a man might surrender to the windings, pit himself against the currents and so get closer to the truth of things, all the while putting himself beyond the reach of the local *kangals*.

The boat, which I had bought in England, suggested a convenience as high-tech and portable as a folding bike. The collapsible craft, to give it another name, actually had established expeditionary antecedents; canvas kayaks had served in the Second World War, and the *Lady Alice*, the transport that had carried Henry Morton Stanley down the Congo a century earlier still, had likewise broken down into transportable sections. The Victorian explorer was on a considerably bigger river, of course, and where he had hundreds of native porters at his command, I currently relied on the bemused goodwill of a Turkish lawyer. The sections of Stanley's boat, so much bigger than the component parts in my bag, built up into a forty-foot steamboat; mine was a one-man canoe weighing just eleven kilos. It was hard to believe that there could be sufficient room for my luggage, little that there was of it, though the more immediate worry was not so much fitting into the canoe as fitting the canoe into the Meander.

For Dinar's ditches had been troubling me from the moment I first encountered them. It was not possible to believe that anything could ever come of their sorry litter-strewn flows and brutal lines. Industrialisation appeared to have done for the historic river that I had discovered in my researches and even now imagined it to be: the river that Cyrus's forces on their way to Celaenae had once crossed by a prototype pontoon bridge almost 200 feet wide; that a nineteenth-century visitor, alive to his readers' reference points, had compared to the Moselle, or to the Forth at Stirling; and that numerous ferry crossings were still serving in the mid-twentieth century. While it might be argued that the Meander must be given time to grow, the complaint stood that it might by now have provided for a canoe at home on the most modest trout stream. So much, then, for the departure that might have been, Trueheroes, Darkeyes and *Wolves' Valley* watchers all wishing me well as I paddled out of town. The only thing for it was to walk on until the river grew big enough to accommodate the canoe.

Turgay Darkeye was sorry to see me leave. 'We love you,' he declared. I appreciated the sentiment, supposing that Turgay spoke for the wider hotel crowd, but it was the parting gift, a box of baklava tied with a pink ribbon, which touched me. I liked baklava, and I liked Turgay Darkeye, the more so for having made me his pastries proxy. Those that ill health barred from such sweet pleasures often tended to begrudge them to others. Diabetes, though it had put him on a parsley diet, had in no way embittered Turgay. It would be a privilege to honour his generosity by eating the baklava, but later, when I might also be able to congratulate myself on successfully negotiating a first stretch of water. I embraced Turgay and set off into the bright morning.

I rejoined the Meander at the confluence of its feeder streams, where I had left it the previous evening, and followed the ditch through Dinar's nondescript outskirts. I passed close to the train station, traversed an empty market area and reached the edge of the town. Here a prison stood by the banks of the Meander.

Turkey has an unenviable reputation when it comes to prisons. The encounter might then have been suggestive, substantiating my fears by confirming the Meander's poor start in life; the tough infancy having apparently led to an inevitable first spell inside. It might, less fancifully, have added up to a tableau so depressing – nick, ditch, concrete, rubbish – as to have stopped me in my tracks.

Except that this prison bordered on the picturesque, its features apparently lifted from black-and-white breakout movies: a single guard in a tin helmet surveying a square compound from a whitewashed watchtower with pointy overhanging roof; a washing line hung with what I took to be inmates' smalls; high wire-topped walls, in the way of a proper jail, but with a gate so oversized it might have been the entrance to a giant's castle; a dinky visitors' waiting room for doting mothers; and, against the outside perimeter wall, an outdoor basin with a mirror hung above it.

The basin felt like the telling detail, indicative, whatever sorry episodes might have taken place inside, of what Turkish society demanded above all else of those released from prison; a certain level of personal hygiene. Turks traditionally put a high value on cleanliness, as their ritual ablutions prior to prayer, their extensive patronage of *hamams* (steam baths), and their prime-time adverts for genital wipes amply confirmed. The thought reminded me that I was a comparative scruff, with every chance of becoming a superlative one during the off-road weeks ahead. I had washed that morning. What I did not know was where I would wash that night. From now, since I could only guess at the next tap, I would do well to use facilities whenever they appeared, starting with the prison basin. I made a point of washing my face there before making my way, free and freshly presentable, out of Dinar.

The river had barely passed the prison when it too went free, slipping from the concrete ditch to run between root-veined banks of earth. For a moment, conditioned by captivity to its linear lot, it held course; then it remembered its name and the freedoms it had known above Suçıkan, and at last it began to deviate, throwing loops, which grew full and fat. Beyond the river, lines of spring wheat shoots unfurled in the sunshine. Shawled women, rears to the sky, bent with their mattocks to weed around spinach seedlings. Willow trees rose along the banks. Coots scuttled across the clear stream, and the wing strokes of rising herons sounded like beaten carpets beyond the trees. Turtles basked on the banks, ditching inelegantly at my approach. Fish showed distinct in the sunlit shallows. It was beautiful but for the last rafts of town rubbish – plastic bottles, aerosol cans, margarine containers and discoloured polystyrene chunks – which had gathered behind the scummy booms of fallen branches.

The river began to fill out, but even as my canoe worries were dispelled, fresh concerns took their place. The arable lands had given way to pasture where fresh droppings signalled sheep – and warned of the dogs that commonly attended them. I gripped my walking pole and hurried on until I reached the relative security of a low bridge where a lane ran. Beyond the bridge the river formed a basin with gently shelving banks, which I immediately knew to be the place. I took out my mobile phone. 'I've found the launch site,' I told Mehmet.

The previous evening had proved a challenging one for Mehmet; he had barely come to terms with my walking before he learned that I was to take to a boat, and while walking was merely unnecessary, cars having made it so, boating was positively outlandish. The people of Turkey have never been notable sailors; the Ottoman Navy, though it might have had its moments, was mostly manned by subject peoples of traditional seafaring lands, Greeks especially. Nor did the Meander, as we have seen, boast much in the way of boats: one legendary ark and some rowing boats, unsubstantiated rumours of marble-bearing rafts, a few cable ferries and the odd fish farmer's dinghy did not constitute a rich, river-going history. Mehmet might have tried to dissuade me but for the discovery that my luggage contained a boat; he was enough of a realist to accept that people who packed boats in their luggage probably meant to use them. It was to his credit that we were yet to finish our fish dinner before he had worked out how he might be useful. 'You find your launch site and I'll deliver the boat,' he had proposed, thereby offering the use of his car without me having to go in it.

When he drew up at the bridge some time later, he was with a friend. Adnan was from the *Dinar News*.

'Your ark,' said Mehmet cheerfully. He hauled the boat off the back seat. I unzipped the bag and tipped its contents onto the grass. The canoe comprised a skin, or hull, of red rubberised fabric. Lightweight metal rods, in elastically connected sections, constituted the craft's basic frame. The bag also contained cross ribs, inflatable tubes and seat, air pump, spray deck and paddle.

'What are you doing?' demanded the portly Adnan. I had expected journalistic inquiry; but the tone from the *Dinar News* sounded more like censure. Mehmet might have left his own reservations behind but had apparently brought backup in this regard. I got the strong impression that a literal answer was not what the newsman wanted; rather than describe the assembly process, detailing how the rods fitted together to provide the canoe with its keel and gunwales, I was instead to justify a project Adnan clearly considered ill-advised. I took the romantic line, explaining that I had not thought beyond following the river to the sea. Adnan looked along my gesturing arm but saw nothing at the end of it to satisfy him.

'Why are you travelling without a friend?' he specified. I clipped the inner cross ribs to the frame, which served to stress the canoe, and considered my answer. I had myself wondered whether it was recklessly dangerous to make the journey alone; but Adnan's objection, I suspected, was rather that it was unnatural to forsake the companionship essential to any enterprise. I liked travelling alone, I replied, though the truth was I suspected my expeditionary tastes were sufficiently obscure to have deterred all potential companions.

A craft of sorts was now taking shape. I fitted the support struts. Then I inflated the air tubes, which lay between the frame and the skin, further stressing the structure and providing buoyancy. The thing had begun to resemble a canoe.

'Do you know how to use it?' queried Adnan. I had done some canoeing, I replied, which was true, but my diffidence only encouraged Adnan to prod the other gaping holes he had detected in my plan.

'Where will you sleep?' I explained that I was depending on the Turkish reputation for hospitality to find lodging in the villages.

'They will not be expecting you. They have not seen canoes on this river. They have never seen tourists on this river.'

'Then I can sleep by the bank,' I replied, patting my sleeping bag; I could think of worse predicaments than spending the odd spring night under the Anatolian stars. I inflated the canoe's seat before beginning to stow my luggage. Bags, rucksack and air pump went into the limited space astern, while the walking pole and the dry bag, in which the mobile and other valuables were stored, went forward. I squashed my boots into the bow, lashed the laces to the frame and snapped together the tubular sections of my paddle.

'And what will you do,' Adnan asked, 'about lunch?' There was nothing like lunch uncertainty, it seemed, to endanger a man on the Meander, and this from one who had clearly missed very few of them in recent years.

'Which reminds me,' said Mehmet. He scurried back to the car to return with Turgay Darkeye's baklava. I wedged the elegant box, tied in a pink bow, as best I could against the rucksack. The effect was less than expeditionary. I embraced Mehmet.

'You must call tonight,' he said, containing his own concerns within a single instruction. I promised to do so, clambered into the canoe and pushed off. I was on the Meander.

I had not owned the canoe for long. Its maiden launch had taken place near my home a few weeks earlier. On that English river I had learned that the craft's lightness, a vital asset when it came to the portages I expected to make, had been traded at a price; the canoe was unstable. The manufacturers assured me that I would get used to the thing with practice; I now regretted that lack of familiarity as I moved with the exaggerated wobble of a tightrope clown out onto the narrow stream. It reassured me that I had seen enough of the river, with its shallow gradient, to feel confident of a forgiving introduction. The Meander was sure, now of all times, to stay true to its name.

It did no such thing. Around the very next bend there appeared a different river. A sudden fall in the land's lie, though it was imperceptible, caused the river's languid curves to tighten into bends. The surface of the water was embroidered with sudden ruffles and swirls. Fallen branches littered the channel. I cursed myself for not having made a precautionary foray. If I had checked

the river for another hundred metres beyond the bridge, I would
have known. But I'd been watching the river since Dinar. And
beyond every such hundred-metre stretch another one awaited,
and another, onwards until the current slackened and the water
turned to salt. Much was to be learned, no doubt, from quizzing
the locals and from checking the available maps, but the time
always came when there was nothing but to go with the river. To
trust the river at one's back for the one that lay ahead.

This, though, was not that time. On this occasion I should
have walked for another hundred metres.

I was still settling into the canoe, finding my balance, when
I felt the narrowing river gather pace beneath me. I sensed a
momentum not my own. I was being led. I looked ahead as a
sharp left turn swung into view. Water broke white over a fallen
branch. I was on the bend in no time. I dug in my paddle astern,
looking to swing the bow round, but the canoe's right flank soon
rose where the water heaped up on the branch. The canoe tipped
onto its side and threw me into the waist-deep stream. The
water was cold. I clambered to my feet. I dragged the canoe to
the bank. I emptied it of water. I climbed back in and went at
the next corner, which I cleared, and the one beyond it too, only
for the next one, in the way of next ones, to arrive. A fallen tree
lay across the river, forcing the flow through a narrow chute
where a protruding branch prevented passage. I reverse paddled
to avoid the chute and went broadside against the submerged
tree. The canoe flipped. I came up spluttering, grabbed my
paddle and the canoe's painter rope, and staggered towards the
bank. Something pink caught my eye; Turgay Darkeye's box of
baklava disappeared down the chute.

I dragged the waterlogged canoe up the bank and overturned
it in a field of young wheat. Adnan had been right. I had thought
too much of my own abilities and not enough of my opponent.

What had I thought by taking a river's ancient name as surety? I had barely started before getting soaked and shocked. And I had lost my baklava.

It was then that I became aware of the snake, a benign creature that spilled its liquid green coils through the wheat shoots at my feet. The snake sensed my presence and froze, not so much to immobility as inanimacy, its raised head an iridescent circlet. I watched the snake; it was some time before it continued towards the river, as it had intended. The creature had disappeared by the time I followed its lead back to the bank.

I walked downstream, searching for somewhere to attempt another launch. Beyond a pair of fields I came upon a clear stretch of low-lying bank. I returned to the canoe, unpacked my sodden luggage and transferred it to the launch site. I went back for the canoe. I repacked the canoe. I put myself back on the river. I pushed off, adrenalised, and clattered down a long ramp of little corrugated waves. The banks of earth and roots rose high, the sunlight strobing through the long grass. I slalomed down a gully to a bend that turned more sharply than I could. My bow slammed into the bank and I stretched to take hold of a passing tree root so that the current did not catch me and spin me round, blind to the river at my back.

There were other such bends. And fallen willows. What riverside willows did, I learned that day, was fall. On occasion, where the banks were high, I was able to find a way beneath the trunk, forcing a route through the foliage to emerge caked in web and leaf, and the dusty, fluff-tufted bracts of catkins. Elsewhere, when the blockage was total, there was nothing for it but to clamber up the bank before working my way back to the water, all the time dragging the laden canoe behind me. The hauling proved exhausting. Once, looking over my shoulder, the boot soles that protruded from the canoe's bow caused me to imagine that they

contained the feet of some stretchered person, and as they were
my boots it was natural I should have begun to think that the
stretcher was for me and that I would not get down the river.

I fought the exhausting river for a long time. Then the current
began to slacken as suddenly as it had run, and over the quietening
water I again heard the chatter of sparrows and the splash of
turtles. The relief was complete. I loosened my grip on the paddle,
flexed sore palms, and looked about me. The woven spheres of
weaver birds' nests hung from overhanging branches. In the late
light seeds had patterned the water's still surface. A lone boy, his
face stippled in shadow, watched me from the bank. I had passed
before he offered the gnomic encouragement that I was heading
in the right direction. The banks had begun to lose their height.
The river yawed gently left before spilling into a still lake, which
the low sun had slicked with gold. Geese flew black against the
mountains. I paddled across Gökgöl, or Sky Lake, past a few
scattered fishery platforms towards the village on the north shore.

Fairy lights twinkled in the trees close to the water's edge, and beyond the insects that played in their vague penumbra could be seen a few tethered dinghies stuck with roughly stowed oars. Among them was a yellow pedalo. It had twin bows, each bearing a wave-cresting dolphin, and flicked tails for sterns.

Outside a concrete building a man with a bull neck, hands on hips, watched me put ashore. The man told me that I had arrived at a *pansiyon*, with a *restoran*. He led me upstairs, and along a corridor lit by unshaded bulbs, to a room that the man made mine by plugging his fingers into the necks of some empty beer bottles and tipping a butt-filled ashtray out of the window. I did not think much of the place, nor of the effort that had gone into readying it for me. It was only when I found a mirror that I thought even less of myself. I was caked with drying mud. There were weed smears, and bits of twig all over my T-shirt. One ear was draped with a spider's web and many catkins had snagged in my hair in the manner of miniature rollers.

I showered, washed my clothes and hung them out to dry. I went downstairs to eat. In the vast dining hall tables stretched to infinity. An extravagant plastic flower feature, which might have adorned the shrine of an Iranian martyr, rose from the middle of the hall. A pall of cigarette smoke engulfed the only other guests, six men in suits arranged around a bottle of *rakı*. Maddened insects flung themselves at the harsh bare lights. The owner brought me a plate of fried fish. He laid it before me, helping himself to a chip as he did so. I sensed not boorishness but deliberate insult.

This was behaviour that the antiquary David Hogarth, who travelled extensively through this region in the late nineteenth century, would have recognised. Hogarth stressed the importance of travelling 'with a certain train of pack-animals and attendants; the Englishman who, proud of his power of endurance, discards all superfluities and travels with what he can carry on his own horse excites no admiration but much contempt in the minds of the villagers. "This is a poor man," say they, and he is shown only just as much of what he wishes to see as will silence his importunity.' The *pansiyon*'s owner had taken exception to an approach he considered not original but aberrant. Gökgöl did not do canoes and river filth. If it was respect I wanted, I should have turned up tidy, in a hire car or, better still, a tour party.

I ate the fish and remaining chips, and stepped into the night. The lake was skeined in moonlight; from the far shore there came the distant honk of geese. The canoe lay in a deflated muddy puddle. I dragged it under cover. Then I kept my promise to call Mehmet.

'You made it?' he said. 'We saw you get wet at the first bend. But we thought it was best to let you get on with it.' I told him I had arrived in one piece.

'Good,' he said. 'We'll be with you in the morning. With a television crew.'

CHAPTER SIX

I was sore the next morning, shaken even, and made myself the waking promise that I would find out what lay ahead before having anything more to do with the Meander. People were commonly lost, after all, in Anatolian rivers; the German emperor Frederick Barbarossa had drowned leading his Crusader armies across the Calycadnus River, the modern Göksu, in 1190. While I could take comfort from the relative risks we seemed to represent – the emperor's horse, its rider weighed down in armour, had none of the buoyancy benefits of a canoe – it nevertheless paid to take care.

So I turned to the maps; I had packed several, largely because no single map among all those I tracked down had struck me as in the least reliable. The theory was that the maps might prove unreliable in their own ways, but with a corresponding range of virtues, so that the whole sheaf, consulted in combination, might just help me find my way. Once they had dried out from the soakings, that is, they had received in yesterday's capsizings. I had the previous evening hung them out along the aerial cable that ran from the back of the TV to the window of my room. From that makeshift laundry line I collected them, crinkly now, and unfolded the one the Turkish military had published.

The map should not have been in my possession. Its unauthorised use was illegal. The more pressing drawback was that it dated from 1944. For all its archival interest

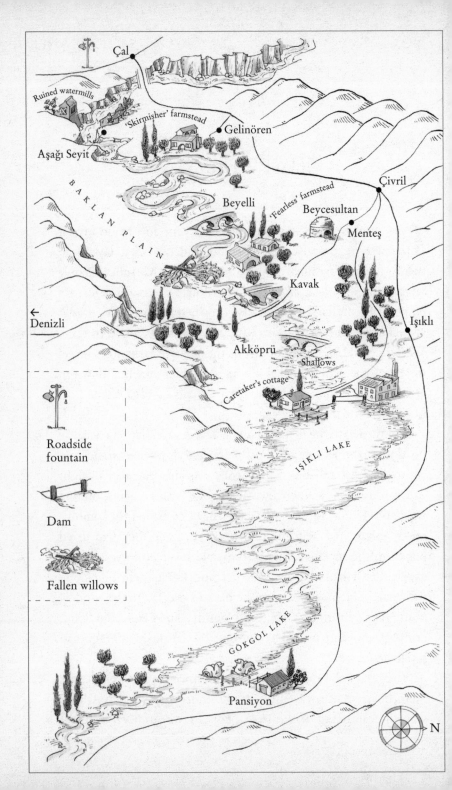

– confirming, for example, that the village of Pınarlı had indeed once been known as Norgas – the map was patently unable to help with any obstructions or dangers that might have appeared on the landscape since the Second World War. The map's great asset, that said, was a scale far larger than anything offered by the competition; at two kilometres to the centimetre, it was sure to provide useful detail, even if much of it might be historical.

According to the military map – once, that is to say, and possibly still – the waters along this stretch of the Meander resembled a pair of lifters' weights, cartoon-like in their unequal sizes, and attached by the stretch of river that ran between them; beyond little Gökgöl the river briefly re-formed before draining into another, larger lake, Işıklı Gölü, whose extent was represented by a wide ruff of marshy tussocks. My practical objective that day was to find my way across the two lakes and in each case pick up the river where it continued beyond their indistinct fringes. To cross-reference the military map with something more recent I returned to the sheaf and selected the pages I had photocopied from a Turkish road atlas, wondering, as I did so, if any motorist had ever unfurled a sea chart across his steering wheel.

Turkish maps were not up to much. They never had been, to judge by one nineteenth-century antiquary, who had found them 'incorrect in the highest degree; in fact, absolutely useless'. My own hunch was that a correlation might exist between the quality of available maps and the historical incidence of invasion across the region they purported to cover. Such a correspondence was liable to throw up all manner of insights into the local insecurities, particularly in the case of much-trampled Anatolia. William Leake, reflecting upon his travels of 1800, recognised that experience had taught the Turks

to view foreigners as thieves, not only, as we have seen, of the
land's ancient artefacts but even of the land itself, maintaining
that the inhabitants were unable to 'imagine any other motive
for our visits to that country, than a preparation for hostile
invasion, or a search after treasures among the ruins of
antiquity'. Anatolia had been subjected, after all, to invasions
by Persians and Macedonians, Romans and Avars, Gauls and
Goths, Arabs and Slavs, Mongols and Tartars, Franks and
Mamelukes, Russians and Bulgars, the British and the Anzacs,
French and Italians, not forgetting the Turks themselves and,
most recently, the Greeks whose invading forces had advanced
from Smyrna up the Meander Valley in 1919. It was therefore
no surprise that the authorities should have come to view those
who sought to know Anatolia's topography with particular
suspicion, and to assume that it was the land itself that the
paymasters of these inquiring individuals – spies, in short –
were after. Maps were weapons, then, no less than armaments.
The army had always made the best maps in Turkey. And it
meant to keep them for itself.

Enter the road atlas, a large-scale, mass-market and informative innovation, which threatened to lay bare every last secret
of Turkey's topography. Except that very little, as I was quickly
discovering, could actually be learned from the Turkish product;
at least in terms of relating the roads, which it covered tolerably
well, to the surrounding landscape. I was quick to notice conspicuous errors in the road atlas's coverage; the railway where James
Mason's gang at Karakuyu had served me tea, and quizzed me
on prosthetic knees, was represented as running round the wrong
side of the Aulocrene Lake, while the Meander was placed on
the wrong side of the road that ran between Dinar and the
village at Gökgöl.

All of which I might have put down to cartographical

inexperience or under-resourcing if it had not been for the military map, and its assertion, even now, that the landscape was not mine to know. Blame *Wolves' Valley* perhaps, but I found myself imagining some clandestine agency of the deep state charged with ensuring that road atlas publishers incorporated in their product a degree of deliberate inaccuracy. Not in their coverage of the actual roads – which was too much to expect, even in the interests of national security – but at least in the bits of cartography that might be accounted of minimal interest to road users; hills and pastures, say, since nobody but shepherds went there, rivers and railways too, and perhaps such strategic installations as power stations, if only because people who bought road atlases for their proper purpose had no business being interested in such things. So it was that a topographical blackout, partial but permanent, awaited the next wave of invaders, wherever they might come from, even if in the meantime it inconvenienced those, canoeists included, whose only design on Turkey's sovereign territory was to pass through it more safely than Frederick Barbarossa.

Beyond the roads, then, I was not to trust the road atlas, even if in this instance it broadly agreed with the military map; two lakes, linked by a short stretch of river, lay ahead. The second lake appeared as much as ten kilometres across, with an unbroken expanse of open water beyond a marshy rim. I had little confidence, however, that this lake might not prove to be an unnavigable swamp. Or a drained expanse of farmland or orchard, the river traversing it by a concrete culvert. Or off-limits in some way that I could not even imagine. I decided to ask the fishermen.

I found a pair of them by the waterfront, scooping up farmed fish with hand nets and tossing them with practised ease back into various pens. It soon became clear, however, that they had put such effort into the acquisition of their fish-sizing skills that they had learned nothing of the river beyond Gökgöl. I tried my luck with another fisherman who was wandering the *pansiyon* grounds in waders, touting a brace of freshly caught, fearsome-looking fish. When I showed interest in the creatures, thinking it might assist my search for directions, the fisherman told me that they were known in the village as *turna*, more generally as the literal *dişli balık*, or teeth fish, and were excellent eating, even at breakfast, and hardly expensive, at least not for me. It turned out, however, that he knew no more than his colleagues of the river's onward route. Beyond Gökgöl the Meander might spill off the edge of the world for all these fishermen cared. The lake was merely their workplace; their travelling they did by the local roads – to Dinar and Burdur, Afyon and Denizli, Işıklı and Çivril – which they could describe with complete reliability. What I heard from the fishermen was the same advice, in short, on offer from the road map, and from Adnan and Mehmet before it; mine was not the way to go.

I retired to the restaurant to consider my position. I breakfasted there not on the local piranha but on bread and olives, and a pan of fried eggs whose yolks had formed a triangle of spheres, perfectly symmetrical, in their unified whites. It was still early, when the hotel man's disdain for his maverick guest seemed half-stoked, even conciliatory, and I felt bold enough to ask him about the way ahead. The man took a biro from his top pocket and began to draw on the greaseproof paper that covered the table, helping himself to an olive as he did so. It was a predictably bad map, but the same cartoon weights could be made out in it; little Gökgöl was connected by a short stretch of the Meander to Işıklı Lake. This appeared to be no more informative than the two printed maps until I noticed that the larger weight, Işıklı, had a decidedly flat end, which the man, lifting another olive, emphasised in bold.

'*Baraj*,' he said emphatically; dam. The post-war landscape had indeed acquired an addition of strategic value – as I might have surmised by the road map's failure to include it – and of relevance to my journey. Beyond this dam, which the man said was easy to spot, the Meander continued westwards – at least when its flow was permitted to do so. The very fact of this first dam, and its intimations of industrial interference, might have registered more alarmingly if I had not simply been content to have found a visible landmark to aim for. I had now got a plan for the day. So I thanked the man, who had just put the printed maps to shame, by offering him the last of my olives.

I was running an eye over the canoe, relieved that it appeared no worse for the battering it had suffered the previous day, when Mehmet and Adnan rolled up at the head of the promised press convoy.

Mehmet emerged from his car unshaven, in sunglasses and an open-necked shirt; it was a dramatic makeover suggestive of a multi-media impresario. As he approached, he threw a thumb over his shoulder at the television van. 'From Afyon,' he declared with the easy poise of one whose influence now extended north across the highlands of Phrygia to Opium, as the provincial capital's name translated, whence he could summon not merely free-sheet hacks like Adnan but fully equipped film crews.

The crew consisted of a middle-aged director, who did his own filming, and a female assistant. This young woman sported an uneven fringe of brown hair and a slight, oddly affecting stoop. But the director, rolling his eyes in frustration, was quick to advertise his immunity to her allure.

'The stills camera,' he snapped. 'You were supposed to bring the stills camera.' With a theatrical flourish he folded his arms and watched his wayward charge make for the van, as if only his close scrutiny would prevent her from falling into the lake, forgetting where she had been sent or returning with the wrong camera. It was a long walk back to the van; long enough that the director

might have punctuated his vigil by making a public acknowledgement of the girl's shortcomings with an indulgent shrug, a
knowing wink, or even some derisive utterance, confirming a
meaner streak in his character. He did no such thing but continued
to watch the girl intently until the rest of us transferred our
attentions, one by one, from the girl to the watching director. As
the impatience drained from his posture and the lines of his face
lost themselves to reverie, it was clear to all of us that the man
was in the grip of something more disabling than a professional
dissatisfaction. By the time the girl drew near, the correct camera
slung across that canted shoulder, he had slipped involuntarily
into some whispered song. Only as the girl arrived among us did
he break the trance and remember who he was supposed to be.

'I shouldn't have to remind you,' he told her. So we set about
making our item for a regional news programme. The director
filmed as I prepared the canoe for the water. I was inflating the tubes
when the girl's shadow briefly fell across the director's shot. 'Stay
right beside me,' he scolded her, but not one of us heard his words
as a cinematographic instruction. The man was in thrall to emotions
that no show of professional irritation could conceal. They came
off him in crackling waves, coursing through the air with an energy
so palpable as to rouse the dogs who shook the strange sensation
from their dozy heads, and the fishermen flexed their fingers, casting
glances skywards to check for thunderheads among the clouds. The
feeling was so all-consuming it was impossible to believe the film
would not convey it; the TV audiences in distant Opium must know
that the foreign canoeist who thought it something to paddle down
the Meander had merely been the sideshow that morning at Gökgöl.

The director declared that he was done except for the footage
he wanted of my departure. He sent the girl back for a fresh
battery and watched her go. In the silence Adnan turned to tell
me that he had fished on Işıklı Gölu as a young man.

'There's nowhere for lunch,' he advised. 'The lake's deep in the middle and the wind can get up,' he said, shaking my hand. 'Keep to the left bank. And that will bring you to the dam.' Adnan's campaign to stop the canoeist, every objection exhausted, had run its course. The assistant returned with the battery, and with some bananas, which she kindly handed me.

'No need to ring tonight,' said Mehmet, who was to follow no further. He embraced me at length. 'Just when you get to the sea.'

I stowed the bananas, made a mental note of Adnan's advice and pushed off. The water was like a screen, and where the blade shed its droplets a faint kink rippled through the reflected willow trees. I had pointed my bow at the channel, enjoying the moment of pure solitude before loneliness began to sour it, when shouts reached me from the shore. It was the film crew. They had commandeered the pedalo. Its twin dolphins were moving out across the lake. Pivoting the canoe to face them, I was reminded how the dolphins of myth traditionally saved men imperilled by shipwreck or storm; and it almost seemed as if that yellow pair, one with a stove-in beak, were bearing the television crew to a higher realm, beyond the social constraints of conservative Anatolia, and onto a stage worthy of the director's passion. He trained the camera on me for a moment before signing off with a raised thumb. Then he briefly rested a hand on the girl's shoulder before joining her at the pedals. They trundled away in a wide arc.

Alone again, I passed outlying fish pens where rope lines, running shallow to stakes on the far shore, chafed beneath the canoe. A man at the furthermost pen had noticed that the tethers were hampering my progress. Holding to the platform with one hand, he worked his way out along the rope to clear my passage, weighting the line until the water drew round his heels. He bowed theatrically as I passed, occasioning a wobble from which he barely recovered.

'Shit!' he exclaimed, putting up a local heron. 'Tea?' I paused, for I was not one to turn down tea, from fishermen on tightropes especially, but it was already past noon.

'I've a way to go,' I declined apologetically.

'All the more reason for tea,' he riposted.

'And I'm not even sure,' I persisted, 'where I'm going.'

The fisherman took rejection with good grace. 'Onwards is where!' he exclaimed. 'The way is clear.'

And with that reassurance I slipped into the channel, settling into my stroke. Reeds closed in on either side, rising green from their fronded bases to a bleached palisade of crackle-dry seed heads. Above their fluffy tops, to the east, I saw sunlit limestone uplands. The rounded summit of an earthen *höyük*, or Neolithic mound, rose from the western plain. Fish broke surface in iridescent arcs. Where ponds breached the reed beds, the yellow bursting globes of water lilies rose on snub stems from foundering pads. Prey birds, alive to the massed clamour of frogs, ranged above the reeds. Egrets trailed their legs, blowsy and vaporous, across the sky. It was a beautiful morning, though the unease I felt at depending upon a poorly drawn map to get through this reedy maze, the scribbled directions of a man who held me in low regard, rather dented my appreciation of the fact.

Beyond Gökgöl, I found myself back on the river where it passed beneath a country bridge, then swung to the north and broadened, its banks ravelling away like stage curtains to reveal Işıklı Lake. The greaseproof sketch had not failed me. The lake's stippled expanse stretched to the foot of the mountains that rose along the shore. Remembering Adnan's advice, I kept left where the shore was banked by a high concrete levee. Işıklı Lake, a one-time marsh where the writ of the season had run without interference, had since become a reservoir. Not that I, having fretted over the apparent lack of water only the previous morning, had cause to complain. The lake teemed, besides, with life; frogs and fish, and tiny water snakes, black and yellow, which fled as the waves from my paddle overran the lily pads where they basked. White storks stood in the shallows, fastidiously immobile. Whiskered terns dipped overhead, their angular wings diaphanous in the sunlight, and above, against the snow glare on the heights of Akdağ, White Mountain, a procession of pelicans passed, their wings in lazy unison, like a half-remembered vision of hands waving from the windows of a passing train. I put ashore where a faded blue boat lay abandoned, the reed-punched hull rotted to wafer, though the gunwale supported my weight, and glad of the birds I ate the bananas in the sunshine.

The west wind got up after lunch. A procession of waves bore down on me as I paddled through the long afternoon. Alert for my landfall, I kept an eye on the horizon where a faint grey rectangle rose from the tree-lined haze. I powered through shallows stuck by drowned trees, past a drift of pochard ducks, the wind ruffling their henna plumages, and at last closed on the building to put ashore in the long shadow it now cast. The man's map had done its job, delivering me to the pumping station beside the dam. Beyond the levee, where I dragged the canoe, smoke drifted from an orchard. Families sat beneath the trees, barbecuing lamb kebabs.

At the sight of me a woman rose from her table and strode across. 'This is State Water Works land,' she announced briskly.

'I hoped I might leave the canoe here,' I replied, thinking to find a room in the nearest town. She threw back her head in the expressive negative.

'I'm following the Meander,' I told her, playing the romantic card.

'You can't leave it here,' she confirmed, walking away. It was then that I brandished the letter I had secured from the state tourism ministry. The effect was instant, halting the woman mid-stride, before she turned to take the letter. At its contents she nodded approvingly. I followed her lead through the long grass in search of the caretaker, dragging the canoe behind me.

I had arranged my own laissez-passer, having been repeatedly struck in preparing for my journey by the prominent role that written permission had played in these parts. Francis Arundell was forever flashing his *firman* – the word originally denoted an Ottoman imperial decree – before he was given leave to proceed. In the Dinar area, where foreigners were regarded with particular suspicion, it proved of special value. 'Returning through the market place, for it was market day,' Arundell wrote, 'we were followed by a Turk, who asked for our firman; and having sent it to the aga, he obligingly gave us permission to go where we pleased.' Arundell was once making out inscriptions when he was interrupted by Dinar locals, 'some with evident marks of displeasure, but "they have a firman" was at once a conclusive and satisfactory answer'.

We found the caretaker outside his cottage where he was scything a knee-high meadow. He had worked his way round two small dozing dogs to leave them undisturbed on their grass islets.

'The man's got authorisation, Mehmet,' the woman said. 'He came across the lake.'

'And where would he be going?' he asked.

'He wants to store the boat for the weekend,' she explained. This Mehmet was much younger than his Dinar namesake. He wore, however, a brimless woollen cap of the kind that the dapper Truehero would not think of wearing, I guessed, until his own Nehir had made him a grandfather, for it was a hat traditionally associated with dotage. The caretaker came from a village further downstream. He had circumscribed horizons, and admitted to knowing nothing even of Gökgöl when I told him where I had paddled from.

'You can put the canoe under cover,' he said, lifting one end and leading the way to a nearby shed. 'Wouldn't want the dogs to eat it.' I thanked him, explained that I would be back in a day or two, grabbed my rucksack and walked out to the road.

The last light was draining from the blossoms in the dusky cherry orchards. Silhouetted hawks perched on telegraph poles. By the road a donkey tugged at its staked tether. A car pulled up and I made space for myself among the rods and nets on the back seat. The driver and his friend, both bank staff, had had a disappointing day by the lake.

'Not a bite,' said the driver. He sniffed the air discreetly.

'Nothing but birds,' his friend confirmed, winding down his window.

'And a red canoe.' I owned up to the canoe.

'So did you have more luck?' the driver asked. I admitted I wasn't a fisherman.

'You were in a boat,' his friend observed.

'I'm travelling down the Meander,' I explained. A lengthy silence followed.

'Let's hope you don't go aground,' said the driver.

The small town of Çivril's main street had high crumbling kerbs, and unlit windows with displays of bubble-wrapped fridges and saucepans printed with vegetable designs. There were several banks.

'His branch,' said the driver, pointing at one of them.

'And his,' said the friend. We drew up by a side street where the driver indicated a building outlined in orange fairy lights.

'Hotel,' he said. 'With a shower.'

CHAPTER SEVEN

A palace once stood a few miles south of Çivril, by a tributary of the Meander, at a site now known as Beycesultan. The palace had long since disappeared beneath a grass-topped *höyük*, along with all trace of the settlement's original name; the tributary now served as an irrigation ditch. I was making my way there the next morning, walking a road that passed through poppy fields, when a kitchen fitter drew up in a van.

Ali was taking his wife and son to visit relatives in the nearby city of Denizli. I squatted in the back of the van where loose screws skittered among the chipboard offcuts, spanners, U-bends, washers and tile samples. There were glossy German brochures but so neatly stacked, with careful folds at the page corners, that I suspected Ali only ordered their designer taps and baths in his dreams, the one place his clients could afford them. Even so I was quick to point out, with the fluent insincerity of the hitch-hiker, that Ali's kit clearly marked him out as a quality fitter. Ali nodded, though he seemed less keen on discussing kitchens than in learning how his lift might spend Sundays back home.

'Well, like you,' I offered. 'Visiting friends or relatives.' A family meal, I continued. A walk.

Unsatisfied, Ali eyed me in the rear-view mirror. 'And church?' he asked. 'I understood Christians went to church on Sundays.' I owned that there were better Christians.

Ali frowned. 'You are a Christian, then?' he asked. 'But not

a good one?' Beycesultan was insufficiently distant for getting
into, never mind out of, exactly what I was; so I merely nodded.

'You do know that there are other religions?' Ali asked. 'Ones
that might suit you better?' I told Ali that I was aware of the
fact.

'Awareness is one thing,' he replied, slapping the steering
wheel. 'But are you actively looking into the matter?' I admitted
that I was doing no such thing.

'You should,' said Ali. 'Everybody needs a religion.' He
handed me a business card in case my kitchen could also do
with an overhaul before dropping me, mildly admonished, where
Beycesultan rose visibly from the plain. The carcass of a king-
fisher lay in the road, one extended turquoise wing tipped with
cobalt and edged, like a condolence, in black.

Mounds like Beycesultan were once dismissed as topographical curiosities, or taken to be the tumuli of ancient nobles.
Advances in archaeology have since dignified these sudden hills
by recognising them as reminders that agricultural civilisation
substantially began in Anatolia. What caused these mounds to
rise from the plains was neither veneration of the deceased nor
geological quirk but patterns of settlement that favoured established sites, as long as some at least of the virtues that had
commended them to their founders – viable communication
routes, water provision, good farming land and security – still
held. There were, besides, obvious advantages in adapting ruins
rather than starting from scratch. So it was, as successive settlements stacked up on the spoil of former ones, that these mounds
gradually acquired distinctive contours and archaeologists
latterly came to recognise them as repositories of the little known
pre-classical past; the beginning, in short, of Anatolian history.

Excavations on central Turkey's Konya plain at one such
mound, Çatalhöyük, duly uncovered evidence of Neolithic

settlement dating back some 9,500 years. The earliest remains at Beycesultan, where excavations were conducted through the mid-1950s, were found to be 6,000 years old while the palace there was dated to around 2000 BC. The building, perhaps eighty metres in length, indicated a culture of remarkable sophistication. With seventy rooms, extensive sacrificial areas and corridors, staircases leading to upper-storey reception halls, and floors carpeted in reeds and corded bundles of hay, it proved unlike anything else discovered in Anatolia. Of this remarkable structure, and of the civilisation that built it, history knew nothing; at least not until the contents of the 10,000 clay tablets uncovered in 1906 at Hattuşaş, 500 kilometres north-east of Beycesultan, began to be understood.

It is with written record, of course, that the archaeological evidence of earlier human existence gives way to history; the history, with the discoveries at Hattuşaş, of the Hatti people, latterly the Hittites, who had their capital there. These cuneiform writings, the earliest in Anatolia, turned out to be the annals and letters of the Hittite kings. The deciphered hieroglyphs told of an empire that spanned central Anatolia and Syria from early in the second millennium BC. One consequence of their deciphering was that a number of the mysterious hieroglyphs inscribed on prominent Anatolian rocks could now be identified as Hittite. If the clay pages gave a first sense of these shadowy inland traders and warriors, then the landscape turned out to have been inscribed with their literal marks of passage and settlement. Hittite routes were revealed, most notably the major one that ran west from Hattuşaş to the Aegean; this route passed right by the city settlement at Beycesultan, which had once belonged, the tablets suggested, to the rival state of Arzawa.

A palatial city, its ancient name unknown, on the great road through the land of Arzawa: history struggles for purchase

beneath such weight of speculation. A tablet hoard may eventually be uncovered to do for the Arzawan civilisation what the
one at Hattuşaş did for the Hittites by providing it with a
spectacular dust-down of its own. Until then, though, we cannot
claim to know the Arzawans except as a footnote in the history
of the neighbouring Hittites, the same people who pushed west
to absorb Arzawa around the fourteenth century BC. The judi-
cious advice might be to leave the Arzawans well alone if it were
not for the fact that the palace they seem to have built at
Beycesultan some six centuries before their conquest by the
Hittites suggested extraordinary possibilities to the site's archaeologists.

In the view of these archaeologists the Beycesultan structure,
though unique to Anatolia, bore a striking resemblance to the
contemporary palace complexes belonging to the pre-eminent
civilisation of the period, Minoan Crete, an island located barely
a hundred miles from the Anatolian coast. The archaeologists
noted similarities in the sacrificial quarters, the central rectangular courtyard, the use of light wells, the corridor layouts,
the hearth designs and the upper-floor locations of the state
rooms. Specific parallels were observed in roofing technique,
with the same distinctive clay layer filling the same sandwich
of packed earth and brushwood, and even in the way the walls
were painted with broad red horizontal bands.

The core question, then, was how these similarities came
about; did the Minoans learn their building techniques from
the Arzawans, or were they in fact the teachers? Which culture
informed the other? Was it the western Minoans, known by
pottery findings to have had settlements at Miletus around 2000
BC, whose builders first pushed up the Meander Valley to offer
Cretan construction know-how to the inland Arzawans? Or was
it rather the case that the same Minoans, learning of the fabled

palaces of the interior, dispatched craftsmen up the broad valley to master these latest techniques and replicate them for clients on nearby Crete? Or was it in fact the Arzawans who took the initiative, exporting their expertise to the cities of the Aegean coast and the islands beyond?

Archaeology was far from providing anything approaching a definitive answer, though the probability was that these neighbouring civilisations had in fact been bartering ideas and techniques for centuries, and that these palaces were effectively the result of a cultural partnership. Certainly, the Western assumption that the backward Anatolian hinterland had long been impervious to the transmission of new ways and ideas was scotched by the discoveries at Beycesultan. The interior had been in active correspondence, communion even, with the Aegean almost from the beginning, and via the Meander Valley. Beycesultan instanced the inherent momentum with which traded or otherwise transmitted ideas, techniques, advances and inventions, even ways of seeing, flowed along the Anatolian conduit; the same process, in fact, by which German tap brochures came that Sunday morning some four millennia later to be in the back of a Turkish kitchen fitter's van.

If the excavations at Beycesultan established any one fact, however, it was the great fire that had engulfed the palace around 1750 BC. The seams of ash uncovered in the digs strongly suggested that the city was sacked, perhaps in the course of a Hittite border raid; they were a timely reminder that conflict was as much an Anatolian commonplace as contact.

I left the road and took a track to the north. A *kangal* was chained to a farm building. The creature had worked itself into a foam-flecked lather by the time I drew level. In the dust it had made concentric semicircles, its ring of paw scuffs fronted by a broken line of crusted spittle to mark the extent of its reach. I hurried on across undulating grasslands to the mound's twin summits. An Ottoman *türbe*, a tent-shaped shrine, had made a final stand against the site's abandonment. Its octagonal walls of stone, brick and inscribed marble rose to a beehive roof fuzzy with wild grasses. The *türbe* had recently been topped with a faux-Victorian lantern, whose base was repeatedly wrapped with a long length of wiring, as if the absence of a power source on this lonely hillside had occurred to the lantern's installer, cuffing his forehead in frustration, only after he had measured out the cable. I entered through an arch of Byzantine marble. A spare, square tomb, rendered in whitewashed plaster, was backed into the wall. It might, but for the carved stone turban at its head, have been the sleeping platform of some hardy anchorite. Haphazard gestures of reverence – crumpled braided cloths and patchworks, thumbed copies of the Koran – topped the tomb alongside such incongruous items as a wooden mallet and a metal file, which I took to belong to the toolkit of a stymied electrician.

A young man appeared in the doorway. He was not the type I had expected to meet at Beycesultan; a passing shepherd, perhaps, or a reverential rustic, but not a man in a well-cut grey coat and modish glasses, a digital camera slung over his shoulder. Ahmet was an agricultural consultant employed on a nearby irrigation project. He indicated the works site, stepping outside the *türbe* to point out a distant scrum of brightly coloured earth diggers clawing at the plain. He had wandered up here in a break from his duties, he explained, to check out what he described as 'the shrine of some dead old sheikh'. Religion, I figured, meant rather less to Ahmet than it had to Ali the kitchen fitter.

'You know,' he asked, 'that our state is bringing a closure

case against the governing party?' I nodded; I had read about the case at the breakfast table of Mrs Darkeye in Dinar a few days before. The case was scheduled for later in the year.

'It must be done,' Ahmet continued. '*Ak* is threatening the nation's secular constitution.' Local mayors were repealing alcohol licences. Mosques were being built across the country. Women proclaimed their right to wear religious headdress in the course of their work or study. Despite his support for the proposed closure, Ahmet acknowledged that such an action could only profit the Islamic movement. He wondered whether a coup was in the offing.

Coups had been a prominent feature of Turkish life over the last half-century. They were the political equivalent of earthquakes and happened about as frequently. As earthquakes were preceded by seismic tremors, so coups tended to be presaged by political ones; Ahmet saw the closure case as such a presentiment. Turks commonly feared coups for the disorder they threatened, for the damage they did to the nation's reputation abroad, but mostly because they emphasised the country's cultural fault lines. It was as if Turkey had so long been warred over as to have ended up, inevitably, at war with itself; Western secularists squaring up to Eastern Islamists along the old fault line between the two worlds.

The coup, that Turkish institution, had conspicuously evolved over the years. The first one occurred in 1960 when a scheming cadre of ambitious army officers, tanks on the streets, arrests and executions, effectively represented Turkey as a banana republic. In a country with democratic and European ambitions, of course, such old-school interventions were an acute embarrassment. The powerful military achieved the same objective rather more subtly in 1971 merely by issuing a memorandum that demanded the formation of a national government. The prime minister resigned accordingly. The military consequently learned to develop subtler arts of interference, in part by working in concert with more malleably pragmatic institutions such as the judiciary and some sectors of the press. In fact, since widespread disorder regularly threatened Turkish society, many Turks tacitly supported army interference as a means of restoring stability. In recent years, however, such support had become increasingly eroded.

The main threat to society had shifted, or so some believed. While the issues in 1960 had largely been economic mismanagement and social repression, had been revolutionary political unrest a decade later and economic collapse in 1980, the so-called 'post-modern' coup of 1997 was in response to something else entirely: the rise of political Islam.

When an Islamic party, Welfare, was able in 1996 for the first time to form a government, albeit in coalition, the military should not have been surprised. It had, after all, actively encouraged political Islam as a counterweight to leftist and separatist ideologies during the 1980s. Now, however, rather than protect the country from economic or social chaos, it was the nation's secular character and constitution that the military vowed to guarantee. Further evidence of Islam's advance into the public sphere – the government's decision to close state agencies early during Ramadan, allowing observant employees to be at home in time to break their fast – finally spurred the military into clandestine action in 1997. The government fell.

Welfare and its leaders were subsequently banned from politics. Political Islam proved hydra-headed, however, duly reappearing under other names – Felicity, then Virtue. When these parties were also banned by the courts, Justice and Development replaced them; this same party, *Ak*, the judiciary was now threatening to close. It seemed less likely, then, that Turkey's Islamic constituency would lose all ideological steam than that its political parties would run out of words by which to name themselves.

A measure of the military's waning influence was that its latest interference, which took place the year before my journey, should have ended in humiliation. In April 2007 a memorandum appeared on the website of the Turkish general staff. The memorandum threatened action if the *Ak* Party pushed ahead with plans to install a pro-Islamic candidate as the next president, a post secularists held sacred on account of the fact that it had been originally occupied by Atatürk himself. *Ak* responded by calling general elections; the landslide majority they won not only endorsed their presidential candidate, but delivered a public rebuke to the generals and to those who would prioritise secularism over democracy. The current closure case represented yet another battle for the *Ak* Party as the military-backed establishment accused it of subverting the secular constitution.

'The Islamists are definitely getting stronger,' Ahmet insisted. 'Ramadan is more strictly observed every year. They have used democracy to get into power. But don't expect them to respect it if it looks like preventing them from staying in power. Which is why I hope the courts stop them. Whatever trouble that may mean.'

I left Ahmet behind me. He was still there when I looked back, sitting in the grass, staring into space. A hawk, light spilling through its splayed tail feathers, hovered above him and the mound of those who had been there before; the early people who had settled by the tributary banks 6,000 years ago, the Arzawans and the Hittites, the Phrygians, the Persians and the Greeks, the Romans and the Byzantines, the Mongols and the Tartars, the Ottomans, their dead sheikh entombed where the past broke surface, and, finally, an agricultural consultant in a raptor's shadow pondering Anatolia's present troubles.

Beyond the muddy bed of the irrigation canal, the fields were stippled with the ragged purple blooms of the opium poppy; the produce of these same fields, now harvested under strict government controls for the pharmaceutical industry, had once fed the widespread addictions of eighteenth- and nineteenth-century Europe, famously inspiring Samuel Taylor Coleridge's *Kubla Khan* and soothing the toothache and travails of Percy Bysshe Shelley. The use of this 'poisonous drug', largely grown in the watershed of the upper Meander and north to Opium, the regional processing centre, was banned in Turkey during the 1820s. But it continued to be harvested for an export market enthusiastic for Turkish opium's high morphine content and for the quality of its preparation. Turkish opium accounted for as much as 90 per cent of British imports of the drug for much of the nineteenth century. The harvested crop was processed into black, paste-like cakes wrapped in leaves, which went down to Smyrna by mule or camel train to be packed in zinc-lined cases and sent abroad.

At the nearby village of Menteş shawled women sat by road-side piles of reddish cherry prunings, which they hacked unceasingly into kindling. A mother in baggy *şalvar* trousers, belted with twine, punched at wet and soapy laundry in a blackened tin; her young daughter, wrapped in a knitted green coat, fed fragments of a tinderised tomato carton into the fire at its base. The men of the village motioned me, meanwhile, to join them in the shaded garden of the tea house. The older men took my visit as an excuse to recall their *Gastarbeiter* years in Europe;

a tailor had found piecework in Paris, stitching jacket linings, and a mechanic had worked shifts in Austrian factories. Their memories had grown indistinct, however, for the villagers no longer went abroad to work.

'Europe doesn't want us,' the tailor said. He was settling back into the sun-splashed afternoon when a van drew up.

'Fish!' yelled the driver as he clambered from the van. The man stood a wooden box by the roadside and topped it with a rough tray into which he emptied the slithering contents of a plastic bag. These tench were greenish-yellow except where livid discolouring around the organs showed beneath translucent underbellies. The man spread his catch across the tray. He then busied himself by arranging the shoal as if it were still alive, turning errant fish among them so that they all presented their sightless stares to those who might buy. The tea house fell silent in the shared suspicion that no amount of presentation could commend these fish.

'More tea?' somebody murmured, waving a discreet hand before his nose. I was reminded of an ancient Phrygian taboo against the eating of fresh-water fish; William Ramsay, travelling the region before trout farms were established here, claimed not to have found 'a single stream which furnished palatable fish, and even where the fish seemed of good quality they were most unwholesome and could only be eaten with the greatest of caution'.

'We call them *kadifer*,' the tailor told me with a grimace. 'From Işıklı Gölu.'

'Ah,' I said. 'The lake I crossed only yesterday.' The men at the tea house showed no more interest in my travels, however, than in the tench. The men of Menteş, though the older ones had been to Europe, knew not what to make of a passing canoeist.

The tailor eventually broke the silence. 'It was all of thirty years ago that the river last had proper water,' he declared. 'I doubt you'll get a boat through there now.'

I had all but given up on Menteş when an old man stirred in a corner of the tea garden. He struggled to his feet, steadied himself against a chair arm, and like the Ancient Mariner, a vision the product of these very fields might even have helped inspire, he fixed a cautionary finger upon me. 'Watch out!' he bellowed. 'Watch out for the old watermills at Aşağı Seyit.'

I dined that evening in Çivril's only restaurant. I was alone among my surroundings; caryatid Cleopatras, spangly chairs backed with enormous satin bows, plastic yukkas and palm trees swagged with year-round tinsel and Christmas bells. A half-size shepherd girl, carved from meerschaum, cradled a basket of plastic blooms and frosted pine cones. Plastic ivy was entwined around the television cables. The walls were embossed with gilt bells, which housed orange art-nouveau light fittings. There were football club pennants, portraits of family patriarchs,

Atatürk memorabilia, clocks and paintings of tumbling rivers. The kebab I ate against such a background seemed hopelessly prosaic. So I followed it with the plate of baklava I had been promising myself since losing Turgay Darkeye's gift to the river.

I wandered into the evening. A spring warmth was in the air. Çivril's park, partially lamplit, was deserted except for a youth preening himself in the wing mirror of his moped. A bronze Atatürk in educational mode clasped the hands of two studious children, books beneath their arms. A sparrow clamped the tip of a discarded ice-cream cone in its extended beak. Beyond rusted tables were brightly painted swings.

The park's main feature was an elevated and oversized amphora, tipped to send an ornamental stream winding through the park. The stream's course ran beneath low hump-backed bridges lined with ornate iron railings. The setting consciously recalled, in degraded form, the paradise gardens of the Persians; the shaded pavilions, the blooms, flowerbeds and fragrant trees, all alive with the murmur of streams and the song of birds, like the parklands by the Meander's banks at Celaenae.

Herodotus acknowledged the particular Persian regard for rivers. 'Rivers they chiefly reverence,' he wrote; 'they will neither make water nor spit nor wash their hands therein, nor suffer anyone to do so.' The same was true some 1,500 years later of the Mongols and Tartars who, though they might have scourged the land and piled up the heads of the inhabitants, refrained on principle from urinating or washing in rivers. It was a reverence today's Turks, with their affection for such names as Pınar and Nehir, and for kitsch paintings of tumbling streams and water-falls in sylvan settings, consciously observed. Except that Çivril's ornamental stream was bone-dry. And rubbish was strewn all along its concrete bed.

CHAPTER EIGHT

In the morning I searched Çivril for a belt of sorts. Along the streets of the country town sprays of budding cherries spilled over crumbling garden walls; cardboard signs marked *zehirli* – poisonous – claimed that the trees from which they hung had been treated with chemicals, as if to caution the cowherds against risks to the health of their wandering cattle, though I suspected that these warnings had in fact been fabricated to preserve the cherries for their exasperated owners.

In the shade of an alley stacked with cement sacks I found an ironmonger.

'For belts,' he explained, 'we go to the *butik*.' This patient man might have been reciting from a Turkish primer. The man's exaggerated clarity, though it cast me as a halfwit, was not so mortifying as his ready surmise that I must be after some fashion accessory. I hastily emphasised my expeditionary credentials, explaining that I actually needed something to cinch tight a rucksack, which I'd been having trouble fitting within the stern frame of my canoe.

'Your canoe no less,' the ironmonger replied with exaggerated courtesy; and standing corrected as to how this customer preferred to think of himself he wandered off into the dusty recesses of his shop. When he returned it was with a functional leather strap, about a yard long, with a heavy-duty buckle.

'For a rifle,' he said, laying it along the counter between us. 'But I dare say it will also do for your sack.'

Back at the dam, I surprised the caretaker in a private exam-
ination, which finally explained the brimless cap I had noticed
at our first meeting. A stooped Mehmet was peering with visible
concern into the wing mirror of his ancient motorbike. He had
removed the cap to reveal an irregularly threadbare pate, tufted
in the way of the terminally ill, which he smoothed with a tentative palm. Mehmet moved to replace the cap the instant he saw
me, though the knowledge that he had been observed soon
caused him to abandon any attempt at pretence.

'It was the shampoo,' he confessed sheepishly, straightening
to shake my hand. 'The advertisement promised to thicken my
hair. Instead, it's made it all fall out. All over the country there
have been people complaining about the stuff. I heard on the
television.' In the coverage dominating Turkey's broadcasting
– items about the etiquette of headscarf-wearing, updates on
the threatened closure of the ruling party, the *Ergenekon* arrests
– I had heard of no such national outbreak of hair loss. Nor
was I in any position to advise, though the caretaker appeared
to think otherwise, fixing me with a searching look that anticipated I might have the solution. I was reminded how country
Turks had habitually regarded travelling Westerners as repositories of medical knowledge. William Leake regarded 'an
assumption of the medical character' as nothing less than a chief
necessity for successful travel in Anatolia; such consultations
were so commonly sought that the sardonic Reverend Arundell
came to regard visits from Turks as 'affording me an opportunity
of displaying medical talent'. Certainly, Mehmet seemed disap-
pointed that I could do nothing for him. It was only when I
told him I had feared he must be properly sick that he acknowledged the implied inconsequence, even the comic value, of his
predicament with a thin smile; one which broadened when I
promised not to say a word. We shook on it.

'Then I'll help you carry the canoe,' said Mehmet. He led
the way to the shed, which he had gone so far as to padlock
over the weekend. I thanked him for the care, true to his calling,
that he had taken of my canoe.

'Not at all,' he replied, lifting the bow and leading off in the
direction of the dam. 'It's just I can't see you getting much
further in it.'

What Mehmet meant did not become clear until we had set
down the canoe and made our way across the dam by the railed
walkway. It was a modest installation, a series of gates and sluices
set low in the concrete levee, but noisy for its size; a considerable crush of water was being drawn from the lake though it
was not being released, it happened, into the river. The torrent
foamed through a sluice and tumbled hectically into an elevated
concrete canalette, which smuggled it off to irrigate the nearby
cherry orchards.

William Hamilton, geologist and topographer, had in June
1837 witnessed a pre-industrial version of the same process not
far north of Çivril, where villagers were 'busy preparing channels and water-courses for the summer irrigation'. The description, though spare, conjured a practice that had obtained in its
generalities beyond Anatolia, even unto the high-summer vegetable gardens of Hamilton's native England; the retrenching by
mattock or spade of the old channels that had previously carried
water from river, spring or tank, or the digging of fresh courses
in newly tilled ground, with soil dykes at the junctions to regu-
late each watering.

Hamilton witnessed the skilled application of a water
husbandry that had continued unchanged for thousands of years,
and with no discernible effect upon the source. It was a view I
envied, given the sickening sight that now greeted me below the
dam. The river was almost empty. Glazed patches of its bed,

humped slicks of mud, had broken surface. No birds, for all their abundance on the adjacent lake, frequented the half-lit mire. The only living things were the midges, dancing in a frenzy over the stretches of standing water.

I stood horrified and recalled the dry, litter-strewn bed of the ornamental stream in the park at Çivril. It now appeared as a presentiment of trouble on the river, and by no means the first: the pumps that had diverted the water at Suçıkan; the concrete ditches of Dinar; the regrets Mehmet Truehero had voiced about his beloved river; Turgay Darkeye's repeated assumption that I could only have an industrial interest in the Meander; and the recurrent doubts, expressed most recently by the caretaker himself, as to how much further I was likely to get. My journeying appeared done, here and now, for the employees of the State Water Works, by the buttons they pressed and the levers they pulled, had diverted every last drop of river water to the surrounding orchards. They had severed the river from its headwaters, terminally decapitating the Meander.

Mehmet was wringing his hands; this empathy was to his credit, as was his insistence that I should not now abandon the river. Mehmet, seeing that my canoe required hardly any water and judging that the river might yet recover, urged me to attempt a launch. With his encouragement I stowed my newly strapped rucksack, shoved the canoe into the shallows and thanked Mehmet for his help.

'Good luck,' said the caretaker, embracing me. 'And remember,' he whispered, pointing towards his head. 'Not a word.'

I drifted out across the stagnant water, my paddle stirring the cesspool contents; particle clouds mushroomed to the surface, painting my wake with grey, cauliflower growths. I followed a weaving course between flats of mud and rock; their exposure appeared quite as ominous as the weed-wrapped ruins of spires and gables that were said to rise from the cracked beds of drought-struck reservoirs. The going was arduous and only with regular shoves of the paddle was I able to punt myself clear of the groundings; high above me, meanwhile, there passed the banks where the springtime flow must once have jostled, tugging at the trailing willow branches, back before the irrigators and their farming clients stole it all for cherry juice.

The river, as Mehmet predicted, had managed a partial recovery by the time I reached the first bridge of the day. Three arches of pale ashlar carried the handsome Akköprü, the White Bridge, across the river. The bridge was Ottoman, though the crumbling footings on which it rested were far older; some of the stones might even have known the weight of the vast column of chariots and carts, horsemen and foot soldiers, greaves and helmets catching the spring sunshine, which had crossed the river here in 401 BC.

Some fourteen centuries had passed since the sack of the palatial city at nearby Beycesultan. The Hittites, having absorbed the
Arzawans, had themselves given way; in the ruins of their abandoned cities another people, the Phrygians, had long since settled.
The Phrygian kings, the legendary Midas among them, had established themselves over much of western and central Anatolia.

By 401 BC, however, Midas had himself passed into fable,
and not in a manner that would have been to his liking. The
soldiers at the bridge knew him, if they knew him at all, not as
the venerated former monarch of the lands they were crossing
but as storied fall guy of the Olympian gods; another victim of
Apollo who, having dealt with Marsyas's musical impertinence,
now turned on the Phrygian king for having sided with the
cocksure Anatolian flautist and gave Midas the ears of an ass,
as if his patently defective hearing deserved them. The Olympians
further reduced Midas by granting his ill-judged wish that
everything he touched might turn to gold; his every touch, it
turned out, of his lips as well as his fingers so that the King
had no sooner enjoyed infinite wealth before he was subjected
to intolerable hunger and thirst.

The Phrygian people themselves had not done much better
than their ridiculed ruler. They had not quite disappeared but
had become subject to the rule of others, occupiers from the
east. Phrygia had since 546 BC been a satrapy, or province of
Persia. In 401 BC it was under the regional command of one
whom we have already encountered among his marching forces
at Celaenae; Cyrus, who had spent a month at his Celaenae
hunting lodge, reviewing his forces and awaiting the arrival of
reinforcements from the Greek lands of Thrace, Sparta and
Arcadia, before he led his forces out of the city and onwards to
the bridge at Akköprü.

To the distant sound of an engine refusing to fire I put ashore, hauling the canoe up a shelving bank pitted with the mud-cast hooves of watering cattle. I strolled up a farm track to the bridge and looked out across the plain to a truncated furrow where a farmer in rubber boots was climbing from his stalled tractor.

The forces under Cyrus's command, following a three-day route that ran roughly parallel to my own, duly reached the river crossing where I now stood. Not that Xenophon chose to mention the crossing in his account of the great march. Its omission from the pages of the *Anabasis* was understandable in that barely a blister had been suffered by this stage of the march. The crossing must have been routine, certainly compared to the many hazardous ones that lay ahead. Many hundreds of parasangs, the Persian measure of distance, and a good many months were yet to pass before the men of the expedition would be called upon to demonstrate the exemplary endurance, fighting spirit and solidarity that posterity was to celebrate.

Those events, destined to play out in the distant uplands of eastern Anatolia, were to be remembered as a classical Dunkerque; in this regard Xenophon would have been technically correct to have called his account the *Katabasis*, or Retreat to the Sea, since the primary events it detailed constituted an evacuation, albeit one of unquestionably heroic endurance, rather than an advance. The doughty forces, finding themselves outnumbered and leaderless following Cyrus's death in battle near Baghdad, were compelled to reorganise and beat a winter retreat over snowy passes and swirling rivers, fending off hunger and hostile tribesmen. The triumphant cry they put up at their first glimpse of the Black Sea's Hellenised littoral – The Sea! The Sea! – has reverberated through Western history.

Back at the bridge and barely embarked on their march, however, the same men could have had no idea that the Black Sea might lie ahead; not the least intimation, in fact, that they were destined to be remembered for anything. Xenophon and his mercenary fellows had not even been informed as to where they were actually headed or whom they were to fight when they got there. They thought to have signed up for a routine mission; the word put about by Cyrus himself was that he meant to subjugate the rebellious Pisidians whose lands lay just east of the source of the Meander. Persia, in short, was merely dealing with one of the minor insurrections to which any vast empire was occasionally subject.

History never ended, of course, though at that time the Persians might have believed that theirs was the one empire that would endure, whatever the successive eclipses of their predecessors in the region – the Arzawans, Hittites and Phrygians – might have taught them. By the fifth century BC the Persians had established their rule over all Anatolia, west beyond Phrygia to the Greek port cities of Ionia, and had even filled the city states of Greece itself with the spectre of invasion.

By this time, however, Greek pride and civic culture were allied with an increasingly sophisticated fighting know-how. There were even those, both in Greece and along the Hellenised shores of Ionia, who sensed beyond Persia's extraordinary power and might something of the Easterners' fallibility. Some dreamed not only of driving the Persians from their own cities but even of uniting one day to push east and invade the lands of the Great King himself. Aristagoras, a Greek whom the Persian authorities had unwisely entrusted with the satrapy of Miletus, in 499 BC rallied the city to rebel by mocking the ruling Persians for the trousers they wore and by claiming that they 'were wont to carry neither shield nor spear and could be easily overcome. With the abject failure of the subsequent Ionian Revolt, an independence bid bolstered by the support of some mainland Greek states,

Aristagoras was proved wrong, though not many years were to pass before it appeared that the man may have had a point about the Persians; at Marathon not far from Athens just nine years later the invading Persians, despite every numerical advantage, suffered a crushing defeat at the hands of the heavily armed Greeks.

For that stinging reverse the Persian kings swore eternal vengeance. In honour of that pledge Xerxes led his armies west through Celaenae in 481 BC. Xerxes' invasion of the West failed comprehensively, however, when the Greeks crushed the Persian trireme fleet the following year at Salamis, consolidating that success with further victories in 479 BC on both shores of the Aegean. Defeat in 460 BC at Eurymedon in southern Anatolia dealt another blow to the Persians, a people who not only wore trousers in battle but were quite willing to drop them, it was gleefully assumed, when otherwise required; vases painted in Athens after the Battle of Eurymedon, probably not intended for family use, depicted a Greek, erection in hand, advancing on the presented rear of a prostrate Persian.

Not that this posture resembled the one adopted by the noble Persian leading his forces out of Celaenae in the spring of 401 BC, though Cyrus's intentions were certainly unorthodox; the satrap had reversed the Persians' traditional direction of travel. Cyrus, though his own forces did not yet know it, was after his own brother, the Great King himself, whom he meant to overthrow and so claim the Persian throne. To secure what he saw as his birthright he hardly relied, moreover, on any significant degree of support from fellow Persians. Instead, he had signed up some 10,000 Greek mercenaries hardened during the Peloponnesian Wars that Sparta and Athens had concluded just four years earlier. On this point Cyrus had been specific, instructing his commanders that they should 'enlist as many

Peloponnesian soldiers of the best sort as they severally could'.
Addressing his Greek mercenaries, whom he held to be better
and stronger than many barbarians, the broad-brush slur by
which the Ionian Greeks denoted the uncultured Asiatics, Cyrus
appeared to believe in his words beyond their morale-boosting
capacity. In Western military prowess, technique and armament,
he reckoned, the East's huge numerical supremacy might now
have met its match.

Cyrus's hired hands, for all their paymaster's confidence,
would no doubt have baulked at the sheer ambition of his actual
plans, not least on account of the footslog the project entailed.
It was for precisely this reason that the satrap had fobbed them
off with his talk of a routine regional mission. Cyrus's stated
plan – driving the Pisidians 'out of his land entirely' – was one
that his mercenaries initially had no reason to question. Until
the day, that is, when he led them out of Celaenae in quite the
wrong direction. Geography had it that the mercenaries must
advance by the great pass at Celaenae and continue beyond the
site of the mythical musical scrap at the source of the Meander
if they were to sort out the Pisidians. Instead, Cyrus led them
north-west, and back to the banks of a river they thought to
have left behind.

Over the plain which these ancient mercenaries had once
crossed there now came a series of increasingly frustrated clangs.
The farmer lay flat beneath his stricken tractor, only his boots
protruding. With every ringing blow of the farmer's spanner,
the storks that had gathered to pick along the fresh furrows
unfurled their white wings in readiness to fly.

Although Xenophon passes over the bridge in silence, it was
here, it is to be assumed, that some among his fellow marchers
must have felt their doubts deepen. It was only logical, given
that river crossings were a primary measure of progress, that

some should have wondered why they had doubled back to one whose famed sources they had already reached at Celaenae. If this was not the way to Pisidia, then the satrap must be leading them, and by a patently roundabout route, against some other foe whom he clearly did not mean them to recognise. Was it here, then, that some might have had the first intimations of what truly lay ahead? That they would be the first Greeks to take the fight, literally, to Persia?

The anabasis commemorated a pointed moment in the process of Persian eclipse; when Greek military power, albeit under Persian authority, set out to conquer Persia just as Xerxes' Persians had advanced on Greece eighty years earlier. Indeed, Cyrus largely followed the very route of his great-grandfather but in reverse, rolling up the Persian advance and with it the last great gesture of Eastern imperial might before the West was to take its turn. The anabasis might initially have been about rivalry between royal Persian siblings; its actual effect, it turned out, was to inspire an era of Hellenic expansionism. The Roman historian Polybius regarded 'the retreat of the Greeks under Xenophon from the upper satrapies, in which, though they traversed the whole of Asia, a hostile country, none of the barbarians ventured to face them' as the chief inspiration for Alexander the Great's Asia campaign seventy years later. The West had learned not only how to defeat the East, but that it must tramp across Anatolia to get at it.

Of all this there was now no sign. Out on the plain the farmer wiggled out from beneath his tractor and clambered to his feet, brushing the soil from his worn jacket. Then he threw down the spanner and set off in search of help, and along the half-ploughed furrow storks hopped out of the irate farmer's way.

Below Akköprü the Meander was severely choked. From the angled trunks of fallen willows branches rose like banister spindles.

I sought out the gaps and pushed through the half-submerged crowns to emerge in a slick of cobwebs, catkins, bits of branch and river weed. Floating branches had boomed rotting reeds into stinking rafts, which I inched through by hauling on overhanging branches. The going was hard, and I began to wonder when I would reach the next bridge.

It was about this time it struck me that the Meander was not proving the carefree experience I had imagined. It seemed I was always in a hurry on this river; today because I could not afford to reach the next bridge after nightfall if I hoped to find lodgings there. Villagers could not be expected to take in strangers if they could not first view them in the full light of day. I felt less like a free-spirited wanderer than a Transylvanian coachman, whip raised against the setting sun, as I dug in my paddle to drive through the willow brakes. The relentless bends added to my frustration, the low sun shearing away from the bow; only when the sun's glare was back in my eyes did I know that I was heading west, towards the next bridge, which was where I was meant to be going. What I really wanted that evening, for all my earlier protestations, was the odd straight stretch of water. But this was hardly the river to want that from.

The sun had set by the time the drone of thinly spaced cars advised me that I was finally getting close. The crossing that swung into view was an arched Ottoman bridge, partially collapsed, and beyond it a concrete replacement carrying the tarmac road. I ran the canoe ashore and made my way across a rough pasture where a tethered horse was staked. The village at the crossing took its name, Kavak, from the poplar trees that rose, along with the spike of a minaret, out of a mean cluster of block-built dwellings and dusty vegetable plots. I met the headman in the lane and asked if the village could put me up. He looked at me.

'We don't have the space,' he said. 'The nearest hotels are in Çivril. But you can leave your canoe in the schoolyard.' He dispatched a young man to help me. Together we walked down to the river.

'Your boat's full of bits of tree,' said Gökhan, bending to pick up an end. We carried the canoe back to the school and lifted it over the low wall.

'And there's a nest in your hair,' he remarked. I thanked Gökhan, shouldered my rucksack and walked out to the road; there was nothing for it but to overnight again in Çivril. The moon was rising above a cooling earth, silvering the willows along the course of the river. I watched a pair of lights bore out of the darkness. As the *dolmuş* drew to a halt I brushed myself down and prepared to board.

CHAPTER NINE

I was back in Kavak early the next morning. A ragged chicken watched me retrieve my canoe from the deserted schoolyard. It flexed its stubby wings to follow me across the empty road and down to the river, apparently caught, in the village way, between seeing me off its patch and shipping out itself.

I launched below the collapsed Ottoman bridge and passed beneath the stained concrete slab that carried the modern road, only to run into the partially submerged remains of yet another crossing. These rotted stumps, all that remained of a wooden footbridge, might have conjured a picturesque past for Kavak if they had not more immediately served as a jagged reef, which threatened to hole the canoe's fabric hull. My main concern, though Kavak might once have been more appealing, was not being stranded in the unlovely place, with concrete crossing and territorial chicken, that it had since become.

I had cleared the village and was making steady progress, relieved that the stumps had caused no lasting damage, when the first fallen willow of the day appeared. I was getting used to these obstructions. I liked to think I was learning to read them; canoe-height clearance, in this case, hard by the right bank beneath a foliage overhang that my seated torso could push through, I reckoned, without too much scrape or scratch. Until something stirred beyond the bank. And then began to growl.

I could barely see the dog through the willows, but was at least relieved to hear a clinking sound. The chain told me that the creature's reach was limited, though what shadowed that conclusion was the realisation that any such restraint was likely to be of a length that the dog might drink from the river, if only to save on water bowls. That necessarily put the dog in reach of the only place where I might pass. When it began to bark I abandoned these considerations and took up a holding position in the middle of the river, there to contemplate the fearsome reputation of Anatolian dogs.

Turkey's dogs had always been a fear of mine, and in this I was not alone. The *Anabasis*, that monument to Hellenic valour, tended to focus on such hazards as conflict and snow drifts, hunger and exhaustion; it made little mention of the ferocious mutts Xenophon and his comrades may have encountered along the way. Large packs, however, of what Herodotus described as Indian hounds were known to have accompanied Xerxes' invasion force across Anatolia on its way to Greece in 481 BC. These creatures were impressive but essentially recreational, there to accompany the Great King when he was minded to hunt – unlike the dogs of Magnesia, a city on the lower reaches of the Meander. When Magnesia's horsemen made war on the people of neighbouring Ephesus, they first threw their enemy's lines into confusion by setting their dogs upon them. Pliny wrote how the people of another city of the Aegean littoral, Colophon, raised entire detachments of dogs to fight alongside their soldiers.

These warring canines had long been demobilised by the time Reverend Arundell set out in search of nineteenth-century Apamea. It seemed, even so, that they went about their civilian functions, as guardians of the sheep flocks, with all their old belligerence. They behaved like outlaw irregulars, taking to the hills where they paired up or formed bands before descending upon any strangers who dared to trespass upon the dogs' self-proclaimed, shifting territories. Nor did they seem much interested in the role they had been assigned except, like nightclub bouncers, for the action it might bring, even to the point of abandoning their woolly charges to take on passing vehicles.

The heavy-set, short-haired *kangal*, which seemed to have taken its colourings, chameleon-like, from the straw and dun tones of the surrounding steppe, resembled the mastiff-type hunting dogs depicted on ancient Persian reliefs; it might have descended from Xerxes' Indian hounds. Modern Turks had found, however, another lineage rather more persuasive for their national dog, much as Turkish names were preferred over Persian ones for their villages, and instead traced the *kangal*'s descent from the dogs of the Turkish nomads who had first migrated to Anatolia in the eleventh century.

The Reverend Arundell, though he did acknowledge that *kangals* were 'rather worrying', preferred to make light of them by emphasising the beasts' 'noble appearance' and 'the brave fidelity with which they guard the flocks and herds of their masters'. More revealing was Arundell's observation, referring to his travels near Işıklı in 1833, that his companion's whip was regularly 'in full exercise against the dogs'. This detail, which conjured the local dogs in all their pack-like ferocity, appeared to concede that Arundell's expressions of *kangal* admiration were worked up retrospectively, and on the safe side of his nightly billets' secured doors.

I had rather more in common with another traveller, William Childs, who proved himself refreshingly craven when it came to the dogs. In 1912 Childs crossed central Anatolia, not far from the very district which gave the *kangal* its name.

'Nothing in Turkish travelling, indeed – neither the filthy khans nor universal dirt, nor risk of disease, nor chance of robbery – equals in unpleasantness this plague of savage dogs,' he wrote. Childs, who was subjected to *kangal* attacks daily, defended himself not with a whip but with a 'heavy, steel-pointed stick'. He eventually took refuge in his *araba* – Childs' 'walk' was supported, somewhat questionably, by an attendant vehicle – whenever a warning 'flock of goats or sheep appeared ahead'.

Born into a time that had rather marginalised the use of whips, I had instead taken my cue from Childs; the reducible walking pole I carried was stout, with a spiked end. How I thought to have truly stolen a march on the man, however, with his dubious cart and driver arrangement, was by taking to the river. That a dog should have blocked my way even here came as a rude surprise. I attempted to drive it back by slapping the water with the flat of my paddle and nosing the canoe forward until I could see something of the creature beyond the foliage; my truncated view was of braced paws, which briefly left the ground with every bark but showed no sign of retreating. I conceded defeat and put ashore on the opposite bank.

I lashed the canoe to a root, grabbed my walking pole and scrambled up the bank. A smiling youth stood beside a field of maize.

'Hello,' said Hasan Fearless. He offered a hand, extending it like a toy soldier. 'You are welcome. We were expecting you.' I had guessed, knowing Turks, that I might be welcome. But I had not expected, as I told Hasan, to be expected.

'We read about you in the newspaper,' he explained. 'In the *New Century*. You will drink tea.' It transpired, then, that Adnan's article had enjoyed a life beyond the *Dinar News*, graduating from that small-town free sheet to feature in the regional newspaper that served the Turkish Aegean and its hinterland. The syndicated article, having outgrown its home town, had burst out of Dinar and raced down the valley, all the time finding new readers, to alert the Fearless family that a foreigner in a canoe was closing on their isolated farmstead. Where there was to be no continuing, it seemed, until he had stopped for tea.

Hasan led the way past the fallen willow, along the bank to a footbridge of poplar trunks clinkered with knot-edged planks. We crossed to a low-built house with a tiled roof above walls of cracked bare plaster. A Turkish flag and a framed photograph of Atatürk hung above a doorway draped with a faded floral muslin. The sepia photograph happened to show the great leader himself emerging from a door, a grander portal admittedly, and flanked by saluting officers. The conjunction was such, however, that it might have been the Fearless family home that Atatürk was leaving, and the Fearless family itself, drinking tea at an outside table shaded by a hanging vine, to whom the leader was doffing his determinedly Western bowler; to Mr and Mrs Celal Fearless, to their teenage daughter Adile, and to Ayşe, whom their son Hasan was to marry the following month. Certainly, it was precisely the sort of family to have found favour with the great social revolutionary, the champion of modern values and the European dress styles that were supposed to complement them, not least because the Fearless family men were free of reactionary brimless hats and because their women went unshawled. It was harder to know, though, what Atatürk would have made of Ayşe's *No More Heroes* T-shirt; a sentiment that seemed not only at odds with the particular surname Ayşe was so soon to adopt but also in defiance of the generally valiant tenor of Turkish surnames.

'Welcome,' said Celal Bey. 'So you're going to the sea, God willing. I was there once. But here is where we have been for sixteen years.' He gestured at his riverside plot, and the blessed sky above, laying a contented palm across his chest.

'Tea, tea,' said Mrs Fearless, pressing a glass upon me. 'The man must be thirsty.' I admitted that I had come no further than Kavak that morning.

'Kavak,' Celal Bey mused. 'My birthplace.' I wondered if the village's last smile had left with him.

'We knew something must be on the river from all the barking,' said Adile. 'Bosti doesn't much bark yet. She's only a few months old.' So I learned to my shame that a puppy called Bosti was what had halted my progress.

'You'll stay for lunch,' said Celal Bey. I declined the offer. I had a lot of river to cover.

'Then we'll make you a picnic for your journey,' said Mrs

Fearless. 'Adile! Boiled eggs for our guest. Three. And some salt. Ayşe! Almonds.'

'You really don't need to worry,' I protested. I had bought bananas and biscuits that morning in Çivril.

'Nonsense,' said Mrs Fearless. She bustled off to pick me some plums. Ayşe, meanwhile, had settled herself beside a chopping block. She set about a pile of almonds, shattering their shells with a mattock. A flying shard landed in my tea. I wondered just what might remain of the almonds once the redoubtable Ayşe was done with them; Hasan would soon know, I rather guessed, what it was to be married.

'Come,' said Celal Bey. 'Let me show you round.' Rows of rocket, lettuce and parsley, arced with soil-stuck willow branches that had supported winter polythene cloches, furled now, grew in early profusion. There were peppers, chillies, tomatoes, aubergines and cucumbers. Beyond were orchards of almond, plum and cherry, and I stood in the shade of walnut trees that the Fearless family had planted just six years before. The farmlands of the Meander valley, accounted the richest in all Turkey, had always been 'the orchard of Asia Minor'.

It was a measure of this abundance that the Roman deity of this river, the eponymous Meander, was commonly represented in a pose of voluptuous plenty, with flowers in his hair and 'a cornucopia in his arms, overflowing with pineapples, pomegranates, grapes and other fruits of the valley'. The bearded god's bounty was acknowledged on Roman coins minted along the river from Apamea to downstream Antiocheia. All through its history the valley has produced a remarkable diversity of highly prized and abundant produce. The upper valley has long been known for its grapes and cherries, apples, capers, wheat, and the poppies whose seed-head secretions once fed the pipes and tinctures of Europe's restless addicts. Along the lower reaches figs, citrus fruit and strawberries, tobacco and cotton, sesame and silk, liquorice and olives have traditionally predominated. The Meander Valley's abundance has commonly proved a source of astonishment; 'such crops of wheat', as one visitor declared, 'as to astound one who contemplates the fact that since the days of antiquity these fields have, without fertilization, fed hordes of Romans, Greeks, Turkish and other nations as empires successively rose and fell. In fields about the river Meander . . . I stood in wheat which, thick as grass, rose above my head.'

Until the twentieth century, when the building of dams began to interfere with the process, this historical productivity was the natural consequence of the rich topsoil silts that the regular winter floods deposited evenly across the plain. This plain had grown, particularly along the lower reaches, to become disproportionately broad and exceptionally flat; magnificent farming country through the summer months but seasonally subject to extensive winter flooding. These floods, though they had once fertilised the valley every winter, also caused their share of disruption. It was said that the god Meander so regularly washed away riverine tracts of land that he was subject to beggaring fines; landowners affected by the flooding, that is, were compensated by payments taken from the local ferry tolls. One historical consequence was that valley settlements, especially downstream ones, had learned to keep back from the flood plain. I wondered if Celal Bey had given any consideration to floods before settling his family right beside the river.

'Floods?' Celal Bey laughed. 'This river's flooding days are done. It hasn't flooded since they built the dam on Işıklı Lake. Believe me, too much rain is the least of our problems. Yours too, though there should be enough water to get your boat through. Though I can't say beyond Çal. And you wouldn't want to be out at night.'

'On account of the wolves,' explained Mrs Fearless, carrying a handful of the sour spring plums Turks are so fond of.

'Wolves?' scoffed Celal Bey. 'Only on Çökelez Mountain, woman.' Mrs Fearless was briefly silent.

'Scorpions, then,' she said. 'Now, let me make the man a sandwich. Adile! I need some baby green almonds for our guest's sandwich. And spring onions!'

'Spring onions! Coming!'

'The wife's right, though, that you'll need somewhere to stay,' said Celal Bey.

'And a cucumber, Adile!'

'Cucumber!'

'See if you can make Gelinören. They're sure to put you up there. Just ask for the headman.'

'Ayşe, tomatoes, once you've done the eggs!'

I jammed the bulging picnic bag in the bow of my canoe.

'You can come through this way,' said Hasan, hauling the branches clear at the bank. I drove the canoe into the gap.

'Thanks,' I said. 'And best wishes for your marriage.' Bosti had followed Hasan to the water's edge. The dog pounced as I passed, but only to lick my ear and I mused that *kangals* were not the monsters I had taken them for. Celal Bey was waiting for me at the footbridge.

'You forgot this,' he said, and reaching to shake my hand he passed me down my walking pole.

I paddled through the warm day and slipped past the country bridge at the hamlet of Yahyalı where I noticed a welcome chafing on the surface of the water; the current, absent since the dam, had resumed. The wonder was where the water had come from, and I sensed secret capillaries freshening the river long after the spring rains had stopped, the skies set fair for summer, even reclaiming water stolen to irrigate the orchards. The fish, flashing bars of black, had returned to the river. Sparrow gangs were out after bedding, stripping the crackle-dry debris that crested the bank-side stands of reed. Nests of weaver birds, felted baubles, hung from the tips of willow branches, and for many reasons – the river's miraculous recovery, my growing confidence in handling the canoe, the generosity of the Fearless family, Bosti's lick – I was happy to be on the river.

A fresh concern was arising, however, by the time I had made a few more kilometres to stop for lunch at the bridge by the village of Beyelli. It related to the third and final map in my sheaf; the local tourism department's one of the province, Denizli, into which I had lately crossed. This map I had until recently ignored, doubting my ability to compute the value of yet more conflicting cartographical information. The previous evening, however, I had given it a cursory glance and could no longer ignore its alarming contents. I now spread the map before me on the grass, weighting its corners with the bags of Fearless almonds, plums and boiled eggs. The map was even less use than the others; its particular deficiency was to demonstrate provincial tourism department thinking at its most wishful. The map had recast the local landscape according to its own agenda. It was dotted with recreational symbols – tents, campervans, horse riders, picnic benches, paragliders, fishermen far better equipped than the ones I had seen, even a waterskiing girl in bikini bottoms and life vest – which bore no relation to my own experience of the river valley. So I might have dispensed with that fantastic map entirely except that the photomontage abutting the province's irregular boundaries – not only of mountains and waterfalls, but of such unlikely attractions as conference facilities and glasses of wine – included a rubber dinghy manned by helmeted paddlers chuting down a white-water rapid above the legend: *Menderes – Rafting*.

I was done with rapids, especially ones as big as those in the map montage. Rafting rapids were not meant to be in the programme. Not on the Meander. Over a sandwich of chopped green almonds and spring onions I carefully considered the evidence. The tourism map's claim was both insistent and specific in that the photo in the montage was supported by a whole series of raft symbols showing repeatedly along the river below Beyelli. Since arriving in Turkey, however, nobody had made the least mention of rafting on the Meander. In fact, rafting on the river seemed even less likely than running into a curvy waterskiing blonde there. I decided a better plan, knowing what I did of Turkish maps, was to ignore this one in favour of my own instincts. I would stay on the shallow river and make, as Celal Bey had suggested, for the village of Gelinören.

It proved a long afternoon, one in which I came to believe that there might indeed have been thrill-seeking rafters on this stretch of river, but only back before the building of the dam by Işıklı Lake. This section of river would have been perfect for rafting, I reckoned, if only the water had not gone missing. The gradient visibly steepened, and the rock-ripped waters that remained ran faster down the tilted bed. The waters rushed across the shallows, grounding the canoe, which clock-handed wildly on stony pivots. Repeatedly I climbed from the canoe and walked my battered boat down the ankle-deep river, and thought how the dam had done for the river, its sloshing tide backed up there to serve the seasonal fattening of the local cherries. The banks rose higher still above my bottoming canoe where once the waters had deepened beneath bobbing rafts. The trough that I travelled was now deep in shadow, and I even feared that the banks might close above me, the river disappearing down a sinkhole just as it had done above Dinar. It was late, besides, and where a fallen willow forced me from the river, up a steep bank, the last of the daylight was raking a meadow of poppies and cornflowers. On the low rise beyond, skewered to the earth by a single minaret, there chanced to be the village. I stowed the canoe in the deep meadow grass and walked into Gelinören.

Clusters of shawled women, mattocks hanging from their rough hands, were returning from the fields. At the edge of the village they parted with abraded nods and made for home, padding down tributary paths grooved by the passing of their own feet. Rising up from the river, and along a path I by contrast could expect to walk just twice, and only so I might return to the canoe, I never felt so rootless. I felt quite as lost as those sorry wanderers of the Phrygian plain to whom one Lityerses in mythical times had commonly offered food and lodging in exchange for help, Kibbutz-style, in his fields along the Meander. Lityerses, according to some sources the bastard son of King Midas, proved a harsh host when it came to those who failed to work their stay. These he decapitated before wrapping their torsos in the same sheaves they had so signally failed to cut and dumping them in the Meander. Lityerses was to meet his match, of course, as mythical Anatolians invariably did, at the hands of some avenging Olympian; it fell to the superhero Heracles, Roman Hercules, to carve up Lityerses and consign him in his turn to the same river as his victims. Modern interpreters of myth have taken Lityerses' end to instance the emergence of a less conditional notion of hospitality towards strangers; one for which Turks in their homes were justly famed and which might, I hoped, obtain in this shabby village, with its minaret, its flat roofs and rubble walls, and the twilit agro-barn that one woman pointed out, in reply to my question, as belonging to the headman.

At the far end of the open barn, with shit-splattered cattle pens to the fore, the headman's house squatted beneath an industrial expanse of sheet-iron roof. Agricultural implements rusted in long grass around the toilet block. The headman was sitting beneath the house's awning, dressed in a threadbare suit and dandling an infant on his knee. Ali Ihsan Skirmisher was in his middle years. When he proudly repeated his name it was to indicate, with a gesture to the infant, that he shared it with his first grandchild. Among fluttering moths I settled gratefully into the rickety chair he now offered.

'And little Ali Ihsan is very beautiful,' I offered.

The child was fine but the compliment was an awkward attempt at ingratiation. I had not forgotten how my direct attempt the previous evening to secure lodgings had been unsuccessful. Time had been when beds were commonly sought in Turkey's villages, and foreign travellers thought nothing of rousing homeowners at any hour. Visitors knew the form; they were confident in the knowledge that the *oda* or village room, maintained at the expense of some prominent villager, existed expressly to accommodate them. In these honoured institutions they commonly enjoyed remarkable displays of hospitality; the archaeologist Charles Fellows was lodged in a house near Kütahya 'when in came nine people each bearing a dish . . . I was informed that it is the custom of the people, strictly enjoined by their religion, that, as soon as a stranger appears, each peasant should bring his dish; he himself remaining to partake of it after the stranger has fed . . . The hospitality extends to everything he requires; his horse is fed, and wood is brought for his fire.' Payment, moreover, was rarely demanded, though some did use money to secure exclusive access to the accommodation. Reverend Arundell, loath to share the 'magnificent fire', the spread mattresses and provisions freely provided at Dinar, bought off the two other would-be guests – 'gaunt, bony, six feet gentlemen, by occupation beggars, and literally heaps of filth and rags' – with a few piastres.

And now it was growing dark.

'What a beautiful farm,' I ventured. Ali Ihsan, inclining his head at my excessive courtesies, frowned in a dignified bemusement.

'If it is that you need to stay,' he said, 'then you are welcome.' He confirmed the offer by calling for a plate of green almonds. A daughter appeared from the house and placed the almonds, served with salt, on an upturned olive oil tin beside us. Six-year-old Yağmur, whose name meant Rain, spun on a theatrical heel and stared fixedly into the dust.

'Why,' this inquisitive child asked me, 'do ants work so hard to collect things in the spring?' I replied that the spring must be a busy season for ants.

'For people too,' said Ali Ihsan whose own son was still out ploughing the fields. Yağmur continued to scrutinise the same patch of ground. 'And why do ants like green almonds so much?' she asked. It was dark by the time Ali Ihsan's wife called us in to eat.

The family gathered around the stove in the main room. We formed a cross-legged circle on the rugs; Yağmur placed me between herself and her inflatable Tigger. I noticed how Mrs Skirmisher and her daughter-in-law, a girl of striking green-eyed beauty, wore their headscarves; they had fashioned them in the manner of high, elaborate turbans, restraining the hair but making no attempt to conceal their faces, necks or throats. I had registered other styles of headscarf among the valley's womenfolk; some knotted them at the chin while others wore them in the way of wimples. They were artless, the traditional arrangements of working women, and were not to be confused with the avowedly Islamic veils that were behind the current political lather. Such veils, the outriders of Islamic revolution and of *sharia* law in the secularists' judgement, no doubt even of public amputations in the opinion of some, were worn pinned close to the face, often crossed at the neck, and were sometimes complemented with a shapeless full-length coat. Even so, facial concealment was rare in this part of Turkey where women and male strangers plainly could eat together, and there was little sign of the sequestering outfits favoured in Arabia and Afghanistan, and I thought it strange that female headdresses should have thrown today's Turks into such convulsions that they meant to close down their government over the issue.

We were helped to a battered pan of Black Sea *hamsi*, or anchovies, their tails turned up like the dried-out bristles of lacquered paintbrushes, and to bread and salad. The anchovies proved popular: Yağmur, hard pressed to keep Tigger from burying his snout in the pan, was admonished by her mother. We ate in a television flicker. When Ali Ihsan had finished he rose without a word, pocketed his cigarettes and mobile phone, and led me outside to his car.

Insects spiralled in the headlights as we drew up among the tractors parked outside the tea house at the neighbouring village of Dayılar.

'He came by canoe,' said Ali Ihsan by way of introduction. 'He's taking it to the sea.'

'Are you carrying your own water?' asked a farmer, stroking his stubble.

'I fill up my bottle along the way,' I explained.

'I meant to float on. After all these years of drought you won't find much of it downstream.'

'Before that, though, you should watch out for the old water-mills at Aşağı Seyit,' another man advised me. It was not the first time I had heard this warning. And when I asked the man what he meant, he lifted a horizontal forearm from the table and angled it steeply downwards, his other hand driving a current before it.

A crescent moon had risen by the time we returned to the silent farm. In the pile of shoes and slippers by the doorway pink-eyed kittens stirred. I washed in a tiny bathroom where the mirror that lay among Ali Ihsan's shaving kit was from the wing of a car. My host dug out some nightclothes for me, a pair of shorts and an undersized cerise towelling robe, which I had not the heart to turn down. Being required to dress like a bantam-weight boxer did not compare with the treatment meted out by Lityerses, certainly, but it was a reminder that there had long been a downside to Turkish hospitality. The hosts dictated terms and had always felt free to call on their guests after dinner; even to make sizeable inroads into the supplies of medicaments and coffee, which foreign travellers tended to have about them. Nor were the mornings much better; Charles Fellows wrote how locals turned up at his door at dawn bearing 'cream and honey as an excuse for remaining to see me dress', while Reverend Arundell was woken one morning at four o'clock by 'smoking Turks, full of curiosity to witness our operation in dressing and shaving'.

We were to share the main room; Ali Ihsan, who had spread blankets for me on one of the divans there, now made himself comfortable on the other one. We both settled down to watch the television. I dozed fitfully, repeatedly surfacing to television noise – football highlights, gunshots, updates on the closure case against *Ak*, more *Ergenekon* arrests – or to Ali Ihsan's explosive snores. It was a long night. And by the time dawn came, I knew it was time to get off the river.

CHAPTER TEN

I rose early and rummaged for the military map, which I carried out into the early light. Beyond the barn the village women were already returning to the same fields I had watched them leave the previous evening. In faded floral *şalvar* and headscarves they re-formed their stooped rows. A male overseer stood by, running a wheat stem between his teeth.

In the night it had occurred to me that the military map could at least be trusted when it came to the gradients; gradients being unlike dams, roads, villages and village names, that is, in that they could not have changed much since 1944, and being of such strategic importance that the Turkish Army's map men had no doubt got them right. Gradients had been uppermost in my mind since the previous afternoon, when I had sensed the valley begin to close, the river quicken, and especially since hearing the warning repeated at the tea house. A glance at the map confirmed my misgivings; brown lines positively tidemarked the river's banks just a few miles below Gelinören. What remained of the plain, patched with poppy and wheat fields, had already begun sliding south towards the town of Baklan; the river, meanwhile, continued west, and the closely contoured uplands through which it carved a course looked like no place for a lone canoeist. I had prepared myself for the possibility that I might have to leave the river, and had not the least regret about putting away my paddle, for now at least, and pulling on my boots.

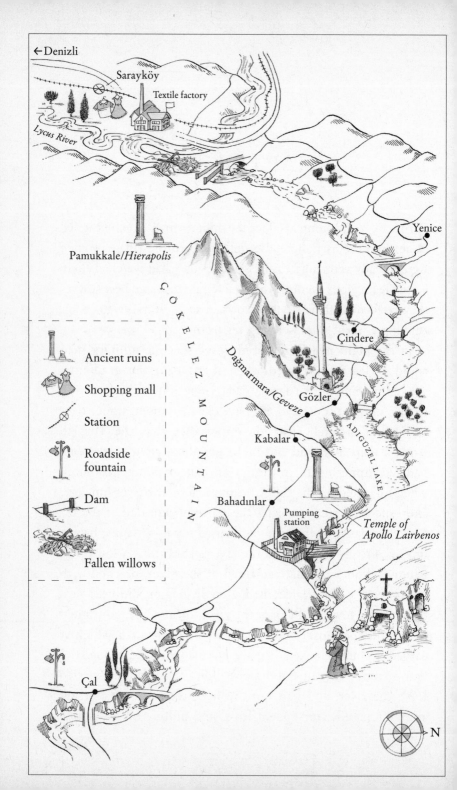

←Denizli

Sarayköy

Textile factory

Lycus River

Pamukkale/*Hierapolis*

Yenice

Çindere

Dağmarmara/*Geveze*

Gözler

ADIGÜZEL LAKE

Kabalar

Bahadınlar

Pumping
station

*Temple of
Apollo Lairbenos*

GÖKELEZ MOUNTAIN

Ancient ruins

Shopping mall

Station

Roadside
fountain

Dam

Fallen willows

Çal

N

I walked down to the river, bagged up the canoe and shouldered it back to the farm.

Tigger had deflated during the night. Yağmur puffed away at
the toy before parking it in the breakfast circle. We ate *yufka*,
stove-warmed sheets of flat bread, with thick cream and tomatoes.
Yağmur, who liked cream, tugged inquisitively at a ringlet of
brown hair. 'How would an ant,' she asked, 'carry cream to its
nest?'

It was time to leave. With a dignified air of apology Ali Ihsan
accepted my offer of payment. He carefully pocketed the folded
notes, promising to put them towards the street light the village
was saving for. Only when I asked if I might leave the canoe in
his care until I could arrange for its collection did Ali Ihsan
realise that I was now without transport.

'But I'll drive you,' he protested. I explained that I meant to
continue along the banks of the river on foot, thanked the
Skirmisher family for their kindness and walked out of the village.

The river's mazy seam ran towards the hills. Across the valley
bottom, cut sticks had been planted four-square, like Zimmer
frames, around gnarled vines whose budding branches were
further supported with frayed ties ripped from old feed sacks. A
white-haired man in a buttoned jacket of faded checks steered a
horse between the scraggy rows, the plough turning the red sandy
silt to level the bold yellow daisies and podded vetches. These
ploughed plots, the vineyards and the stands of spring wheat
initially showed as regular blocks. As the valley narrowed, however,
and the rocky heights closed on the river, so the confined fields
and the vine rows lost their shape, running liquid to the flat land's
broken edge as if to seek out every available indent.

By the time I reached Aşağı Seyit, a sun-struck sprawl of
rutted lanes and slumping tiled roofs, rising red bluffs had closed
on the river. The path, forced from the riverbank, rose out of

the gathering gorge and I followed the faint score of its track across pine-covered slopes. The river fell away but its roar increased. I heard its torrents clattering through the choke of trees. I had done the right thing; if I had not made the decision to leave the canoe, then there was no doubt that I would have abandoned it rather less voluntarily by now.

It was then that I heard bells; not the church peels that the Ottoman sultans had once banned as an infidel affront to the muezzin's sacred call, but the arrhythmic clank, thin as knocked pots, which alerted herdsmen to the whereabouts of their charges. The sound, generally accounted bucolic, triggered more alarming associations in my case. Just as the sight of flocks or herds had caused William Childs to make for the safety of his conveyance, so the bells had me grabbing for my walking pole. I was braced for snarling *kangals* when a pair of placid cows appeared through the pines; the herdsman who followed in their wake wished me peace, which I returned, before the two of us lapsed into bemused silence. Company came as a surprise on this lonely hillside, and it was some time before either of us could make sense of the other: a stick-wielding foreigner, without apparent purpose and on a path where foreigners were not seen, and a local herdsman, face weathered to a walnut, and wearing a ripped T-shirt with English words printed across the chest:

Inside From The West World
X-Position
Mission Available
Loading

'You're travelling alone,' the herdsman remarked; this was a familiar observation among a people who regarded solitude as unorthodox as recreational walking, and solitary walking as cause for outright suspicion.

'So are you,' I countered peevishly. I was contemplating the message on the man's T-shirt – which made no more sense to me, despite every linguistic and educational advantage, than it could have done to its wearer – when the herdsman threw an impatient arm in the direction of his cattle; one went with the cows where he came from, the gesture implied, while the apparently purposeless wanderings of strangers, without cows, might legitimately be called to account.

'I'm looking for the old watermills,' I offered.

The herdsman pointed into the gorge. 'There were several along the river,' he said. 'They were abandoned back when the electricity came. People don't go there mostly.' Nor should I have thought of doing so if it had not been for the tea house warnings. I was curious about the watermills. The locals spoke of these mills as they might have referred to old mine workings or to the quicksands of tidal flats, to ice-covered ponds or the craters of rumbling volcanoes; I sensed it might pay this visiting canoeist to understand the local view if only because watermills meant no more to me than innocuous echoes of a pre-industrial past, a stock feature of picturesque period landscapes, high wheels turning harmlessly within the barred confines of their leats. I asked the herdsman the way to the mills.

'You'll find a path down a little further on, where the slope eases. But there's not much left of them.' I had thanked the herdsman and was continuing on my way when I heard his voice above the bells.

'Is Turkey beautiful?' he called out. Reassured by my fulsome reply, he turned and with his stick rapped the rump of a lingering cow, hurrying it towards Aşağı Seyit.

Where the herdsman had advised I descended across a

rock-strewn meadow of wild flowers and waist-deep grasses. A thick wall of foliage lined the river. With my pole I hacked at the tangle of briars, hollyhocks and dog roses until I had made a hole through which I could poke my head. The river, half-lit beneath the green canopy, surged past in forbidding white braids that slapped at the banks. Feeling for the bank with my feet I discovered a choked channel, perhaps a metre wide, which ran beside the river. I knelt and picked the moss from the channel's sheer sides to reveal concrete. It was a leat, and a mill had once stood where the water-course disappeared into impenetrable thickets. Downstream I could make out the broken walls of several other mills.

It was clear what distinguished these mills: the lack of the trademark vertical wheels, and the fact that they were not regu-larly spaced, in the way of more temperate lands, but were conspicuously clustered, as I now remembered the ones along the banks of the Marsyas at Dinar had been. Anatolians, when they first learned to put their river gods to work, soon discovered that they must resign themselves to a fitful supply of aqueous muscle. It was in accordance with the region's unreliable rains that they designed their mills – water, its fall maximised, turned the paddles of a horizontal wheel whose rising spindle directly rotated the grinding stone up in the milling chamber – and learned to locate them where water flowed fastest. As Canadian bears grouped at waterfalls to gorge themselves on migrating salmon, these mills were traditionally gathered to catch the best of the current; in the case of the millers who served the Baklan Plain, this was along the steep stretch below Aşağı Seyit. Every rural Turk knew by instinct that watermills were found where the land fell away; the foreign canoeist had to work out for himself, however, that the cryptic warnings issuing from the tea houses were to be equated with the brown lines on the map.

These so-called 'Greek' mills appear to have originated in

the region; first attested at Byzantium, they were one of the transforming technologies of the Hellenistic Age. That period of Western pre-eminence, which marked the end of the ancient Persians, is generally considered to date from the moment that Alexander the Great crossed the Hellespont into Anatolia in 334 BC. It was not until the following year, however, that the age's scope was truly confirmed when an ancient oracle identified Alexander as the man who was to subdue all Asia.

By the time of his arrival at Celaenae the young Alexander had already subdued the coastal cities of western Anatolia. On a rising reputation the brilliant Macedonian commander now marched out of Celaenae, as the Persian Cyrus had done sixty-eight years before him, to rendezvous with his forces further north. At Gordium, ancient capital of the eclipsed Phrygians, Alexander made offerings at the Temple of Zeus. There he happened upon a sacred object, which figured large in the Phrygians' founding myth.

It was a farming wagon, its wheels solid timber discs, which spoke, like the sturdy carts of the South African Boers or the early settlers of modern America, of a national pride that was at once peasant and pioneering. The Phrygians' forebears were said to have come, like Alexander, from Macedonia. These ancestors, the story went, had been advised that they were to take as their king him who first appeared to them in a wagon; and in that same totemic wagon the peasant who duly turned up, Midas, led his people out of Macedonia to their new home in Asia.

This legendary journey appeared in several key respects to presage the one that the ambitious Alexander was now in the process of making; early Macedonians, though history might have since swept them away, had once made their mark in these parts. These correspondences, in which Western dominion seemed prefigured, perhaps caused Alexander to heed an oracle that appeared to confirm the same ideas; he who could undo the famously insoluble knot of

the wagon at Gordium, that is, would rule over the East. The
Gordian Knot was undone, either by the power of the sword or by
subtler contrivance, and within ten years Alexander had conquered
Persia and extended his control beyond Afghanistan to India.

It was left to Alexander's generals, following his death in the East,
to cement Hellenic rule across the region. These generals, though
they were eventually to sunder Alexander's vast inheritance by their
competing claims to it, nevertheless established a Greco-Macedonian
dynasty flush with the wealth of Persia's plundered treasuries. The
Seleucids, as they were to be known, set about extensively redevel-
oping the native and Persian settlements of Anatolia's archaic age,
especially the cities that guarded the great road along the Meander
Valley. Kings like Antiochus and Seleucus renamed many of these
lavishly restored cities after themselves or similarly honoured
mothers and wives such as Apama and Laodice. They commissioned
splendid gymnasia, council buildings, libraries and medical schools,
on gridded plans and amidst an abundance of two-storey colonnades. Fine houses went up; the first closed drains and private piped
water systems appeared. Public spaces were landscaped. Not only
watermills but also aqueducts were built. Schools were founded,
and the arts and sciences – geometry, astronomy, philosophy, rhetoric, oratory and drama – were rigorously studied. A uniform system
of Greek law was established. Athletic training, often undertaken
naked, grew rapidly in popularity. Greek began to marginalise native
languages like Phrygian, Lydian and Carian. Subject peoples, the
more readily assimilated at least, took Greek names that they might
more easily pass among the influx of Westerners: these settlers
included veteran soldiers who had been apportioned generous plots
of land, administrators, magistrates and merchants, architects who
refashioned the temples and artists who carved cult statues, in the
Greek style, so that native gods were gradually absorbed by the
Olympians. The Greeks extended a Hellenising skein of language,

culture and thought into the Asiatic interior, and the meaning of those fabled Anatolian reverses was fully revealed. The defeat of Marsyas and humiliation of Midas at the hands of Apollo, and Lityerses' decapitation by Heracles, demonstrated that West had finally bested East, and could now do as it wished with it.

The sorry experiences of those mythical and legendary natives echoed, in fact, the actual plight of the Anatolian peoples. The Phrygians and their regional neighbours had plainly suffered under Eastern dominion as they were to at Western hands, at least to judge by the experience of Pythius, the world's second richest man, whom this narrative last encountered offering up his fortune in the service of the Persian war machine. The Celaenae tycoon, who came from the neighbouring Anatolian region of Lydia, rashly assumed that his generous offer somehow afforded him special pleading rights with the Great King. Since his five sons had all been drafted into the Persian ranks, the Lydian tycoon thought the oldest at least might reasonably be excused from service in the invasion of Greece. Xerxes was outraged. Pythius's oldest son did not go to Greece but only because he rapidly became in no condition to do so; the youth's carcass, cleft on Xerxes' orders from head to toe, was left by the roadside to remind the King's serving subjects of the fate that would-be draft dodgers should expect.

By his action Xerxes reminded this family of prominent Lydians that they were nothing but his absolute subjects, their purpose to serve his merest whim; and that Anatolian peoples such as the Lydians or Phrygians, Pisidians or Lycaonians, almost as obscure to Xerxes as they appear to us, represented an underclass that was born to subjugation. Xerxes quite forgot how the Phrygians under Midas, and the Arzawans and Hittites before them, had in their time all created viable Anatolian empires of their own. Anatolians were ethnic elements that were to be subsumed either into his empire or, if it came to it, that of his Greek enemies, the great

Xerxes even going so far as to claim that his invasion must end in one of two ways: 'that what is ours be under the Greeks, or what is theirs under the Persians; there is no middle way in our quarrel.'

In all this any notion of an independent Anatolian identity appeared comprehensively lost. An all-or-nothing duality, East versus West, was at play, one that Xenophon reflected in the *Anabasis*; the account, after all, of a Persian leading Greeks against Persians, and latterly of retreating Greeks fending off Persians. The Anatolians, who might truly have felt the land to be their own, tended towards invisibility in the *Anabasis* where they were largely dismissed as barbarians; the term, first used by Homer to denote the babble-speaking Carian peoples whose lands lay immediately south of the Meander River, progressively broadened in scope to include all Anatolians, all Persians and peoples ruled by Persians, all Asiatics, and finally all uncivilised foreigners. If Xenophon specified Anatolian races, it was only because their moral deficiencies served to highlight Greek virtues: the pesky Pisidians whose red-herring role was to conceal the identity of an enemy more worthy of the Ten Thousand's attentions; or the Lydians, the original retailers, whose effeminacy led them to wear rings in their ears and whose only talents were profiteering from their management of the mobile markets that provisioned the expeditionary army, and making prostitutes of their female children. The Anatolians had been so long marked down as subject peoples, destined to lose their languages and identities in favour of superior ones, that it was no surprise European antiquaries of the nineteenth century should have largely considered them beneath notice.

In the afternoon I reached a bridge, where I followed a rising road out of the hot valley. At the first village, Yukarı Seyit, a foun-tain stood by the road. The fountain began impressively enough, with a marble base, sponsor's name and lugubrious inscription

– Some evening some time I too will fade with the sun – but grew increasingly gimcrack towards the latter stages of its construction; it was finished with offcut bathroom tiles, carelessly grouted, with the sort of push tap usually associated with public toilets, and furnished with a pink plastic mug. Turks traditionally fulfilled the charitable acts their faith required of them by the provision of such fountains; those who worked the land benefited from these fountains to perform the holy ablutions required of Muslims before prayer, though the proximity in this case of the village mosque, with its own fountain, suggested that personal prestige might rather have influenced the siting of this one. I filled the pink mug and drank deep and, the prospect of my own fading temporarily deferred, I continued footsore along the empty road.

A town of sorts eventually rose out of the land. Çal, standing at 850 metres, was a forlorn place. Beyond a few apartment blocks, dirt lanes wafered away to wilderness. Children in blue tunics

silently padded across the pine needles carpeting the schoolyard.
A queue of farmers trailed from the town's cash machine. Tractors
trundled past. The only place to stay was at the Forestry Directorate,
a compound of block buildings behind a barbed-wire fence, the
walls hung with long-handled fire beaters and red-painted buckets.
The directorate had a guest wing where I found a bed that was not
broken, and set about washing my stinking clothes in a large
saucepan sneaked from the communal kitchen. I hung my laundry
over a railing and looked out over the grounds. Potted saplings,
pines and firs, stood in long rows where a man walked a hose. His
care recalled the roadside signs – 'To Every Village a Forest' – I
had seen; and I wondered why it should be that the Turks looked
after their trees rather better than their rivers.

The guest wing was free of visiting foresters, so I sought out
diversion on the streets of Çal. Most of the townsfolk had disappeared from view, and the only activity was in the internet café
where the shadows of careening cars and jinking footballers flickered
across the pale faces of young men. Beyond the pavement a donkey
chewed at its staked tether. I was making for an early night when
music reached me from the pine trees in the town's park. The
music had an experimental, arbitrary quality, layered as it was with
dissonant phrases that were soon submerged beneath ones that had
no business keeping their company; snatches of oboes and violins,
electronic keyboard riffs, a volley of drums, a falsetto voice, each
confronting and consoling the others in what I took to be some
intriguing musical face-off. For just an instant I thought I had
stumbled across an avant-garde soirée; the descendants of Marsyas
himself defying their peasant expectations by what they had made
of themselves. It turned out that the noise came from a makeshift
combo of mobile phones. A group of youths were slouched beneath
the pines, spitting out the husks of sunflower seeds, while they
passed the time comparing ringtones.

CHAPTER ELEVEN

It rained through the night, and at Çal's Forestry Directorate the rows of saplings slumped in their black polythene pouches. The clatter across the roofs ceased at dawn, and from a clearing sky the sun soon began to retrieve what water the earth was yet to absorb. Steam heads were rising off the meadows by the time I reached the river, and villagers and their tethered horses evaporated to wraith-like outlines in the vineyards, the blossoming apple orchards and vegetable plots.

It was an enchanting scene, at least until the mist lifted to reveal the concrete canalettes, and the concrete posts with their metal spreaders that ran support wires along the vine rows, and the tractors, if only of the few who could afford them and the diesel costs. Rural Turkey was industrialising, shedding its picturesque ways, and I regretted that the earth-dug irrigation channels had not the carrying capacity of the canalettes; that the makeshift vine props I had seen the previous day did not provide the support of the concrete posts; and that no horse could pull a plough like a tractor. Much had gone the way of the watermills but the main regret, I guessed, of those who still hitched plough to horse, and who gazed upon the tractors of their luckier neighbours, was that they themselves were yet to be spared the grind that passing foreigners had always thought so appealing.

The Meander had made a decisive change, meanwhile, in

direction; running up against the foot of Mount Çökelez, it
turned sharply to the north. The river would not trend west
again, as the military map revealed, until it had cleared the
hoop-shaped gorge it had in its own slow time scoured around
the base of the mountain.

What the military map did not show, of course, was that much
of the same gorge had since disappeared beneath the lake, which
had backed up behind the hydro-electric dam they had built
near the village of Adıgüzel during the 1990s. I knew of the
lake, which I meant to reach that evening, from the other maps;
the tourism one had it as nothing less than the haunt of the
curvy blonde on waterskis. The farmer at the bridge thought
not.

'You'd be lucky to find so much as a fisherman there,' he said.
'And you won't get through by following the river.' He stamped
the mud from his boots. 'What you want is the asphalt.' He
pointed at the marvellous innovation beneath our feet before
lovingly tracing its route up the valley's western flank, detailing
every bend with a calloused finger. He was wading into a stand
of maize when I thanked the farmer for his advice; it was a useful
reminder that tough terrain lay ahead as I approached the most
remote stretch of the Meander. Unlike both the river's headwaters
and its broad lower valley, astride the ancient highway and richly
described since the time of Herodotus, this conspicuous midway
kink had remained unexplored into the nineteenth century.

It was easy to see why, most especially to those travelling
not down but *up* the Meander Valley, the European antiquaries
among them, who typically ventured inland from the coast
by the valley road that brought them to the lower side of
Mount Çökelez. There they arrived at a defining junction;
the great road continued into the interior by the Meander
Valley's natural easterly extension – the valley of the classical

Lycus, the Meander's main tributary – while the Meander made off into the high canyons behind the mountain.

Only in 1826 did a European, Reverend Arundell, first think to leave the well-trodden road for the route of the unexplored river above its junction with the Lycus. 'I was now entering upon the principal object of my journey,' Arundell wrote with expeditionary anticipation, 'to discover the course and sources of the River Meander.' Leaving the highway's broad valley and turning north into the shadow of Mount Çökelez, he soon found himself on 'a pathway not a foot wide, and sloping towards a precipice of great depth'; the road was 'at best extremely intricate, and scarcely distinguishable'.

The Meander's unknown course evidently attracted other scholars' exploratory instincts. In 1835 William Hamilton declared that his 'first object . . . was to examine the course of the Meander between its junction with the Lycus' and the river's headwaters; to explore, in other words, the river's wilderness wanderings around the back of Mount Çökelez. No sooner had he begun, however, than Hamilton 'became fully alive to the difficulties of getting through this part of the country, intersected as it is by so many deep fissures, as I may almost call them'.

This lost world, now threatening to close about me, had remained little known as late as the 1930s; at that time the few tracks that served the Çal region, considered too rough even for carts, were passable only by donkeys. Even now the metalled roads were sufficiently novel that the local people could not imagine that anybody might harbour a preference for the same footpaths that had so wearied their forebears. I suspected the farmer's enthusiasm for the asphalt was the reflex response of one who had not trodden the old ways for many years and knew nothing of their condition, and could conceive of no circumstances in which a foreigner could possibly have any interest in following them: remaining loyal, if the farmer must know, to the river, if not to the canoe, which was why I turned my back on him and his road, and crossed the bridge to the right bank where a rough track ran beside the tumbling river.

This track dwindled before ending at a gate; the gate was easily climbable, though it did carry a crudely painted sign which read PIG TRAPS ON THIS LAND. The sign might have sounded a sincere caution, as the cardboard ones slung from the sprayed cherry trees in Çivril had perhaps done; the fact, however, that Turks specifically disliked pigs, creatures proscribed by their religion, gave rise to the same nagging suspicion – that these particular porkers had been fabricated, along with the dire prospect of being trapped alongside them, to dissuade people from passing over the gate.

It had been my experience, that said, that the only Turks intent on keeping people out were the military, and this they did with formidable fences and signs of unmistakable intent. The rest seemed perfectly happy, proud even, that I should wander their land at will, and it was a measure of their refreshingly unfenced approach that only fallen willows and invitations to drink tea should so far have blocked my way. I therefore read the sign to indicate that I was perfectly free to proceed, but that there were pig traps on the land, which is to say that I advanced gingerly through the field, toeing aside the wild rocket, with its faded lemon petals, to check for the least glint of gaping iron jaws or even for a brush-covered pit, set with stakes, the better to do for the unholy swine.

The field proved quite empty, and beyond the ruins of a remote farmstead, where a rusted children's swing was lashed by lengths of electricity cable to the bough of a walnut tree, the valley drew decidedly to an end. The river now squirted into a high-sided ravine, and the only way onwards was by scrambling up a steep slope and grabbing at the holly oaks, thick with dusty webs, which thrust from the crannies. Here, where the sun could not reach, land crabs sidled away; from the safety of rocky recesses they swivelled yellow eyes to watch me pass.

I found myself on a narrowing rise. The deepening ravine fell away to my left while to my right rose a sheer rock face set with the regular shadows of the arched or rectangular entrances that had been cut there. Many of these cell-like caves, patently hewn by hand, were now inaccessible; they must once have been served by ropes or by timber footholds in the form of driven pegs, which had long rotted away. I managed to reach the lowest cave where I ran a hand across the rough rounded roof, expecting a sandstone sufficiently soft and powdery to have encouraged the cell's excavator to take it on. This rock was seamed, however, with quartz; it was a granitic gneiss so unyielding as to suggest an occupant committed to a life lived, whatever effort the readying of his quarters might have cost, on that especial ledge. Other than this evident determination there were no further clues to conjure the cowled reclusives who had once settled these remote rocks. Nothing but an old ash pile and the single quill of a porcupine, banded brown and white, now lay on the floor of the hermit's cell.

It was then that the slope opened up. Among the remains of stone terraces I pictured the anchorites, grateful for a break from the chiselling, taking turns at tending produce they had once raised here. Now only a sunlit sweep of dandelions stretched to the ravine's edge. Martins rose from the river and winged over the grasslands, careless of the breeze that bludgeoned the yellow-black swallowtail butterflies there. A stork soared on fixed rectangles, its pink legs trailing, and I followed the flit of its shadow far below me, crumpling and unfolding across the contours like the shadow of a descending aircraft observed from its own cabin.

Then I came to a track not tramped into being by ancient usage, but machine-made and newly graded, which coiled downwards to draw up beside the river. On the far bank stood a pumping station, which was reached by a footbridge of planks nailed across a pair of stripped poplar trunks. The path, confronted by the cliffs that reared before it, crossed the bridge to continue along the far bank, but not before it had run beneath the high gate at the far side of the bridge and wound its way across the pumping station compound. It was only when I reached the gate, finding it locked, that I was reminded what bridges were in fact for.

For during my time in the canoe, free as I was to paddle between the banks, bridges had served not as crossing points but as something else entirely; they were the exits where I might leave the river for the roads or tracks the bridges carried. I had accordingly come to see bridges as junctions – which generations of watering cattle had perfected by trampling the adjacent banks to gentle shelves, foliage-free slopes, as if their mission had always been to assist the landing and launching of river craft, and their need to drink merely the consequence of the effort it had taken them. Here was a reminder of the actual use for which bridges had been built, for crossing rivers; but only, in this case, by those who had legitimate business with the pumping station on the far bank. I was stuck.

Nor was I the first; river crossings had historic form as prominent obstacles to Anatolian journeying. There were the mountains, of course, but the challenge they represented was embodied in their sheer substance. Before many bridges had appeared – early ones, around roughly 500 BC, were constructed on pontoons – most rivers subjected travellers to delay, effort and expense even as they allowed tantalising views of the far bank. Their modern equivalent was negotiating the remote border post, the difference being that the river crossing was not merely tiresome but fraught with danger; this danger being the last thing, of course, that Barbarossa was to discover before he was pulled under by the weight of his crusading armour. As today's travellers hope to find border officials in tractable mood, so ancient ones held out for favourable fording conditions; waters, in short, which did not rise above the chest, and a current sufficiently weak that men might stay on their feet. Thales, the great engineering philosopher of Miletus, gained renown for reducing a river that blocked the advance of an army intent on taking on the Persians; his solution was to dig a canal, splitting 'the river into two streams, which were both easily fordable'.

The Persians preferred to dispatch magi, their priestly wonder workers, to propitiate the deities of the river; on Xerxes' Greek campaign they even sacrificed white chargers to the waters of the River Strymon. When the forces of Cyrus's anabasis succeeded in crossing the Euphrates at Thapsacus, where the river was generally reckoned unfordable, the active support of the gods was presumed. On that same great march can-do types occasionally engineered ingenious solutions to the problems the rivers posed; a man from Rhodes offered to transport Xenophon and his comrades across a river in eastern Anatolia, 4,000 at a time, on a pontoon bridge made from the inflated skins of local livestock. Elsewhere on the same expedition the men filled their tent coverings with hay and made floats of them by stitching them tight.

Whereas I got to call out, prosaically enough, in the hope of attracting the attention of a key-wielding attendant; to decide, when none appeared, that safety considerations prevented me from attempting to wade the turbid river; and to retrace my steps to the bridge where the farmer had shown me the only way forward earlier that same day. I followed his finger's course through a long afternoon. I passed the hours pondering how perspectives – on everything from asphalt to watermills, on the various uses of bridges or trowels – were what distinguished us.

The rising road wound through fields, scattered villages and scrub-covered rocks, beneath a black sun, and not a vehicle passed. At length I grew weary, and my head drooped to fix stupidly at the asphalt I had thought to avoid. Only the accumulation there of cowpats signalled my approach to a final village. Beyond the crusted shit and the stir of flies I plodded unsteadily into Bahadınlar. At the road bend was a village shop, tiny and half-lit, where I found Cola and a packet of biscuits. The news of my arrival spread through the village. Murmuring men crowded the open door of the shop, the only light source, so that I paid in gathering darkness.

'Who is he?' somebody inquired.

'Give us some light!' the shopkeeper protested. 'I can't see the man's money.'

'Is it Peter?' another villager asked. I drained the Cola, wondered who this Peter could be and shouldered my way though a crush of soil-streaked farm labourers.

'Maybe he's here to see the tourism place,' somebody suggested.

'The tourism place?' I asked, instantly interested. A young man in a torn suit jacket, checking the time on his wrist, stepped forward and offered his hand.

'I'll show you,' said Mehmet Halil Blessed. In no time we were heading north down a rough track in the village *dolmuş* while Mehmet Halil asked me if I knew said Peter.

'Peter,' he insisted. 'The historian from England.' We passed between fields; then, at the plateau edge, the land ran wild and the track plunged down the steepening slopes of the Meander Valley. It flattened off at a promontory where a hill protruded from the valley slope. The driver pulled up. We climbed through the breeze-blown grasses to an eroded summit and looked out over the crumpled vastness of the empty land. The ravine lay far beneath us. I looked back to the high-sided gorge, with its mysterious hewn rock cells, where I had walked that morning. Beneath us the river widened into a silvered expanse, which zigzagged between myriad capes and headlands. I had reached the lake, my day's objective, where there was no sign of the waterskiing blonde. Instead, the remains of a classical site – marble blocks, monumental stones, chunks of carved architrave and column drums – lay scattered along the hilltop.

'The tourism place,' said Mehmet Halil. 'Peter came here some five years ago.'

And others before the mysterious Peter; an archaeological research team led by William Ramsay and David Hogarth had discovered the site in May 1887. They travelled up the Meander Valley by train, Turkey's first railway having been extended a few years earlier as far as Sarayköy, the town at the south-west corner of Çökelez Mountain. At Sarayköy, however, the modern world's advance was abruptly halted, and the team continued their progress to Çal on horseback. There they learned 'of the existence of ruins in or near Badinlar, three hours away to the north', and were duly guided to what Hogarth described as 'the site of a small temple situate on a conical eminence' above the Meander gorge. 'Only the platform on which the temple had stood remained in situ,' Hogarth wrote, 'and very few fragments could we find of columns or cornice: such as remained of the frieze showed by their formal ornament the Ionic of Roman period.' Beyond the memorable setting there was not much, in short, to be seen; it was remarkable, given the more extensive classical sites in which the region abounded, that the remote site should have detained the scholars. Yet something caught their eye; the discoveries made at the temple were to provide an extraordinary insight into the workings of religion at the end of the first century, when the temple's extant remains were dated to.

Almost half a millennium had passed since the conquests of Alexander. Through the intervening centuries the Emperor's Seleucid successors established an avowedly Hellenic culture across the region. They warred as much among themselves as with others, however, and thus did much to hasten the dynasty's decline. The rising power of Rome, in harness with its regional client, the adjacent Anatolian kingdom of Pergamum, inflicted a series of defeats upon the Seleucids, who agreed humiliating terms at Apamea in 188 BC; the payment of massive war indemnities and the cession of western Anatolia, the Meander region included, to Pergamum. When Pergamum's last king died heirless in 133 BC all his territories passed to Rome. Under imperial rule, the region was formally established as the province of Asia. In the Meander's lavishly refurbished cities, at Apamea, Laodicea and Tralles, Hellenic culture was soon partnered by Roman writ. Out in the sticks, however, the old ways largely endured; what Ramsay and Hogarth discovered at the lonely temple site below Bahadınlar, a large number of inscribed stone slabs or steles, revealed an impressive cult to the local god Apollo Lairbenos.

The pagan gods of Anatolia had long been conspicuously

diverse. Native deities, often Hittite or Lydian, jostled for influence with popular incomers from Zoroastrian Persia, like Mithras, Isis and Osiris from Egypt, and established Olympians such as Apollo. What decidedly crowded the devotional landscape, however, was a strong variant tendency among the established archetypes; the likes of the moon god, Men, and the great mother goddess, popularly known as Cybele or Leto, came in local versions, growing epithets, or prototype surnames, to indicate their particular constituency communities and distinctive powers. Apollo cults in particular flourished across western Anatolia where the god not only practised his established talents – the guardianship of a pure musical tradition, as we have seen, along with prophecy, harvest, sun worship and medicine – but had also sprouted specific, often pointedly singular functions; one, Apollo Smintheus, slew mice and was represented accordingly, a triumphant heel poised above some cringing rodent, while Apollo Culicarius made it his business, like a divine spray, to repel mosquitoes. The meaning of Lairbenos has not been established; it probably referred to the people of these uplands, the Lairbenes perhaps, whom the god held in his tyrannical sway. For the inscribed stones uncovered in the vicinity of the temple site compellingly cast these Lairbenes, for want of a better name, as victims of Apollonian harshness, as the land's mythical figures had been before them.

These inscriptions were to prove hard, hard as the herdsman's T-shirt that had so baffled me the day before, to decipher. They were in Greek, which all through the Roman period continued to denote refinement and education in these Eastern lands, but rendered by a people whose linguistic carry evidently did not reach far beyond their native Phrygian. Ramsay, expert in Anatolian epigraphy, described the inscriptions as 'mis-spelt, corrupted, distorted so much as to be sometimes unrecognisable', while Hogarth remarked on 'the extraordinary barbarism of their orthography and etymology'.

What the decrypted steles eventually revealed, nevertheless, was a people in thrall not only to a fancy foreign language but also to an excessively ritualised theocracy. By their inscriptions the Lairbenes sought absolution for their sins, which were apparently many, and at once confirmed themselves as obedient subjects of the god. Their steles resembled the legion testimonies heard in charismatic churches, at once confession statements and oaths of loyalty. The Lairbenes admitted to all manner of transgressions: the theft of sheep, of clothes from a bathhouse, and of firewood from a sacred grove. One individual had consumed improperly sacrificed goat meat; another had had sex while in the service of the temple. A lie had been uttered that somehow related to the sacred pigeons housed in the temple precinct; there had been a failure to attend divine service. The author of one stele owned up to having masturbated – if his coy euphemisms were correctly interpreted – while the hapless Apelles even felt compelled to admit that he had once contemplated sex with his wife at a time when such thoughts were evidently proscribed.

Many of the inscriptions bore witness not only to the actuality of divine power but also to the fact of a deity willing to deploy it; the contrite Lairbenes commonly acknowledged having suffered some kind of retribution for their transgressions. These chastisements the rationally minded Hogarth mostly identified with ailments such as the 'disease, perhaps malarial fever, which always hangs about the valley'. According to the subject mind it was Apollo who brought the sickness, as Ramsay well understood. 'When illness struck an individual, especially fever, the unseen fire in the body,' Ramsay wrote, 'he searched his conscience to find where he had sinned, confessed, made atonement, and recorded the circumstances as an example.' So it was that one Sosandros, having 'sworn falsely, and being impure on that account', and having been chastised, warned 'that no one should despise the god Lairmenos, since he will have my stele as an example'. Another, Kleonymos, 'punished by the god set up this tablet even as he punished me, for my oath, for consciousness of guilt, and for pollution. I warn all that none should slight the god.' An institutionalised guilt, general and visible, appeared to hang over this Anatolian tribe.

We made our way across the hilltop, passing the information board the tourism department had lately erected, and looked out across the view, which the dam had transformed over recent decades; what qualified this beautiful prospect was the fact that these wild waters, now tamed, had been herded into a body of water where they were condemned to mill until their time came to turn turbines.

What was left of the shrine, however, the extensive platform, the stubs of columns and plinths of statues, the fallen pediment festooned with fruit and foliage and the odd in situ stele, remained much as they had been when Ramsay and Hogarth first found them. In this respect the hilltop site had lost nothing of its resonant atmosphere. In my mind I was able to retrieve the scattered stones, and raise a colonnaded portico, with coffered ceilings, above the platform. By the sacred groves, thick with roosting pigeons, I laid out the courtyards and furnished them with the deity statues, long since removed to museums, and with the steles, numerous as gravestones, where local consciences were laid bare. At the temple I caught my first unmediated glimpse of the native Phrygians who had hitherto been excluded from the history of their land. Among the incomers – Persians, Greeks, Jews, Romans – Anatolia's own now appeared. It felt, however, like a sorry entrance.

History could only know these people for what they admitted to having done wrong. It was from their criminals that most societies wrung formal confession statements, and from their marginalised that they demanded oaths of loyalty; the steles showed that the average Lairbene habitually endured both. The fate of these people was to read divine displeasure in their every misfortune. The assumption that they had brought their trouble upon themselves duly led them to the deluded belief that they could do something about it; if only, that is, they could work out what they were supposed to have done wrong.

For by the imaginative range of their confessions the Lairbenes appeared as much to propose possible misdemeanours as to acknowledge them. These people willingly owned up, in a language not their own, to any conceivable transgression; anything to lift the fever, to prevent more deaths in the family or losses of livestock, to protect the crops from hailstorms, or otherwise to guard against loss of livelihood. The confessions had the look of statements given under duress; the work of sorry souls racking their brains not for the truth but for the words their torturers might wish to hear. I sensed, and not for the first time, a people stalked by victimisation.

Mehmet Halil was tapping at his watch to signal some unknown commitment. We made our way back to the *dolmuş*.

'Does he know Peter?' the driver asked over the straining engine. Peter was the last foreigner, it now transpired, to have visited the temple site. He had been here fully five years ago, and had not stayed long. It seemed, even so, that the villagers had invested this Peter's visit with particular significance. His name was invoked to substantiate the outside world's interest in the temple, bring tourists to the tourism place and thereby transform local livelihoods, as it had done at the great archaeo-logical site at nearby Hierapolis, which I meant to visit over the next few days. I was no coach load, of course, but could perhaps be said to constitute a start in the process. It may be I was thought worthy of cultivation. The *dolmuş* had not reached the village, where a shawled woman slapped a stick against the threadbare rear of a donkey bundled with vine prunings, before Mehmet Halil was inviting me to stay.

He lived at the end of a cobbled alleyway, among scruffy chickens and vegetable plots, on the first floor of a small stone house. Steps rose to a raised patio; an ancient marble column, fitted out as a heavy roller, served for flattening the mud floor. Mehmet Halil welcomed me with a sweep of the arm but this familiar gesture of village hospitality had a contemporary twist, concluding with a motion that indicated the particular socket, the one that worked, where I might charge my mobile phone. He lit a brushwood fire in the open hearth and dispatched a cousin to get vegetables. The young boy returned with lettuce, green peppers, spring onions and tomatoes gathered from a nearby plot. When Mehmet Halil went off in search of a chicken, I therefore thought to hear the frantic wingbeats of a cornered bird followed by the rude termination of its protesting squawk. He reappeared, however, not with plucked feathers trailing in his wake but with a family pack of frozen drumsticks he had picked up at the corner shop.

Mehmet Halil arranged the drumsticks across the hearth, poured cups of home-made wine and told me about his life. He was born in Bahadınlar and had attended the village school until he was thirteen. He did not have a proper job and had no prospect of one. With only occasional farming work, Mehmet Halil was in no position to attract a wife. The unspoken probability was that he would grow old in the village, without a family of his own.

'Eat up,' he urged, tapping his watch as he laid a plate in front of me. 'And then we'll go to the tea house.'

Night had fallen by the time we left Mehmet Halil's house. We made our hurried way through the village beneath a crescent moon, passing beneath the enormous spread of an ancient plane tree, its trunk sundered by lightning strikes. The region was renowned for its great planes; on his invasion march Xerxes had halted not far from here to admire such a tree before bedecking it with golden ornaments raided from the imperial war chest and furnishing it with a troop of guards. It was all of 900 years old and sacred, according to Mehmet Halil, who might have told me more if he had not been so keen to reach the tea house.

In no time he was steering me into a large room, the walls bare but for the commercial calendars of tractor parts distributors, suppliers of fertilisers and animal feed, their tear-off stubs some two months out of date, where a few flat-capped men and youths were warming their hands around a central stove. Most of the village's men had already parked themselves, however, before the television, with only the strewn husks of sunflower seeds to show where their chairs had once formed conversational clusters. These chairs were now arranged in neat rows, five deep, before the screen; we were among the late arrivals, pushing through the door with a sort of premiere excitement, who dragged chairs across the bare boards to join the audience. With a last look at his watch Mehmet Halil motioned me to sit beside him. The talking stopped and the clink of tea glasses fell still, and through the window the sound of cattle briefly carried.

'*Wolves' Valley*,' whispered Mehmet Halil.

The steles discovered around Bahadınlar, dated to the end of the first century, do not appear to have featured in earlier ages. Around that time, then, something caused the Lairbenes – some signal shift in their relationship with their god – to make these public displays of their legion transgressions. It was as if, in fact, Apollo Lairbenos and the god's pagan sponsors sought overt confirmation of civic devotion; the old guard reassuring itself by this insistence that the Lairbenes affirm their subject status. The cult of the gods, complete with imperial imprimatur, was reconfirmed; but in the face, of course, of the new creed that was sweeping Anatolia.

That creed, in William Ramsay's judgement, had already left its mark among the Lairbenes. For one stele inscription appeared to admit to an offence not of ritual but of actual religion, as if its author had in fact been flirting with a dangerous heterodoxy. The inscription, Ramsay reckoned, amounted to a forced recantation of Christianity.

CHAPTER TWELVE

Mehmet Halil had neither a spare room nor much spare space in his own one. I bedded down where a wife should have been, as Mehmet Halil would certainly have preferred it. In the proximity of strange male company it was I, that said, who had trouble sleeping. My thoughts drifted back to the squealing tyres, the poly-wrapped bricks of banknotes, the reflector sunglasses, the shiny black gloves and the practised fitting of pistol silencers that had featured in that evening's episode of *Wolves' Valley*. An agent of the state had morphed into a gang boss, and viewers in the Bahadınlar tea room and across Turkey watched transfixed.

Wolves' Valley reflected a profound national cynicism; it was as if James Bond had agreed to allow some evil genius's bid for world domination – so long as they cut him in on the proceeds. The Turks had long trusted the 'Father State', as they once referred to it, to protect the national interest at any cost, even if it meant deploying agents in a range of clandestine operations. Such activities were typically legitimised as confirming a heroic tradition in the service of national salvation: the training of guerrilla units and caching of weapons, for example, whereby the Turks under Atatürk had prepared for successful resistance after the Ottomans' defeat in the Great War, and the secret provisions made during the 1950s to prepare for possible occupation by Warsaw Pact forces. Many Turks also acknowledged, albeit with rather more ambivalence, that such shadowy forces had been responsible for many of the killings committed in south-east Turkey during the Kurdish insurgency of the 1990s.

This trust was shaken, however, when the extent to which the state was mired in common criminality became explosively apparent on a wet night in 1996. A black Mercedes – *Wolves' Valley* to a tee – left a hotel in the resort of Kuşadası to collide with a lorry hours later near the town of Susurluk. The car was found to contain: a high-ranking police commander; an MP who had made a fortune hiring out his private armies in actions against Kurdish separatists; a heroin-smuggling gangster wanted by Interpol; and the gangster's girlfriend, predictably enough a former beauty queen. Three died in the crash – the only survivor, the MP, lost all memory of how he came to be in the car.

Which was prudent, given that it excused him from explaining either the company he had been keeping or the contents of the Mercedes' boot: pistols and silencers, quantities of cash, a diplomatic passport in the gangster's name and a host of other incriminating documents. Ensuing investigations revealed that the gangster held a whole array of diplomatic passports, identity cards and gun licences; he had been operating as the state's assassin, and in return had been permitted to continue his heroin-smuggling and money-laundering activities unopposed. The state not only sanctioned the extra-judicial executions of its enemies – those businessmen suspected, for example, of funding the Kurdish insurgency – but did so in a partnership richly rewarding to its criminals. Many Turks were not so naïve as to assume that their politicians and policemen were all above suspicion. What shocked them was the complicity revealed in the wreckage of the Mercedes. It was no longer possible to distinguish – in

Turkey as in *Wolves' Valley* – between criminals and agents of the state.

The more immediately relevant question, come the morning, was what lay beyond the lake I'd seen from the temple ruins. More river rafting, according to the tourism map, as well as biking along the riverbanks, horse riding, and the chance to sample local wines in long-stemmed glasses, perhaps at one of the picnic tables handily sited along the trail. Mehmet Halil thought not.

'Beyond the dam?' he gruffly echoed my question. 'Another lake. Leading to another dam.' He forked some tomato slices onto his breakfast plate. 'And below that they're building yet another dam.' The entire gorge at the head of the loop had apparently been given over to a series of reservoirs; vast quantities of river water, stored heads of hydroelectric energy, which stepped down the sheer-sided canyons to power the flickering light bulbs of the neighbouring towns of Buldan and Sarayköy. The tourism map did not include bulldozers and heavy machinery, it seemed, in its coverage.

I was being progressively distanced, I felt, from the river. Since there was no way through the gorge, not even on foot, I had no choice but to continue by the lane which, all three maps for once agreed, shadowed the gorge for its entire length. This road would return me to the Meander once it had reverted to a river, below the dam they were currently building, and not far from the town of Yenice. At Yenice, that is to say, I could think about retrieving my canoe.

'There's a hotel at Yenice,' added Mehmet Halil. After a run of largely sleepless nights I could do with a room of my own, I reckoned, and determined to reach Yenice the same day, though it was at least forty kilometres away. I packed at speed. Mehmet Halil, aghast at my offer of money, embraced me as I strode out into the morning.

The narrow lane ran through fields flecked with green
shoots. Hunched villagers dug fertilising hearth ash into the
red earth around the roots of their vines. The day had already
turned hot, and the clouds were floury wisps above the distant
gorge. There were few buildings and I spotted the roadside
hut long before I reached it. It stood beside a mulberry tree
and in the shaded interior there was an armchair, shabby but
serviceable, with a clay washing bowl set in the earth floor
beside it. Two old amphorae were propped against the rough
stone walls, with wooden lids hand-fashioned in the shape
of table tennis bats. I lifted one; the amphora brimmed with
water freely offered as Mehmet Halil's hospitality had been,
and I drank deep, wondering about the plainly good person
who must come, if I waited long enough, to replenish the
water, pat the dust from the chair where I now sat and rinse
the plastic cup I now drained. It was a kindness, apparently
anonymous, and one that required repeated attention; the
tap fountains, which entailed no such maintenance, appeared
by comparison like monuments to the beneficence of local
worthies. The regular readying for others of this place was
all the more affecting because most of those who might once
have stopped here no longer even noticed it, passing as they
did in their *dolmuş* seats or on the trailers of tractors. The
world sped by and ever-dwindling numbers, the odd indigent
or itinerant, came to the hut for its shade and water. It could
not be long before the place fell into disuse and yet another
ruin would mark the landscape, and plastic bottles thrown
from passing windows would instead indicate where travellers
got their water from.

For now, however, a stranger's care had sanctified the
contents of the roadside amphorae. The State Water Works
might be busily turning the last of the canyons into

hydroelectric stores, but the water that came chilled from that earthen darkness felt like the gift of life. It lightened me on my way and in that marvellous morning I glimpsed the lemon flash of a golden oriole among the trees outside a place called Kabalar. It was a plain village, a bare cluster of block-built houses, but in the little square a woman stopped to learn who I was and where I was headed. Women in rural Turkey did not generally accost male strangers. Perhaps it was because she was decidedly matronly, beyond all that, or that she had learned to see things differently during her years in Switzerland where her two children now worked as an architect and in the computer industry; prosperous and married, with children of their own, ambitions fulfilled in a way, I feared, that Mehmet Halil was not to know.

All morning I followed my shortening shadow across the silent uplands. I passed through hillside pine forests. In the chill braids of a milky stream I bathed my feet, the current sweeping the sweat towards the gorge as I laboured onwards to reach the village on the high slopes. It was a cluster of flat-roofed hovels and whitewashed cottages where poplars in their spring brilliance rose like Day-Glo fireworks. The village was now called Dağmarmara, or High Quarry, though the military map knew it as Geveze, or Windbag, a plain silly name proving quite as unacceptable, apparently, to the modern bureaucrats as a foreign or religious one might.

The village was empty. The flank of a sleeping dog heaved in the shade of a blue water bowser. Beyond it, where a wide plain ran to the horizon, I left the road. A path led through scattered plots of corrugated soil. Among those irregular strips, their straight edges giving way to violin curves where boulders and scrub oaks intruded, I found the villagers of Dağmarmara. An elderly couple weeded a field of thyme; a gang of women, their hoes abandoned, hitched up their baggy *şalvar* to squat around a blackened teapot in the shade of a pine tree. In the wake of a slow tractor a disc plough trailed neat lines of tobacco seedlings. Seated workers, the women in floral shawls and the men in brown rubber boots, topped the plough. They slipped the seedlings into notches on blades that revolved to release them upright in the newly turned soil. I asked where the crop would end up.

'Izmir!' exclaimed the moustachioed patriarch who sat at the wheel of the tractor. 'And where might you be going?'

My answer caused him to smile. 'Ah, Yenice,' he enthused and at my good fortune threw up his arms. It was a gesture that did wonders for the hotel there, instantly furnishing it with foyer and ornamental fountain, and I lengthened my stride against the sun.

I was making for the minaret I had spied in the west. It appeared from a rift in the plain, where I thought to rest and drink tea in the village of Gözler. Clearing a final limestone bluff, however, I saw that there was to be no tea. The minaret, patterned with blue-glazed bricks and rising to a round balcony, stood amidst a ruined village. Fields enclosed by low broken walls, waist-deep in thistles, edged the abandoned settlement. The minaret rose from the tumbled walls of a mosque whose roofs had been scavenged for building materials; I reckoned it might just be climbable.

I had never been up a minaret, which felt like an omission; the question was whether it was wise that I should begin with a derelict one. The mosque had been reduced to a pile of bramble-choked rubble and a fig tree thrust from the arched doorway at the minaret's base. Beyond the fig tree, however, the minaret's staircase looked reasonably sturdy. I had often been struck how minarets commonly defied their slender fragility to

outlast buildings they had once served – like the legendary one at Jam, Afghanistan – no doubt because the modesty of their roofs, in this case a steep cone of stainless steel topped by the traditional star and crescent, preserved them from the ingress of rain. Even so, it was only the consolation of a memorable epitaph – *Died in a Minaret He Himself Had Caused to Collapse* – which finally persuaded me to push past the fig tree, hung with spiders' webs, and start up the cramped spiral.

The stairs of rough concrete proved solid. I had soon ceased to worry about the structure of the minaret. By the time I had climbed all of its eighty-eight steps I was instead thinking of the muezzin who had made the same ascent, five times daily, to pronounce that Allah was great, and that there was no God but

He; whatever others, long since banished, had once claimed for numerous other deities from Apollo Lairbenos to the god of the Christians.

A sunlit archway gave onto the balcony where the parapet had partially fallen away. So I halted there and looked out over the land's deep folds and the limestone outcrops. From my high outlook I now saw that one other building had survived amid the wreckage; it was a stone house of some distinction, which must once have been home to the village landlord or *ağa*. The house, squarely built, with thick walls, Gothic window arches and a sagging roof, stood within a walled garden where a *kangal* had been chained to assert an absent owner's claim. The creature was less anxious to defend the property, however, than itself – and from the falling tiles which the roof regularly shed. Smashed tiles lay across the garden, leaving not a single patch of clear ground; not one so big, that is, that a *kangal* might safely shelter in it. It appeared that the dog had been suffering in this way for months. In the process the traumatised creature had come to survey the sky whence it had learned to expect strikes. It now caught sight of me there and, taking my high tower for the haunt of a tormenting deity, it gave a long whine of submission, and I figured I might finally be done with worrying about *kangals*.

I passed the village of Çindere, which clung to the plateau rim high above the half-built dam, in the late afternoon. Wicker baskets heaped with fresh-cut meadow fodder stood in the dusty lanes, and the road beyond the village began a sweeping descent. The watered western flank of Çökelez Mountain was thick with pinewoods and with the lilac blossoms of the Judas trees. Bleached jade poppies stood slashed with ragged purple petals. Box beehives the colour of old denim patterned the hillside meadows. The only traffic I encountered was a pair of donkeys bearing an elderly couple to Çindere. He sported a coal-black flat cap, a fob watch hanging from his tattered purple waistcoat, while his wife wore a high turban, extravagantly tied, and patterned in ivory and gold. They were mounted on embroidered saddles, with high wooden pommels, and the firewood sticks they had gathered protruded from their saddlebags, feed sacks reinforced with stitching, like desperado musketry. They were magnificent.

'You're out late,' the man observed, glancing over his shoulder. His meaning might have been mundane, that he doubted I would get a lift, but I had the thrilling sense he might once have used the same utterance to warn against ruffians and brigands; that a lonely road, the light fading, even now remained no place for strangers. I told him that I was making for Yenice.

'Ask for the hotel,' he said, kicking at the flanks of his donkey. I now saw a low-lit bar, heard a piano and even fancied a line of flagpoles at the front.

It was an evening among the heavens. The last sunlight was so low among the plane trees that it caught the undersides of the leaves. The long shadows grew indistinct and a lowland warmth rose up the road to meet me. I plunged through woods and fields, and had almost reached the valley floor by the time the lift came. The tractor came barrelling out of the gloaming, a wide-eyed driver staring down the beam of the one functioning headlight. I clambered gratefully onto the trailer and had barely sunk to the wooden boards when we were clattering over a bridge. The Meander slid beneath us. I glimpsed lines of current, stronger than I had expected, which were scored in silver across the chipped surface of the river. The headlight illuminated a rusted sign bearing a message I had not yet seen on the Meander: *Entering the Water*, it said, *Is Dangerous and Forbidden*.

The tractor drew up in what I took to be a poor part of Yenice (alt. 263 metres). There was a scruffy park and a broken sequence of street lights, and the little shops, open to the street, sold bags of crisps and disposable razors. A youth emerged from a barber's shop. He introduced himself as Menderes, which I took as a good sign. I told Meander that I was very pleased to meet him and wondered if he could direct me to the hotel which I understood to be in the town. Meander thought not.

'Hotel?' he queried, and went to check with his friends in the barber's shop. He then returned, shouldered my rucksack and led me down the street. When he stopped and wished me goodnight, it was not before an illuminated building, with flagpoles and landscaped flowerbeds, but at an unlit concrete block. On the wall, in red paint, was scrawled the word *OTEL*.

CHAPTER THIRTEEN

I rose early, delaying only to arrange the retrieval of my canoe, before I walked down to the river. It was a first opportunity to return to what was, after all, my theme. The river, besides, was my way out of Yenice. The little town and I had not got on.

It did not help that the travelling had done me in. Three long days of walking had left me sore and blistered. My rucksack reeked of river rot. The broken nights in villagers' bedrooms had left their mark. I was weary to the point of seeing things, though not the standard mirages; regular drinks from the roadside fountains and clay jars had at least spared me the shimmering lakes that parched travellers thought to drain in single draughts. That I was able to stay well watered had only made space, however, for more banal visions; of the neat and prosperous outlines, in fact, of quality accommodation. The shame of it was that I wanted nothing so much as somewhere nice to stay. The same softness at my centre that had caused me to hold out, however remotely, for the likes of waterskiing blondes now deluded me that an oasis of country comfort awaited at Yenice.

It was therefore a disappointment to discover that the hotel there did not even run to a name. The Turks might have borrowed their word for hotel from the French, as the absent 'H' in their phonetic rendering signified, but they had learned little else from those hoteliers par excellence. Turks, who preferred to bestow hospitality rather than to sell it, had always been better at opening their homes to visitors than at running hotels for them; this was to their credit, of course, though the consequence was hotels like the one at Yenice.

Hotels needed names, I reckoned, no less than people did. The lousiest establishments had them. When the water supply failed, or scurrying cockroaches gleamed in the harsh flicker of naked bulbs, or the midnight mutterings along the corridors betrayed the tawdry travails of fellow guests, the one consolation was the magnificent presumption of a place that called itself, say, the Silk Palace. A hotel without a name, on the other hand, trampled the least illusion that it might have foyer or bar – or, for that matter, carpets, breakfast or bed sheets. Or even resident staff.

I had found the hotel locked the previous evening. So I pushed the bell. A man eventually answered the door, which was made of industrial metal, but not from the other side; a dictum, I vaguely recalled, had once impressed me with its solid advice that the only door worth stepping through must be opened from within. It was out of the night, and to the clack of his walking stick, that Hüseyin instead appeared, summoned by some impro- vised relay of messages. I followed the elderly man through the door and up the half-lit stairs, which he took one at a time, levering himself on his stick and pausing to draw my attention to a notice in his own hand that he had posted there.

'No drinking, no smoking, no making noise on the order of the Council's manager,' it decreed. Into one corner Hüseyin had squeezed a subsequent commandment. 'No eating seeds' it read, and I pictured Hüseyin ankle-deep in sunflower shells, stick and broom to hand, resolving to rain down ordnance on those who would litter his floors.

I ate in a nearby kebab house. An aged mute, all gestures, came to sit with me. My journey seemed to awaken old, scurrilous memories in the man, who, throughout my meal, scrawled picaresque bullet points – '1976', 'Baghdad', 'Rotterdam', 'Lorry', 'Dutch girls!' – across scraps of newspaper torn from my tablecloth. He laid them neatly beyond the chipped rim of my plate, even reordering them there, like the parts of a jigsaw puzzle, in the conviction that a minor adjustment was all that could be keeping me from taking a proper interest in his own wanderings. Out on the street a youth sidled up, collar raised, to advise me in a lascivious whisper that there were girls working in the nearby beer hall. Travel allowed all manner of liberties, of course; the one that then mattered, however, was the freedom to leave Yenice without looking back.

So to the river; the road that led to it sported a tattered pink bunting of oleanders, the first such flowers I had seen on my journey. The surreal, even discomfiting colour that they brought to sun-bleached landscapes had never endeared these botanical flamingos to me but the fact that they favoured Turkey's lower elevations meant that these plants for once functioned usefully, as an altimeter, to remind me of the contours I had shed since Çal; almost six hundred metres, more than half the Meander's overall fall, in just sixty or so kilometres, which meant a descent some ten times steeper than the river's overall gradient. In time, of course, the river would achieve a more uniformly steady rate of descent; through geological time, in fact, steadiness had been its guiding ambition. It was a physical law that running water, which had shaped these lands from the first raindrop's fall, sought only such constancy. By the brush of its gathered current the Meander had been gradually eroding the irregularities, boulders and pebbles alike, along its bed. It was in thrall to a process that must always continue. The river was destined in some unimaginably distant future to run down a uniform incline, and in its progress to that smooth ramp erase all evidence of the dams men had once built when they thought themselves masters for ever of the river's power.

We were now reunited, the river and I, at a sunlit bridge beyond the oleanders. The surprise was the weight the Meander had put on. I was aware that various tributaries had since thrown in their lot – most notably the Banaz River, which drained the lands north of the gorge – but I had feared the dams were sure to have absorbed them, even reduced the river once more to a sorry trickle. As it was, the Meander certainly looked to carry me out of Yenice, which was fine, but at a considerably greater speed than I might welcome; it was clear that the river's steep descent continued. A racing current tore down it, bearing trails of spume ripped from the riffling crests of the waves lining the stream's V-shaped sides; waves that jostled but never advanced, the water sliding beneath the frozen form of the rucked surface. I followed the rip current downstream, and passing through the vineyards that lined the banks, I scanned the river for the reassurance to relaunch there. I walked a long way before I found it.

It was midday by the time I got back to Yenice. On the main street, where tractors hauled pesticide sprayers, the man I had phoned earlier that morning was standing by a taxi. He pointed at the bag he had left by the door of the hotel. It was my canoe.

Around AD 47, roughly half a century before the Lairbenes had set about erecting their steles high above the Meander, a ship had docked at the port of Perge on the southern shore of Anatolia. Among the passengers were two men, Paul and Barnabas, who headed north into the interior. The road was long and the men were vulnerable to all manner of dangers, with nothing to propel them but an absolute conviction, which they meant above all to share; that gods were not multiply incarnated, in fact, in Roman emperors, Macedonian generals and Persian kings, in the deities of the Olympian pantheon, in the sun and moon, in rocks and trees, but singly, and in a carpenter from Nazareth in Galilee. A new faith had set out to seek its fortunes in the uplands of Anatolia.

The young religion would duly have to contend with that dense crowd of pagan deities, Apollo Lairbenos included, which it so utterly denied. First, however, it must survive its own mother religion, Judaism, whose orthodox elements had from the very beginning sought to smother the unwanted offspring. The Pharisees, Judaism's self-appointed guardians, dismissed as a charlatan the Jew who had been crucified some fifteen years earlier in Jerusalem, and those who proclaimed him the Messiah they condemned as blasphemers against the Law of Moses. Paul, himself a Jew, had once been a prominent persecutor of the Jesus sect; it was as Saul, name of the first king of Israel, that he had set out some years after the crucifixion to inveigh against Jesus's followers in Damascus.

The scourge of Christianity never got there; on the road to that Syrian city, and in a demonstration of the new faith's potency, he was recast as its foremost advocate. This transformation appeared miraculous, though the man's biography, however poorly documented, suggests that divine intervention merely hastened a conversion its subject might in time have managed independently. He who stumbled out of the light had not so much been transformed, that is, as restored from aberrancy; he was the natural product of a cultural background that militated against orthodoxy. For Paul, though an avowed Jew, was not of Judaea. He was instead from Tarsus in south-east Anatolia. A diaspora Jew, possibly the product of the same imperial policy that had in previous centuries settled Jews and their Ark legends at Apamea and elsewhere across Anatolia, Paul was necessarily shaped as much by contact with the codes and cultures of the Hellenist Roman Empire; his newly adopted name may even have been the form he had always preferred in his dealings with non-Jews. Through his upbringing in Tarsus the world of the Gentiles had touched Paul, and through his calling he now set about reshaping that world fundamentally. This process – the early advance of Christianity – was to begin along the same great road that rose in the Meander Valley, ran through the pass at Apamea and some eighty kilometres east reached Antioch in Pisidia before continuing to Iconium (modern Konya) and the provincial towns of Lystra and Derbe.

There had been increasing contact between Gentiles and Jews since the conquests of Alexander in the fourth century BC. Just as the ruling Seleucids and their Roman successors had settled Jewish colonies across Anatolia, so Greeks were increasingly stationed across Judaea. It was predictable, of course, that each people should have found fault with the customs and codes of the other. A chief issue was male circumcision; what Jews regarded as the very mark of their covenant with God, the Gentiles abhorred as vile mutilation. A ban in the second century BC on their rituals had caused the Jews to rise against Seleucid rule. Rebels had forcibly circumcised captured Gentiles; the authorities had responded by slaughtering Jewish mothers along with their circumcised infant sons.

Other Jews and Gentiles rubbed along rather better, however, and in learning Greek Paul was by no means alone. Many such Jews were schooled in rhetoric and philosophy. They frequented the gymnasium and the theatre. Their culture, abraded and adapted, arrived at an accommodation with that of the ruling Greco-Romans.

The striking thing was the extent, given the Jews' subject status, to which this syncretic process operated in reverse. Many

Gentiles admired the Jews for their prosperity and the influence it bought in, for instance, securing top seats at the theatre or prime plots for the raising of synagogues. Others seem to have been attracted by the moral vigour and clarity of the Jews' faith; one God, unquestioned and for ever, which perhaps left Hellenist paganism's overlapping collage of oddly constituted deities looking like the wonkiest kind of bet hedging. Certainly, sufficient numbers of Gentiles had come to revere the One God of the Jews as to acquire a particular designation – God-fearers – at the very time of Christianity's emergence.

These lapsing pagans, as we may call them, are known to have frequented the synagogues, discoursed with Jews and even partaken of some rituals in a tentative experimentation with Judaism; this unestablished monotheist minority was in the market, then, for a faith it could call its own – though it was not, finally, to be that of the Jews. Judaism had no missionary interest in receiving outsiders. It insisted upon absolute adherence to the Law of Moses, circumcision included, which deterred many God-fearers from converting. The fact of these spurned monotheists may explain the apparent facility with which Christianity took its earliest steps, in Anatolia especially, where Gentiles and Jews freely mingled from Miletus to Apamea, from Ephesus to Iconium.

For the Christian message – that the Messiah had indeed come, and that all *this* faith essentially required of its adherents was that they believe in Him – was appealing in its simplicity. Where Judaism barred its doors, in short, Christianity's stood open. This same line Paul and Barnabas preached on their arrival at Antioch in Pisidia. If the message played well with the God-fearers who had gathered to hear him at the synagogue, however, it outraged many Jews by defying their assumption that the new faith was no more than a minor offshoot of Judaism, and its followers unconditionally subject to Jewish law. Paul's riposte was to accuse the Jews of rejecting the word of God and declaring his missionary intent in one of the New Testament's most resonant phrases: 'lo, we turn to the Gentiles'. So Christianity first broke with Judaism at Antioch in Pisidia. The new faith spoke, of course, to a constituency, the God-fearers, which was predisposed to hear it; Christianity was yet to set its sights on the multitudes who worshipped the pagan gods of imperial Rome, and therein lay the greater prize.

Paul, recalling the dangers he had faced on his missionary journeys through Anatolia, wrote of beatings and stonings, and of being robbed. First, though, he mentioned the rivers.

At Yenice, I saw why. The river ran fast, and even if it had broadened, allowing me at least some space to manoeuvre, I was unconvinced that my decision to return to the water was a sensible one. Just below the bridge, where an open stretch of gently shelving shingle edged the Meander, I therefore reassembled my canoe with particular care. I checked that every last rib was clipped securely into place. I adjusted the inflatable tubes to achieve the perfect balance of rigidity and pliancy. For stability, I ballasted the bottom of the hull with the heaviest kit items and fitted the inflatable seat as low as possible. I made sure to lash down every last object. Then I retired to the shade of a nearby scrub oak. I was practising with the paddle there, summoning strokes I had not used for days, if only because I might now need them in a hurry, when a tractor appeared from the direction of Yenice. The driver had barely glimpsed me before he braked so abruptly as to spring moulded ingots of sun-baked mud from his tyre treads. He was not accustomed, it seemed, to seeing foreign boatmen on the river. When he lit a cigarette and sat back to watch, however, even thinking to cut his engine, I had the uncomfortable sense that something more than mere curiosity had brought him to a halt; the feeling, as I slid the canoe into the shallows, that the driver guessed he might just be in for a treat.

The shallows were slack, though there was not much of them; they barely contained the canoe. I was still settling into my seat when the current's braided rim snagged the canoe's wavering bow and began coaxing it onto the water. I back-paddled, grounding the stern on a mudbank while I took stock. Beyond the stretch of open shingle thick foliage soon crowded the banks. Willows tumbled out over the water. To clear that wet thicket, and the trailing branches that tore white strips in the stream, I must take the current on. I settled my hips, seeking balance, and suddenly, as if to catch the current unawares, I drove the canoe hard across the stream. I held a fighting line until the last moment; as the current threatened to overwhelm my faltering forward momentum I dug in at the stern, spinning the bow to face downstream. I caught the outermost willows, busted through, and slipped out onto the river. At my back the tractor moved slowly off.

I had safely launched. I had denied the tractor driver his entertainment. The way ahead looked wide enough, moreover, to take a fallen willow and leave space for a passing canoe, which had been my particular hope. It was this formula – one willow's height plus one canoe's width – that it came down to; that much river and I reckoned my progress was assured. On a growing sense of confidence I surrendered to the current, paddling only to correct my line through gouts of rising turbulence, which spread bubble-strewn slicks across the stream, and I raced through the spinning vortices. The banks slid by in a blur of trees, reeds and stands of purple-topped thistles. Up came a bridge, a thing of two roughly equal halves comprising a hand-some Ottoman span, all pointed piers supporting keystoned arches, and the crumbling concrete slab it met midstream. It was a typically Turkish repair, inelegant but serviceable, which I took at the time to have been caused by a typically Turkish instance of long-term neglect. I was later to discover, however, that the damage to the bridge was deliberately done by locals intent on halting the advance of Greek forces in the war of 1919–22; a preview, in short, of what modern history had in store for the river and an early intimation of the devastation that was to descend upon the Meander Valley from almost a thousand years before that final war.

As it was, I had barely seen the botched bridge before the current had slung me through one of the arches and swept me downstream. I was not far beyond the bridge when the banks began to steepen. The reeds that lined them thickened with every moment. A familiar gloom settled upon the river. A drowned cow, a yellow plastic tag stapled to its ear, floated upright among the willow brakes; it had swollen like a drum and lost one eye to the birds. In my seat I hunkered down and raced downstream where a heron, half-lit, rose gracelessly from a dead tree, taking the last of life with it. For a moment I thought I might be swept down a riverine plughole. In this darkening netherworld I tore round a bend where the channel came to an abrupt end. At two fallen willows.

These trees had once faced each other across the river; and just as they had chanced to grow in each other's shadow, so they had merged in their falling, the splintered branches of their half-submerged crowns meshing mid-stream. The blockage they formed was total. From one bank to the other the trunks ran a uniform boom where a grey scum rose in agitated wavelets, and the few plastic bottles that had collected there, fretting against the sodden, peeling bark, bobbed furiously against the pull of the ducking current. I braked hard, back-paddling and at once turned the canoe tight. But I was too late. The canoe broadsided the willows with a thump. I felt the craft flex alarmingly. Then the current kicked in, the hull rode up the trunk and the canoe began to tip, and it occurred to me that I had miscalculated the river's vital measure; a canoe's width plus the height of *two* willows, then, being the requirement if one was sure to pass.

The canoe did not quite capsize. Its rising edge caught against a branch, wedging it at an angle while the current boiled around it. But the boat was taking a battering. It had begun to ship water over its lower gunwale. I instinctively pushed against the trunk, thinking to swing the bow upstream, even as I knew I had no hope against the current. I leaned along the canoe, grabbed at a willow branch and heaved hard. For a moment nothing happened. Then something gave and the canoe, its fabric skin squealing in protest against the willow, began to bump along the trunk. I pulled again and again, and the current began to lessen as I closed on the far bank. The canoe finally slipped back onto an even keel.

I was breathing heavily as I ran under the bank, a high palisade of plainly impenetrable reeds. There was no way I could get myself off the river here, nor begin to extricate the canoe. The only possible exit out of this trap was upstream. What now signified was not the river's width but the rate of its flow. To escape the river I must paddle the canoe at a speed to outrun the current. Otherwise, I could only wait for the current to weaken, which might take days, while my own weakening proceeded apace.

I faced the canoe upstream, the stern resting against the willow boom, and pondered my escape. The current ran weakest by the banks; but by running among the foliage I would be likely to snag the paddle and lose vital headway. I sighted my bow accordingly, taking a line to clear the willows and reeds, drew down a deep breath and drove in the paddle. For a moment, there was nothing but the frantic churn of water. Then, slowly, I felt the stern ease free of the willow and the same backdrop that had fled past minutes earlier – trailing branches and dead trunks, desiccated reed tops and weed tresses – now inched into reverse. I began to make gradual ground, but I was sprinting. It was no time before I needed to rest. I grabbed at an anchoring branch so as to bank the few yards the flurry of strokes had earned me. In this manner I made my way upriver. The paddling spurts soon began to shorten, the rests to lengthen, and all the while the reed stands stretched along either bank. Something bumped against the canoe; it was the cow's bloated corpse, idly spinning in the current, as it slipped downstream.

I must have covered some 200 metres, and was drenched in sweat, when I saw the plastic irrigation pipe. Broad and blue, it ran down the left bank. To install it, the farmer had cleared a passage through the reeds before trampling the bank to a moderate gradient. I had noticed such pipes on the river's upper stretches and cursed them for the ecological damage they did in depleting the water levels; I now blessed them, and irrigators all, and with a final dig of the paddle drove the canoe into the reeds beside the pipe. I clambered unsteadily up the bank, dragging the canoe behind me. At the top my legs gave way beneath me and I found myself lying in a damp field of green barley.

For some time I did not move. I looked up at a blue sky scored white by gliding storks. A rim of mountains was cloaked in a grey haze. When I finally got to my feet I found the barley stood to my midriff. The crop fringed the river into the distance. One thing at a time, I told myself, starting by traversing the field and clearing the fallen willows. Then I could try to find a way back onto the river. I offloaded the rucksack and stowed the paddle. The rucksack was heavy on my shoulders; it was sodden on account of the water the canoe had shipped. I flipped the canoe until the water had

drained out. Then I wrapped the painter round my fist and ran
it over my shoulder before setting off across the field. The canoe,
its fabric skin sliding over the smooth green stems of the flattened barley, moved with ease; more easily than I did, sinking
to my ankles with every step. Into the field the irrigation pipe
had delivered not only me and my canoe but also considerable
quantities of water – which was, after all, its purpose.

   The sun was spiralling out of the sky by the time I trudged
past the fallen willows that had blocked my way. Beyond them,
however, a fringe of impenetrable reeds ran unbroken to the
horizon. The river remained quite out of reach. I continued on

my way, insects about my ears. When I looked back, the canoe's wake through the parted barley resembled the runner marks of an Arctic sled, stretching out of sight. The barley finally ended at an earth rampart, which ran at right angles to the river. Thistles grew all over it. With my paddle I hacked a way over the top to discover the earth was spoil freshly dug from an adjacent irrigation canal. The way to the canal's banks was clear, and the canal ran unchecked back to the river. I wept, but not for long, because the sun was low. Then I repacked the canoe and launched on the canal.

I noticed it the moment I rejoined the river; the current had spent itself. In the course of my progress through the barley the river's bed had finally levelled out. The plummet that had begun at Çal, and had caused the river to lose more than half its overall fall, had ceased. The Meander no longer tumbled down its crevice; it had cleared Mount Çökelez to turn sluggish in a broadening valley.

Through the thinning willows I now spied an expanse of low-lying meadow and copse; the emerald and jade tones of another valley, wider, and out of the east, lying roughly at right angles to the Meander. This was the valley of the Lycus, the historic road's continued route into the interior; the effect of the Lycus's approach was to head the Meander, at first gradually, from its southerly course. Beyond a final bend the tributary closed on the river and was lost in it without ceremony, but not before nudging the Meander further towards its original bearing. I felt the river turn until I was paddling into a setting sun. I was back where I was meant to be; heading west.

I had completed the great hoop; the Meander, its wilderness wanderings behind it, now rejoined the same arterial route it had last touched at Dinar. That the river was once more in the company of the railway and the main road prepared me

for the roar that rose from the bridge; refrigerated pantech-
nicons, speeding Mercedes, police vehicles and gleaming overnight coaches streamed beneath the road lights towards
Sarayköy and Denizli. The carts, thyme fields and plough-bent
villagers of the uplands already felt like a fond dream.

The surprise was that somebody should have marked the
Meander's return to the modern world with something so
fitting as a riverside factory. A chimney-topped edifice sat
behind its security fence, belching smoke into a darkening
sky. A sign, which announced the Meander Textile Factory,
bore a stylised wave, which appeared to claim a harmonious
association with the river. From where I sat, however, the view
was of a one-sided, even abusive relationship. What I initially
mistook for the chimney's reflection in the water in fact turned
out to be its submarine counterpart; a broad pipe from which
a heavy brown effluent, gold along its edges, spread out into
the water. The river now changed colour, and it began to
smell.

I passed under the bridge and beached on a shabby shore
in the half-light. I rolled the canoe into a stand of wheat,
shouldered my rucksack and crossed the bridge where another
discovery struck me by its aptness. Beside the road, at the
point where the Meander turned west, an outlet store had
lately been built. The store, now closed for the night, was
plastered with Euro-style brand names: Puma, La Notte,
Tivolyo, Colin's, Loft and Sevenhill. The lights from the
main road revealed shelves of trainers, racks of T-shirts,
jackets and belts, and bins of footballs. The window also bore
the reflection of an itinerant of the sort – mud-caked shoes
and trousers, dripping rucksack hung with bits of barley and
willow – that factory outlet stores tended to discourage.
Hearing somebody call out, I turned to the sight of an

approaching pair of security guards in pressed blue uniforms and feared the worst.

'Tea?' one asked. The men led me into their office and made me their honoured guest, sitting me in a chair before a bank of screens that displayed the several views provided by the CCTV cameras; my trail of mud was clearly visible in a number of the images. The guards were too intent on enthusing about the outlet store to notice my filthy state; they described how the store, which had opened six months earlier, had attracted gawping crowds of wide-eyed shepherds, housewives and imams alike, and from as far as Nazilli and Burdur. They brought me more tea and regaled me with the news that Galatasaray, an Istanbul football team, had been crowned Turkey's champions the previous day. I in turn asked them about the river.

'No problem,' said one. 'At least as far as Feslek.' One of the guards, who was going off-duty, offered to drop me in nearby Sarayköy (alt. 153 metres) where there was a hotel.

From Antioch in Pisidia Paul and Barnabas journeyed east to Iconium where their teachings once more stoked hostility among the local Jews. The two men fled to Lystra, a modest country town, where Paul miraculously caused a cripple to stand. The locals, who spoke the regional Lycaonian, took the two strangers for gods and prepared to sacrifice an ox in their honour. Paul and Barnabas rent their clothes to express disapproval of these heathen ways. 'We are also men of like passions with you,' they exclaimed, 'and preach unto you that you should turn from these vanities unto the living God, which made heaven, and earth, and the sea, and all things that are therein.'

Christianity thereby set its sights on the pagan world.

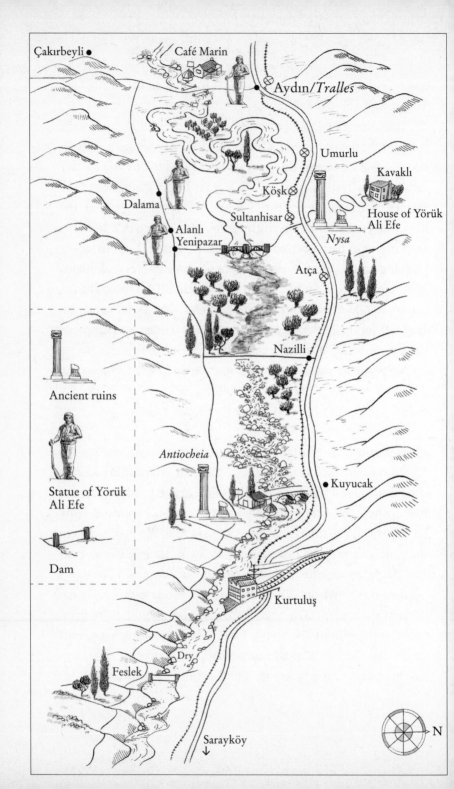

Çakırbeyli •

Café Marin

Aydın/*Tralles*

Umurlu

Kavaklı

Köşk

Dalama

Sultanhisar

House of Yörük
Ali Efe

Alanlı
Yenipazar

Nysa

Atça

Nazilli

Ancient ruins

Statue of Yörük
Ali Efe

Antiocheia

Kuyucak

Dam

Kurtuluş

Dry

Feslek

Sarayköy
↓

N

CHAPTER FOURTEEN

In the year 110 the Roman governor of the Anatolian province of Bithynia wrote to Trajan, alerting the Emperor to a growing Christian presence in the region. The cult, having at first found few takers beyond the urban God-fearers, had since flourished across Anatolia's pagan hinterlands. The likes of the Lystrans, the Lairbenes too, had evidently been listening.

Not only were these increasingly numerous Christians of all ages, as the governor's dispatch reported, but they appeared immune to such deterrents as denunciation or trial. As well as prohibition and sometimes brutal persecution the authorities had also tried promotion, staging lavish spectacles in honour of the pagan and emperor gods, but their efforts seemed only to spur Christianity's advance across western Anatolia.

In the Lycus Valley – at the three cities of Colossae, Laodicea and Hierapolis – some of the first Christian missionaries had been operating for fully half a century; from around the time, in fact, of the letter that Paul, then under house arrest in Rome, had addressed to the people of Colossae.

Paul's 'Letter to the Colossians' served to steer the new religion's initiates with an impassioned blend of instruction, succour and correction. It also included some specific requests: that its contents were to be circulated among the Laodiceans, and that the people of Colossae should be sure to read the separate letter, since lost, that Paul had sent to Laodicea. These orders might have been passed over as nothing more than routine reminders of the need to foster common understanding among neighbouring Christian communities; particularly, that is, if Paul had addressed such a letter to the third city, Hierapolis, or specified that the other letters were also to be circulated there. That Paul contented himself, however, with merely passing on the respects of a fellow evangelist to the Christians of Hierapolis suggested that such differences as existed between the cities might merit investigation.

Of the three it was certainly Colossae and Laodicea that had the most in common, even if Laodicea – sumptuously endowed by the Seleucid kings, the residence of the Roman proconsul of Asia, home to a distinguished crowd of rhetoricians and the like – had outgrown its declining neighbour by the middle of the first century. For from their comparable locations on the valley floor the two cities had both prospered from the trade that flowed along the great highway, from the richness of the soil and from manufacture, particularly of garments woven from local wools prized for their softness and for 'their dark or raven colour'. The two cities were extensively Hellenised, moreover, and their cosmopolitan settler populations, Jews and Greeks especially, made for a devotional diversity.

Hierapolis, just six miles from Laodicea and as far again from Colossae, was distinctively different, with a conspicuously elevated, even sanctified setting on the southern slopes of Çökelez Mountain; a fitting location for the 'holy city', which even under Roman authority remained, in the words of Ramsay, 'the centre of native feeling and Phrygian nationality in the valley'. At Hierapolis paganism's roots ran deep.

The devotional piety that characterised Hierapolis was heavily cut, moreover, with a cultic, even orgiastic sensuality. For though the city's patron deity was Apollo, the same Lairbenos who had tyrannised his subjects from the nearby temple above the Meander on Çökelez's northern slopes, the primary influence largely resided with fecund Cybele: the Anatolian Earth Mother, She of the all-over dugs, whom by conflation the Ephesians knew as Artemis. For Hierapolis had long been a focus of an inherently Phrygian devotion to the primal life force. Women once honoured Cybele by serving as prostitutes, a sacred calling, in the courtyards of her temples. An ancient cult of the phallus had widely prevailed, one that a modern tourist trade in graphic clay figurines acknowledged. These satyrs, with their impressive erections, made tacit reference to a dark, chthonic deity known as the Echidna, which had risen from the earth's bowels at Hierapolis to impregnate the Mother Goddess and so spawn all life; to this swollen-cheeked dragon serpent the local population was once in thrall. Conception's special association with Hierapolis was reinforced, though the protagonist this time was female, when the third-century BC epic poet, Quintus of Smyrna, located there the ravishing by the moon goddess of mythical Endymion; the beautiful shepherd caught the eye of the goddess, Selene or Luna, who dosed him with some divine Rohypnol before subjecting the stupefied youth to a prolonged bout of procreation.

These unbridled associations and their attendant rites the mannered Greeks and Romans sought to moderate. They set about civilising Hierapolis with a veneer of seemliness, in part by promoting the healing properties of the city's famed thermal springs. This reminder, that the gods could restore people to health as surely as they made the transgressors among them ill, played a significant role in the recasting of Hierapolis. Under the aegis of medical deities like Aesculapius and Hygeia, who shared image rights on the city's coins with Apollo, the sacred massage parlour and place of conception progressively morphed into a halfway respectable health spa.

What did not change was Hierapolis's essential opposition to

Christianity, to the point that the circulating there of letters that championed the subversive faith may well have been as foolhardy as the hawking of bibles in modern Mecca. The particular instructions Paul included in 'Colossians' may evidence, then, the care with which the new religion's proselytes trod in that bastion of paganism.

Not that Christianity's hagiographers, strangers to stealth or strategy, would have it so. According to the apocryphal 'Acts of Philip', excised by the New Testament's fourth-century editors, no doubt for exceeding plausibility's outer limits with mechanisms such as talking leopards, pagan Hierapolis spectacularly surrendered to Christ in the course of a productive visit by two of his apostles. John, fresh from a successful crusade against the Artemis cult at Ephesus, came with Philip to the city where 'the men of the place worshipped the snake and had images of it'. The natives proved predictably hostile; they bound Philip, piercing his wrists and thighs, and also vowed to drain every last drop of John's blood, to mix it with wine and serve it to the Echidna. When they came to take John, however, they found their hands had been paralysed. Philip turned up the heat by calling upon God to open up the earth and swallow the entire place, 'about 7,000 men, save where the apostles were'. Things had turned apocalyptic, even by apocryphal standards, by the time the risen Jesus appeared over the city. He rebuked Philip for his wrath and condemned the apostle not only to die but to endure a chastening delay of the statutory forty days before being admitted to Paradise. Jesus then released the 7,000 citizens of Hierapolis from the abyss, excepting from his mercy only the city's wicked authoritarian, the Roman proconsul, and the dreaded serpent itself.

So it was that Christianity took the city; the impressionable minds of the time could best account for the coming of a new age, and for the passing of the old one, by resort to the reductive certainties of fantasy epic. I had a hunch, however, that the 'Acts of Philip' might yield a more rational explanation for the same historical process, one Anatolia had repeatedly experienced, when I set out for Hierapolis the following morning.

Along the busy road out of Sarayköy sunlight streamed through the windows of the crowded *dolmuş*. It flashed on the cheap watches of the grizzled farmers, and with every pothole it jolted up the ginger twine binding the cardboard boxes with which the shawled women had immured themselves. Beyond the orange groves snow scraps glinted on the heights of Babadağ, Father Mountain, which faced Mount Çökelez from the south side of the valley. The *dolmuş* drew up at Denizli, the modern city that occupied the slopes above Laodicea's column-strewn ruins, and I transferred to a vehicle where I suddenly found myself among foreign tourists. The sight of all these elderly Germans and young Italians, the first Westerners that I had seen on my journey, caused me to bridle, and some time passed before I had worked out the stimulus to this powerful adverse reaction: it was the money belts and the padlocked rucksacks, and the guidebooks the tourists now consulted, apparently to guard against being overcharged for the cost of the bus ticket, which was about £1. After all the kindnesses I had received – from Mehmet Halil Blessed and Ali Ihsan Skirmisher, from the Fearless family and Mehmet Truehero, the proffered handfuls of green almonds, the tractor lifts, the fountains and clay jars, the gift of baklava and the glasses of tea – this default defensiveness added up to an affront; the assumption that they must expect trouble in Turkey had caused these visitors to don their travelling riot gear.

Not that such concerns would keep them from Hierapolis, a site firmly established on Turkey's tourism trail. For the place the Turks called Pamukkale (Cotton Castle), and eighteenth-century travellers Pococke and Chandler knew as the abbreviated 'Pambouk', now came with that top-drawer tag: World Heritage Site. Richard Chandler was certainly impressed. From his camp-site at the foot of the cliff below Hierapolis he witnessed a view 'so marvellous, that the description of it, to bear even a faint resemblance, ought to appear *romantic*'. 'The warm waters here,' concurred Richard Pococke in his comparatively sober register, 'are the greatest natural curiosities in Asia.'

The bus passed restaurants and souvenir kiosks, to draw up somewhere near Chandler's one-time campsite. We removed our shoes and in the manner of pilgrims proceeded up the flank of a dazzling white hillside. Over the millennia, Çökelez's thermal springs had covered the hill in a thick calcareous deposit, which one early visitor compared to the shell of cuttlefish; this observation, visually accurate but no more appealing for that, Chandler improved upon by evoking the wider scene as 'an immense frozen cascade, the surface wavy, as of water in its headlong course suddenly petrified'.

To Quintus of Smyrna, however, the remarkable landscape at Hierapolis evidenced nothing less than the spillage that attended unbridled fecundity. 'There,' the poet related, 'Luna had once descended from the sky to Endymion, while he was sleeping by his herds; that marks of their bed were then extant under the oaks; and that in the thickets around it the milk of cows had been spilt, which men beheld still with admiration; for, such was the appearance, if you saw it very far off.' This description, though it ascribed the milky puddles to the leaking udders of Endymion's neglected charges, was sufficiently suggestive as to have left Quintus's readers in no doubt that they were in fact the surplus secretions, in keeping with the myth's insistent theme, of the loved-up swain himself.

The chemical reality, as Quintus conceded, was that the landscape was in fact formed by 'clear or warm water, which in a
little while concreted round about the channels, and formed a
stone pavement'. That pavement, braided with rivulets of water,
now lay beneath our feet. The steaming water spilled turquoise
from the rims of scallop-shaped pools, which projected from
the slope, rounded like art-nouveau balconies or nightclub stacks
of cascading champagne glasses. The tourists, their trousers
rolled, composed themselves into photographic poses among
the so-called travertines. As ivories may denote piano keys,
coppers coins, so the Turks did not distinguish between these
signature formations and their substance, a marble-like stone
formed from water-borne deposits of carbonated lime, which
even today was quarried across the region.

Some five years earlier, in a factory east of Denizli, such a
block of travertine was being sliced into floor tiles when a fossil
was fortuitously exposed. The surviving section was from the
skull of an early human. It was estimated to be several hundred
thousand years old and was rich in identifying clues; a prominent
brow ridge suggested that the subject was probably male, the
degree of cranial closure indicating him to be aged between
fifteen and forty years. Lesions consistent with tuberculosis were
discovered, furthermore, in the skull. Susceptibility to tuberculosis in prehistoric times is generally associated with the
inability of dark-skinned people to create sufficient vitamin D.
The palaeontologists therefore suspected that their man must
have come from Africa.

Among such warm pools, where the tourists now took photographs, a distant wanderer had once lain down to die. I had not
thought that our distant forebears might be embedded among
such rocks, in the manner of ammonites, and even inhabit our
banal surroundings – the tiles of shower walls, the floors of

kitchens and car showrooms – with such haunting proximity.

These travertines, rich in association, had on an earlier visit impressed me as a one-off natural wonder; they were the most remarkable manifestation of a process that also turned earthen irrigation channels into lime-faced runnels, coated the paddles of the nineteenth-century watermills along the Lycus River so that they needed daily descaling, and left even today a crusty glaze across the paintwork of washed-down vehicles.

In the course of my journey down the Meander I had, however, come to see these calcite formations in a different light; as yet another, albeit extreme, manifestation of the surreal and suggestive featuring that characterised the wider landscape. Across these topographical borderlands steaming streams turned to milky stone as rivers ducked underground by shadowy swallow holes to emerge reborn from grottoes and caves. Springs bubbled into sudden lakes. Against the constant rumble of seismic activity – which lightning storms, like natural *son et lumière* shows, were said to attend – age-old *höyük* mounds, sheer-sided gorges and gigantesque plane trees proliferated. These bizarre features extended beyond the river valley. To the north and east, in the Phrygian high country and across Cappadocia, rose rock formations the Turks knew as fairy chimneys but which convincingly resembled giant toadstools, over-sized hay stooks and, most compellingly, phalluses on a scale worthy of the Echidna itself. To the south, in Lycia, the perpetual fire that vented from a singular hillside betrayed the lurking presence there of the fire-breathing monstrous Chimera. Back at Hierapolis, meanwhile, a gaping hellhole known as the Plutonium allowed the egress not only of the rampant Echidna but of gases so pestilential that asphyxiated birds had once plummeted from the sky.

The region's volatile geology was noted by Strabo who wrote how 'nearly the whole of the country about the Meander, as far as the inland parts, is subject to earthquakes, and is undermined by fire and water'. It was a land where nature had apparently tired of its more quiescent conventional role, as seasonal master of ceremonies, to emerge as an act in its own right; a wilful and spirited bill-topper, which accounted for the ubiquitous sacred groves, holy springs, river gods, sacrificial rites, underworld presences and other manifestations of an entrenched nature cult. The paradox was that Christianity had by the third century made more headway here, in Phrygia, than anywhere else. By some counter-intuitive process, though the landscape bristled with pagan installations, Phrygia of all places had proved the new religion's beachhead.

All manner of reasons have been suggested to explain this striking advance: chiefly, that the sheer profusion of the pagan gods, and the availability of a manufactured deity for every eventuality, might have seemed unduly pragmatic, cynical even, compared to Christianity's devotional constancy; that paganism's view of sin, an outward contamination one might salve by sacrifice, by sprinklings of water or blood, was plainly otiose, even intellectually simple-minded, compared to Christianity's intriguing proposition that sin might lie within, and it might even be within one to combat it there; that paganism generally promised to deliver in this life, which it but arbitrarily succeeded in doing, while Christianity could never be known to fail, at least not demonstrably, in its pledge to deliver in the next; and, finally, that the imperial persecutions, which one second-century theologian called the seed of the church, had by claiming high-profile Anatolian victims, among them saints as familiar as George and Valentine, dotted the landscape of the third century with the chapels of local martyrs, which were to serve as rallying points for the Faith.

In the case of the Lycus Valley, however, the timely

occurrence of a momentous natural event may have been quite as influential in Christianity's advance as all these factors combined; the massive earthquake that was known to have levelled the region in AD 60. There may be no rational way of accounting for much in the 'Acts of Philip', not least talking leopards, but the gaping abyss into which Philip cast the population of Hierapolis may preserve a memory of the catastrophic rupturing of the seismic fault which attended the great earthquake, a fault which even today visibly runs through the site.

The same earthquake's dramatic effects may also inform some of the Christian legends associated with nearby Colossae. There the local pagans, pantomime villains to a tee, had attempted to destroy the church by diverting the course of the River Lycus. They had not reckoned on the Archangel Michael who, invoked by the local priest, struck with his staff a rock, which duly gaped open to accommodate the rushing waters. The city was subsequently known as Chonae, or funnel, in honour of the sudden appearance of the subterranean sluice that saved the church and thereby caused the Church to flourish.

The earthquake appeared as a sacred endorsement, then, of triumphant Christianity; by the same logic the local pagans could hardly fail to read anything but divine displeasure in the spectacular disappearance of their settlements and rivers alike. Nature, the very pulse of Phrygian paganism, had itself overthrown the lands, even the sacrificial temples, of its own devotees. Here, then, was one cause of the chill foreboding that passed among the pagan gods and their agents, and which we have already sensed on the northernmost slopes of Çökelez Mountain, where the devotees at the sanctuary shrine of Apollo Lairbenos were made to feel the additional weight of their increasingly insecure god's tyrannical hand.

Apollo, it happened, was represented at the Hierapolis

Museum, though no such end-of-days uncertainty dogged his image. On the panels of a frieze recovered from the city's theatre the god appeared at the height of his authority; he was at the headwaters of the Meander, overseeing the flaying he had ordered. As a beast hung by trussed hocks from a meathook the bound Marsyas was being stripped of his skin.

It was an image that had proved resonant through ancient times, serving a purpose primarily political rather than purely artistic. Representations of Marsyas in his agony, images and statues alike, were tacit reminders of the natives' subject status. Like CCTV cameras, patrolling police squads or Big-Brother posters, they were an integral part of the age's security apparatus. They were a blunt expression of imperial, and Apollonian, power.

That power derived from the god's broad portfolio of interests – music and justice, the sun and the harvest – but it was on account of his prophetic expertise that Apollo especially prospered. Devotees endowed lavish oracular temples to the god who knew the future, most famously at Delphi in Greece, but most numerously along the littorals of western Anatolia, where they spent fortunes securing access to his advice.

Given this prophetic knack, it is tempting to assume, of course, that Apollo of all the deities must have foreseen that it could not last; that he and his power must die as the gods of Arzawans and Hittites, Persians and Phrygians had died before him. The devotional momentum, for one thing, was evidently with Jesus Christ – though the first signs of Apollo's decline were instead implicit in the voices that began to be raised on behalf of a rival from an older tradition: Marsyas. In a process that started around the first century BC the satyr who was once regarded as deserving victim began to be represented as freedom's symbol, especially in Rome where he came to symbolise plebeian rights. His statue was raised in the forum, the centre

of Roman political activity, where it became a focus for demon-
strations and served as a poster board for anti-authoritarian
verses. The power struggle between the common people and
the elite, which came to dominate Roman political debate, was
mirrored by the contest between Marsyas and Apollo; coins
carried satyr and god, one on each side. One coin, minted in
80 BC, represented Marsyas as wearing the *pilleus*, or Phrygian
cap; this item of headgear, originally denoting little more than
the Eastern otherness – barbarianism, in short – with which the
Anatolian lands were closely associated, came to be recast as
the badge of freedom, an association it was to retain even until
the French Revolution. Ovid was repeatedly drawn to side with
Marsyas, and in later evocations of the story it was increasingly
easy to tell where the sympathies of Dante, Titian, Caravaggio
and the like substantially lay. The appalling fate of the tree-
bound Marsyas even came to stand as a non-cruciform version
of Christ's passion. It was inevitable, of course, that the satyr's
reinvention as redeemed martyr should have exposed the divine
disciplinarian as amoral torturer.

Despite this onslaught by an increasingly politicised urban
underclass, Apollo and his agents clearly recognised Christ as
the main threat to their authority. Apollo, whose local proxy had
defended his patch by wringing public loyalty oaths from the
Lairbenes, now deployed his extensive oracular influence to
shore up his embattled position. Apollo's oracles began actively
to champion the piety of ancestral belief. They then went on
the offensive, advising supplicants as to how they might deter
family members who had shown an interest in Christianity and
increasingly cutting their prophecies with sideswipes against
'those who have forsaken the ways of their ancestors'. They
condemned those who worshipped the mortal remains, torn and
broken, of Jesus Christ. With the passing of the centuries,

however, these utterances looked like desperate attempts at self-justification.

It was in the year 303 that Apollo made one of his last recorded utterances. The Emperor Diocletian asked Apollo's great oracle at Didyma, near the mouth of the Meander, what he was to do about the increasing disobedience of the empire's Christians. The oracle's response was that the impious hindered Apollo's ability to provide advice. On the court's insistence that the oracular reference to the impious could refer only to the Christians, Diocletian acceded to demands that the minority faith be exposed to state-sanctioned persecution. Apollo thereby put his name to the razing, slaughter, burning and boiling that followed. The trademark cruelty that had begun with the flaying of Marsyas was not to save him; ten years later, as Christianity was first legalised across the empire, it was apparent that Apollo's final utterances had merely foretold the end of Apollo.

The city's healing gods had fared better, if only because their sacred pool retained its former function. A large sign confirmed the various conditions that the pool's thermal waters were known to benefit; these included diseases relating to 'head function', blood pressure, obesity, chronic gastritis, constipation, catarrhal diseases of the upper respiratory tract, bronchitis and inflammatory rheumatic disorders. In a case, in short, of blisters and weary muscles, a dip could do no harm.

The one-time home of nymphs and dryads was occupied by coachloads of the tourists who daily descended upon Hierapolis; swim-suited Russians swam briskly past, exhaling in chesty Slavic satisfaction, as I settled upon the weed-festooned flutings of a half-submerged column. Plumes of tobacco smoke rose from tables across the poolside patio where waiters brought tea

and beer. In the warm water I lazed for the first time in weeks
and let my thoughts drift.

I reflected how the sacred pool had continued in use all
through the centuries of Hierapolis's ruination. A local *ağa*
arrived to bathe, it so happened, at the time of Richard
Chandler's visit in the 1760s. It proved a fraught encounter; the
ağa, backed by 'a considerable retinue', proved implacably
hostile, alleging that Chandler 'had knowledge of hidden
treasure, and had already filled with it the provision chests,
which he had seen by our tent'. Of this imaginary hoard the
ağa demanded a substantial share. Chandler's party, 'apprehensive of immediate violence', fled without delay.

I wondered what had prompted me to recall this episode,
which appeared historically remote, until it struck me that the
same misunderstandings and suspicions persisted even today;
they were evident, indeed, in the money belts and padlocked
rucksacks I had noticed that very morning. Westerners persisted
in the traditional view that Turks were roguish thieves – as Turks
maintained their equivalent assumption that Westerners were
diabolically clever ones whose educated noses always led them
to treasures hidden on lands not their own. Just as Westerners
had learned to keep their possessions close in Turkey, so Turks
knew not to sell trowels to their guests.

The Westerners were way off in their preconceptions, as my
own experiences had so comprehensively taught, but the Turks
were no more correct in theirs; it was the locals who had caused
the greater destruction, though largely out of ignorance rather
than malice, of the land's ancient treasures. Visiting antiquaries
and scholars were commonly horrified by the extent to which
inscribed stones, even statuary, were blithely recycled as building
material. Charles Fellows once noted a statue – the 'beautiful
body of a child, about a foot or eighteen inches long, with one

arm over its breast' which had been 'built into the wall of a house; the head and legs had been broken off'. Carved pieces were commonly mutilated to adorn gravestones; stone cutters traditionally set up shop at 'quarries of white marble wherever the remains of a temple are to be found'. Fellows also noted a headstone hacked from 'a robed female statue of white marble, stuck head and shoulders downwards into ground; the projecting feet had been broken off, but the folds of the drapery showed that the statue must have been of good Greek workmanship'. At Denizli Reverend Arundell watched a 'stonemason, who was chipping most unmercifully a beautiful frieze, to accommodate it to a Turkish tombstone'. Troughs and cisterns were recycled from 'pedestals, capitals of columns or tombs'; roadside wells with 'Attic bases of columns perforated, and placed over the mouths' as copings were commonly encountered. Inscribed blocks served as hearths and doorsteps.

This wholesale destruction of artefacts continued into the twentieth century, and with the connivance of the Turkish state. William Guthrie, commissioned to seek out and copy ancient epigraphs across Anatolia during the 1930s, ruefully conceded how 'in the advancement of civilisation the making of roads comes before the preservation of ancient monuments . . . Many an inscription is ground up for road metal, and more go into the walls of the Government's schools which are springing up.' Inscribed stones poked from newly built railway platforms. In one village Guthrie was called over 'to where building was actually in progress to see, before it took its place in the wall, a little tomb-relief, a quaint representation of a native art which must have been almost untouched by Greek or Roman influences'.

After my soak I dressed and continued my tour of Hierapolis. The staff of the Italian Archaeological Mission, guardians of the city's Roman heritage, were busy erecting interpretive notice boards. Red poppies bloomed between the quake-shaken ashlar seats of the theatre. Mottled lizards, motionless but for their pulsing throats, clung to the carved mouldings of fallen architraves. I walked north until I had cleared the main settlement where I followed the course of an ancient processional way through the ruin-strewn grasslands. It led to a Byzantine building: an impressive octagonal hall, its dome long since collapsed, with arched doorways leading to a ring of outer chambers. It was the martyrium, or sacred burial place of St Philip, which appeared to acknowledge that a further fact – the apostle's death at Hierapolis – was preserved among the fantastic details packed into the apocryphal 'Acts'. The martyrium, which dated from the fifth century, was designed to lodge the pilgrims who increasingly visited the holy place through Christianity's early period.

These pilgrims, weathered from the long road, had no doubt followed the path up through the remarkable travertines. They continued beyond the great baths and the sacred pool to pass a colonnaded building, which they no longer had cause to notice. For the few who now entered the Temple of Apollo did so with the same furtive discretion that the first Christians must once have shown in Hierapolis – if, that is, the pagan temple had not already been closed or requisitioned by the adjacent theatre for the storage, say, of props and other such stage devices.

CHAPTER FIFTEEN

I breakfasted at the outlet store where the security guards had entertained me some nights before. Amid the chrome and glass of the café, stacks of plastic serving trays shook to the celebratory beat of Galatasaray's footballing triumph. The boy at the till, whose T-shirt declared *Dance Hall – Fervent*, rang up my double portion of *börek*, a steppe lasagne of sorts that was filled with crumbly white cheese and parsley, and my glass of black tea; the very first tea, in fact, that I had paid for on the entire journey. The purchase appeared to signal the end of the exemptions I had enjoyed in the uplands, as the thyme fields had given way to factories, the fob watches to T-shirts and the horse-drawn carts to refrigerated lorries, at least until my bottle of mineral water brought the boy up short. He set the water aside.

'You don't want to buy that,' he advised, pointing out the fountain on the patio at the front of the mall. With its futurist taps and stainless-steel case, this minimalist dispenser was of a part with the café. It might have furnished the open-plan offices of some metropolitan design agency. Even so, the fountain did a job no different from the clay jars of the back roads. At this mission post of Westernised retailing they could not bring themselves to charge for the drinking water they themselves stocked. Heartened, I filled the steel beaker I found at the fountain and crossed the patio of polished travertine, where the ghosts of wandering hominids lay compressed, to eat at a sunlit table.

In the upturned canoe, which I had left in the wheat field below the bridge, spiders had set up home. I shook them free, wicking away their cobweb skeins, and dragged the dewy craft down to the water. It was only now I noticed that the river had broadened considerably since absorbing the flow of the Lycus. Remembering how Cyrus's Greek mercenaries had required a bridge supported by seven pontoons to get them across this stretch of the Meander, it seemed safe to assume that fallen willows, however diabolically they might combine, would no longer block my progress.

The river had also recovered the trademark character it had comprehensively lost all through the gorge; the largely undeviating arc of its steep descent now gave way to windings more expansive yet than the ones that had waylaid me back in the first days of my journey. The loops that now carried my canoe north and south, even back towards the east, were more capacious than ever. This was to be expected; it was along the broad lower valley that the Meander most famously strayed, expressing its freedom by following a course so convoluted that 'the letters of the Grecian alphabet', as one seventeenth-century traveller observed, appeared inscribed in it. What struck me was that rivers and humans covered the ground in oddly antithetical ways – the same steepening gradients that put the twists and turns into men's mountain roads and paths, that is, being precisely what led rivers to straighten. The converse was also true; where the ground levelled off, and the kinks disappeared from those footpaths and roads, was where rivers began to wander.

Rivers were not subject, of course, to turned ankles or brake failure, theirs being a life free from all fear of falling; but while this immunity might account for the headlong descents that rivers favoured, it did not explain why the broad plain should cause them to lose all sense of direction, this river most dramatically, as it did that morning.

Men had speculated as to the reasons for the Meander's windings. Strabo thought it might have something to do with the soil, which he described as 'dry and easily reduced to powder, full of salts, and very inflammable'. The underlying principle was, in fact, one of differential; what caused the outer wheels of a cornering vehicle to revolve more quickly, covering a greater distance in order to keep up with the nearside ones, similarly encouraged a river's flow to run fastest at the outer bank – thereby causing the greater scouring to occur there. This erosion necessarily deepened the curve at the far bank even as the silt scoured upstream was deposited on account of the comparatively slack current along the near one; these two forces working in concert, in short, were what deepened the river's bends. The slightest kink in a river's course was subject to this cumulative process; a silt transfer, working like strong liquor, which caused the river to weave across the plain.

Not that the Meander's mazy twists disturbed me that morning. In fact, I hadn't felt so happy for a long time. I was quite content, mindful of the trouble I had had on the Yenice stretch, to follow wherever that wide and sedate stream took me. It particularly pleased me that the river had come to resemble the one I had initially imagined. As the canoe bow swung through the compass bearings, so my mind wandered free, for once without the least practical consideration to dictate its direction, and the river I travelled at last proved true to its name.

I had often wondered, knowing all that it had come to mean in modern contexts, what the river's name had originally signified. Its etymological journey had begun in one of the original and no doubt interrelated languages, now all but lost, of the ancient regions where it flowed; from its sources the Meander passed through Phrygia before leaving that land to form the historic boundary between Lydia and Caria – at about the point where I now found myself. Since none of the recovered Phrygian, Lydian or Carian inscriptions makes mention of the river, the earliest surviving form is the Greek Maiandros, which carries no hint of the name's original meaning. All it gives us is a distorted echo of how the word might have sounded – but an echo that may not be beyond restoration. One verifiable fact about these ancient languages is that their place names commonly concluded with 'anda', as this cluster of vowels and consonants is best transcribed, which raises the intriguing likelihood that the modern English version of the river's name may happen to be a pleasingly phonetic match with the original.

I had had reason to think about the river's name and the evolution of its etymology the previous evening. I found myself at an empty kebab restaurant in Sarayköy where the waiter, making an exception for the foreigner, sent out for beer, which arrived in a brown paper bag, prohibition-style, along with the whispered request that I keep it beneath the table.

The forbidden brew went down well. In fact, those surreptitious sips on top of the afternoon's long soak at Hierapolis soon reduced me to a kind of meditative stupor in which the restaurant's décor had my glazed attention. For a long time I scrutinised the kitsch wall painting of a silvered tumbling river spanned by a timber bridge before transferring my attention to the patterned paper border, discoloured and peeling, which ran round the restaurant walls. I had noticed the same pattern at Hierapolis, where it was engraved across the old masonry, and around the border of the doormat at my Sarayköy lodgings; a repeat sequence of rectilinear spirals, like a succession of cresting waves, and widely known as the Greek key. Since at least the first century BC, when Virgil used the word to describe a cloak hem's decoration, the pattern has also been known as the meander.

This ubiquitous band or border motif and its related variants are known to have occurred from China and the South Sea Islands to Mexico. It is with the ancient Greeks and their Roman successors, however, no doubt for the prominence of their decorative legacy – their stonework, pottery and coinage, of course, as well as their clothing – that the pattern is most closely associated. It was a common motif on glazed pottery as early as the eighth century BC, and had acquired identifiable associations by the fifth century BC; on vases featuring the Minoan myth of the Minotaur the pattern signified the Cretan labyrinth where Theseus had tracked the monstrous bull. A more recent, anthropological assertion is that the pattern simply reflected the age-old design naturally created by woven reeds along the edge of a handworked basket. Others saw stylised serpents, adjudged the pattern a symbol of infinite cyclical recurrence, or even detected in it an ideogram of the human face.

The most oft-invoked association, however, was with water. The pattern commonly decorated the walls and mosaic floors of Greco-Roman bathhouses. The columns and walls of ancient temples, traditionally sited on holy springs, also featured it. Most compellingly persuasive, however, was that the pattern, however stylised, patently represented water not only as the cross-sectioned wave but from another, equally archetypal perspective: as a rectilinear rendering of a meandering river's aerial view. These associations confirmed an ancient reverence, which somehow appeared to have survived in modern Turkey, to judge by the girls' names – River, Spring, Rain – and the roadside taps and clay jars, even the textile factory's logo and, finally, the instinctive reluctance of the boy in the *Dance Hall – Fervent* T-shirt to sully the stuff, and his common humanity, by selling it to me.

It was an exquisite morning. Across a blue sky storks beat upstream until their white plumages were lost against the high snows of Babadağ. The river coiled broad and clear across the plain, gradually trending towards the valley's southern edges. Wild olives, hazed in the swaggering lowland heat, grew from the reddish rock slopes. A fig tree, choked in vines, murmured with bees and cicadas. I passed beneath a bridge where a red-ruled marker post showed 2.5 metres of water, and with a jolt of joy I figured that nothing could now stop the brimful river from delivering me to the Aegean.

It was then that I came to a place signposted as Feslek, a name that was vaguely familiar, where the black gates of a regulator reared lock-like between the banks. At the base of this metal barrier churned a bolus of rotted weed, plastic bottles and discoloured chunks of polystyrene. From the walkway running along the top a man was waving me in the direction I had come. I paddled upstream to put ashore at a shingle shelf. I dragged the laden canoe through the knee-length grass of an untended olive grove, thinking to return to the river below the gates until I saw what lay there. The river had disappeared.

The locals had repeatedly warned me, of course, that I would find no water on the Meander; but as this had usually turned out to mean insufficient water to allow passage of whatever craft it was that they imagined me to possess, invariably something larger and more deep of draught than my canoe, such statements had soon ceased to alarm me. The security guard at the outlet store had clearly meant it, however, when he told me that there was no water at Feslek. Beyond the regulator there was not so much as a puddle. The damp seam that ran dark down the middle of the riverbed was flanked with a peeling crust of dry mud. I remembered how Mehmet, the tufted caretaker at the Işıklı Lake dam, had at least been on hand to offer encouragement the last time anything like this had happened. There was nothing positive, however, that this watchman could possibly say to a canoeist. The only utterance was my own.

'Gone,' I intoned, slack-jawed.

'Gone,' the watchman confirmed. 'For hydroelectricity and irrigation,' he added, motioning that I follow him across the walkway. Here the water disappeared in a high-pressure tumble, just as it had done at Işıklı, but this time in sufficient quantities to fill two broad concrete canals. Beside the brimming canals stood a sign. *Let's Keep Our Water Clean*, it urged. I asked the watchman if he knew of any plans to open the gates.

'Oh, only if they need to meet irrigation demand downstream,' he said. 'Or' – he wrinkled his nose – 'when the rubbish needs flushing through.'

'How far do you reckon before there's water in the river again?' The watchman cast an open palm up the empty river bed, as if I must find out for myself, though the gesture appeared to concede that it might be a while. He offered tea to see me on my way.

It increasingly occurred to me that the story of the region had for some time been following my own progress down the Meander, and in good chronological order. The river and its history unspooled as one. It was therefore fitting, consolingly so, that I should have run out of water just as I came up against a major historical blockage. The Byzantine Age, a millennium, roughly calculated, appeared as much a challenge to the continuance of my Anatolian journey as any drained river bed.

For from their first appearance in the fourth century the Byzantines had always appeared an exclusively metropolitan lot, with no easily imagined place out in the Anatolian provinces: the very name by which they are known to the modern world exclusively associates the people of the Eastern Roman Empire – ever the *Romaioi*, or Romans, as they styled themselves – with the great city of Byzantium. The empire takes its very dates from their occupation of the city on the Bosphorus which their founding emperor was soon to rename in his honour; what began with Constantine's adoption of the city as his capital in the year 324 ended with Constantinople's loss to the Turks in 1453. It is no surprise, then, that urban backdrops should materialise unbidden in any evocation of the Byzantines: the gilded chambers of Constantinople's Great Palace, for example, or the offices of the holy Patriarchate, or the domed interior of the Haghia Sophia basilica where these chamberlains and tributes, presbyters and patriarchs performed their arcane rituals, intrigued and pointed ring-laden fingers grown long with the endless scoring of obscure philosophical points.

All of which inevitably consigned the Byzantine legacy across the Anatolian provinces – the land they knew as *Romania* – to a corresponding faintness. In the Meander Valley, in fact, it appeared to the modern traveller that the Byzantine centuries had been subjected to a campaign of concerted erasure. No trace remained of the evocative objects – icons fashioned from heated wax, painted books of purple parchment and silver ink, gilded iconostases and gold altar cloths – which were the stuff of their culture. Then there were their structures, which Turkish archaeologists had not always respected in their haste to uncover the classical ones beneath them. In the process of the Byzantine decline and extinction many churches like that of the revered St Michael the Archangel at Colossae had been sacked; others had been turned into mosques. Going back over my journey, the only expressly Byzantine remains I had seen were the monastic cells hewn into the cliffs of the Meander gorge, and the martyrium of St Philip at Hierapolis.

These ruins were not much to go on. They did serve, however, to confirm that the sacrifices of Paul, Philip and the rest had borne fruit in Byzantine Anatolia; Christianity had triumphed there. They might even have been cues as to the particular character of that society – the pilgrims who made devotions to martyred apostles, and the penitents who found fulfilment in the ascetic example of Egypt's Desert Fathers, the devout and the marginalised retiring to remote monasteries and hermitages to lead lives by turn communal and solitary. So I now perceived those abandoned rock caves as home to communities committed to poverty, spiritual wealth and the service of the sick and the indigent. I pictured the monks who lived out their lives after the examples of the blessed saints, in prayer, study and contemplation, in the tending of their plots and the pounding of grain, in treating the sick and in giving alms to the poor. The land prospered under the tenure of Christianity's guiding principles.

Except that this is to ignore the faith's zealous aspect, which had been increasingly to the fore from the moment Christianity was legalised in the year 312; the time had come to turn on the pagans who had once persecuted the early Christians. From the end of the fourth century, when Christianity was declared the Roman world's only legitimate religion, religious dissent was no longer tolerated. In the sixth century the Emperor Justinian, builder of the great basilica of Haghia Sophia in Constantinople, ordered: 'If any unholy or defiled pagan does not make himself manifest, whether living here or in the countryside, and run to the churches with his household, that is to say wives and children, let him submit to the aforesaid penalties, let the revenue confiscate their property, and let them be given over to exile.'

The work that occupied some Byzantine monks, then, was the razing of pagan temples. John, Bishop of Ephesus, set about converting the pagans of the lower Meander in the year 542. 'When God opened the minds of [the pagans] and made them know the truth,' he wrote, 'he aided us in destroying their temples, in overturning their idols, in eradicating the sacrifices which were offered elsewhere, in smashing their altars defiled by the blood of sacrifices offered to pagan gods, and in cutting down the numerous trees which they worshipped, and so they became estranged from all the errors of their forefathers. The saving sign of the cross was implanted everywhere amongst them, and churches of God were founded in every place.' Over a period of thirty years the bishop reckoned that he and his shock troops had forcibly converted some 80,000 pagans.

Even so, the old beliefs endured. When a city north of the Meander Valley, Pergamum, came under siege in 717, a sorcerer persuaded some desperate residents that they might spur themselves to a last-ditch defence by sacrificing to the pagan gods. A pregnant woman was found and killed, her foetus boiled in a cauldron in which the citizens sought divine protection by dipping their right hands prior to taking up arms. These diabolical rituals prevented neither the city's fall nor the slaughter of its citizens; a chronicler of the Pergamum siege judged that the god of the Christians, appalled as ever at such pagan atrocities, had allowed the city to be overrun.

It did not occur to this Christian chronicler that the besiegers must have seen it differently; the men who fought their way into Pergamum were not Byzantines reducing the last outposts of paganism, but raiders from the Arab lands who inevitably credited their success not to the retributive

Christian god but to the active support of their own, newly revealed one. In Byzantine Constantinople Christianity might have continued to reign supreme for over a thousand years. Across much of Anatolia, however, the Christian centuries appeared abbreviated by the persistent paganism at their back and the advance of Islam before them. Christ's enforcers, as events at Pergamum in 717 revealed, were yet to eradicate the last of the pagans before the first of the Muslims swept in from the south.

I drank tea with the watchman and left the bagged-up boat in his care. With a supportive slap across the shoulders, the watchman saw me on my way. There was nothing for it but to continue along the river on foot.

The going was not good. With every step the crusted mud yielded to a fetid green smear. I slid and stumbled down the silent course. The leaves of the bank-side willows were brown and brittle; their roots poked from the collapsed banks like rusted cables. Desiccated tresses of river weed, brittle and grey, lay as they had once streamed upon the water, seawards, a sun-cast memory of current. The birds had fled but for a single heron, which stabbed at the putrefied remains of a turtle. The State Water Works had turned the Meander into a stinking gully, a rubbish flush, and then they had erected a sign that lectured the local people on the need to keep the water clean.

I stumbled on, tired and outraged, until a square grey building rose above the banks. It was a hydroelectric station. Above the protruding metal pipes and sluices the words *Abundance Energy* were painted large across the walls.

CHAPTER SIXTEEN

I had barely returned to the path the following morning when the river got some of its water back. The diverted flow, having passed through *Abundance Energy*'s turbines, rejoined the Meander immediately beyond the power station; just not enough of it to float a canoe nor even, apparently, to stop a man from crossing on a moped.

I watched the man squeeze his aged machine through a gap in the cobweb-starred trees and brambles lining the far bank. Then he sped down the slope into the Meander's bed, barely slowing for the water. The same river that Cyrus's expeditionary Greeks had crossed only with the aid of seven pontoons – and which an impressive Roman bridge, all six stone arches of it, had once spanned at nearby Antiocheia – this man now forded without wetting his shoes.

From those shoes, and from the man's flat cap, tattered suit and even his moped, all colour had long since leached. Only his face and hands, a deep varnished walnut, relieved the monochrome effect. With a sharp twist of the throttle the man gunned his moped up the bank, trailing blue exhaust, only to brake at the sight of me. He wished me good morning, offering a calloused hand.

'You must be the foreigner I read about in the *New Century*,' he said. 'Except they said you were travelling by boat.'

'For that I'd need water,' I replied tartly. I was curious for my part how long it was since the farmer had first been able to cross the Meander on two wheels.

'On and off, all through the drought years,' he reflected. 'Just twenty years ago these fields regularly flooded in the winter. Back in my childhood, in the 1950s, the current even in summer was so strong that our parents only let us swim if we promised to stay close to the banks. The only way across in those days was to wait for the ferry.' The farmer described a flat-bottomed timber raft with a knee-height gunwale, a stout fixing post and a wide stern, of the sort that had operated at various points along the Meander's lower reaches. This transport, which the local ferrymen winched across by a cable secured between the banks, was typically capable of carrying perhaps twenty passengers, along with a cart, some livestock, or even the occasional motor vehicle.

By effectively the same arrangement earlier travellers had crossed the Meander. What Richard Chandler called 'a triangular float, with a rope', Richard Pococke detailed as 'a sort of boat like a sledge in shape of a half lozenge, the sides of it not being about a foot high. They tie vine boughs together, which are about an inch and a half diameter, and from ten to fifteen feet long, which are fixed across the river; a post in the boat rests against it, and keeps the vessel from being carried down by the stream and by the help of this three men pull the boat from one side to the other.' Such river crossings had not changed in their essentials between the mid-1700s and the mid-1900s; from the 1950s, however, industrialisation had begun transforming the valley.

As for the drought, this was not the first I had heard of it. Since Dinar the lack of water had been the talk of the tea houses. Farmers and smallholders glanced skywards and with a shrug gave themselves up to Allah's plan; they submitted to the caprices of divine will, at once absolving their fellow men of responsibility. The statistics might confirm that Turkey had indeed received less rainfall than its customary portion in recent years, but it was also the case that just ten kilometres upstream the Meander brimmed with two and a half metres of water. The real problem was the concrete culverts, which smuggled away every last drop, and the vast volumes of river water retained behind the dams at Adıgüzel and Çindere, not forgetting the additional waters that would be withheld to fill the dam now being built there. I had barely begun to fulminate against the dams, culverts and regulators, however, when the farmer began to lose interest. He who had been pleased to reminisce now appeared awkward, apparently finding his time to be short. I was in mid-flow when he wished me good travels, kicked his moped into life and drove off into the morning, casting a beseeching look at the cloudless sky.

Back, now, to the Byzantines and the faintness of the impression they had left beyond the city; a more substantial bar to sensing their presence in provincial Anatolia may in fact be that they were often short of Anatolian provinces, at least ones they could unconditionally call their own. The Byzantine emperors who went east did so not to tour peaceable provinces but to contest ones they had recently lost.

For the peace secured under Roman rule had begun to fray by the sixth century. Anatolia once more found itself overrun by invaders, and not for the first time from the Asian East. A thousand years after Xerxes had crossed into Europe the camp-fire plumes of the latest Persian dynasty, the Sassanids, rose from the eastern shores of the Bosphorus. Then the Saracen Arabs, newly aflame with the revelations of the Divine Prophet, poured through the Taurus Mountains, the formidable rampart at Anatolia's southern rim, during the seventh and eighth centuries. They swept north beyond the Meander Valley where they sacked cities such as Pergamum, and on three occasions even besieged Constantinople itself.

These regular *razzia*, or raids, might have marked the very seasons in Anatolia; every spring the Saracens came from the south and every autumn, as the mornings turned chill, they led their spoil-laden camels back to homes in the Levant and Arabia. In their wake they left smoking ruins, tumbled apses and trampled fields, the communities reduced by slaughter and abduction, and stripped of provisions and what few valuables they possessed.

The Arab raids certainly brought depopulation, dread and hunger, but the country Byzantines learned to endure; the Saracens would pass as surely as tax collectors, locust swarms, earthquakes and conscription officers. Insecurity had always appeared in the weave of the contested land. The raids, though they continued for centuries, only confirmed the fundamentally conditional nature of Anatolian existence. A consequence of the Byzantines' forbearance, stiffened by their faith, was that the Arabs failed to maintain a permanent presence in Anatolia. William Ramsay went so far as to claim that they 'never held a foot of land beyond Taurus outside the range of their weapons at the moment'.

Those Byzantines who by chance or by their age survived the *razzia* were left to pray for a few years' grace. They wished only that they might be granted time to rebuild their churches and restock their herds, plant their fields and replenish their granaries, repair their threshing floors and raise their walls, and all the while watch their boys put on fighting sinew. They knew they must expect to fight again. If anything gave historic purpose to the provincial Byzantines, it was their achievement in denying the Saracens, at their own great cost, the Anatolian platform whereby they might finally have reduced Constantinople. The city was the very key, of course, to the continent beyond, and the Saracens' failure to take Constantinople stemmed the Arab advance into Europe, diverting its flow to the south, along the coast of North Africa, so that Islam would first penetrate Christendom not by the eastern marches but by its Iberian underbelly. The forgotten heroics of these provincial Byzantines, their memory all but erased across their Anatolian lands, were to have the most profound effect upon European history. Without them, the Arabs might have made the West their own as Alexander had made the East his a thousand years before. As it was, the Arabs were to leave only the faintest mark upon Anatolian culture.

Which could not be said of the next lot of invaders – whom Byzantine fortitude could do nothing to deflect. They came this time from the vast Eurasian steppe, which lay north-east beyond the Caucasus Mountains and the Caspian Sea. These grasslands, irregularly watered, turned from green to tawny with the seasons. Any settlements that sprouted there withered under the alternating effects of summer sun and winter freeze; a shortage of natural defences left the rest vulnerable to sack. The only thing for it was to travel light and chase down the sudden sweet greening beneath the rain clouds where the

herds might grow sleek and rich in milk. To this end alone
the steppe people roamed, no doubt in the familiar orbit of
their forebears, but unburdened by sentimental attachment
and only for so long as the ancestral lands continued to serve.
In times of drought, or if a succession of good years had so
swelled the herds that the traditional pastures could not
sustain them, the nomads were suddenly gone, the steppe
coughing up whole tribes and hawking them in the direction
of whatever settled peoples happened to lie in their path.
Some centuries before, just such a migratory paroxysm had
carried the Mongolian Huns and the central Asian Avars
westwards, shunting into the tribes they encountered there
through the fifth century; the people they displaced, the Goths
and Vandals among them, duly overran the Western Roman
Empire. Something similar was now about to befall the
Byzantines in the Roman East.

In the Anatolian lands that were destined to bear their name
the Turks had first registered only as a conscripted element
among the Sassanid and Saracen raiding parties; a hardy steppe
people who made excellent soldiers. These Turks originally
hailed from the mountain fringes of the distant Gobi Desert
– from that secret valley of legend Turkey's more fervent nationalists now knew as *Ergenekon*. The temptation was therefore to
assume that the Turks had taken a very long run-up in breaking
down the Byzantine door. In fact, they had meant no such thing;
with only a modest name for metal working to distinguish them,
and the watering whims of their sky god by way of propulsion,
these animist nomads had seemed more interested in escaping
their Chinese persecutors than in entertaining the least ambitions towards territories in the distant West.

By the eighth century, however, a complex combination of
motives, unspecified but no doubt rooted in the exigencies of

grass and ground, had energised certain tribes of Turks and
caused these pigtailed nomads to muscle their way across the
eroded ranges of central Asia and close on the Persian borderlands. Here, they honed the skills for which they were
renowned, as horsemen and archers, and meantime discovered
the foil for their martial zeal in the militant creed now pulsing
out of its Arabian hub. The Turks took readily to Islam; the
males, from sultans to soldiers, were thenceforth to favour the
name of the Prophet, which their language rendered as
Mehmet.

So the Turks' wanderings, no longer in thrall merely to the
seasonal cycle, acquired a missionary sense of direction. With
Persians and Arabs they came to contest not only the pastures
on which they once had solely depended but the settled lands
too. These steppe skirmishers now acquired the weapons and
wherewithal to take cities. To the sound of the kettle drum, to
the swish of the scimitar they took on all comers. By the eleventh century a federation of Turkish tribes known as the Selçuks,
named for their founder, held sway over much of Persia. In
1045, with their first incursions into Anatolia, the Selçuks set
their sights on the grasslands of Byzantium. Twenty-five years
later, they had raided beyond the headwaters of the Meander
to reach the Lycus Valley. In the nave of the great basilica at
Chonae, built on the site of the fabled church St Michael the
Archangel had once saved from the diverted waters of the
pagans, these Muslim raiders now shook off their steppe dust,
stabled their war horses and made plans to stay.

Ploughed fields ran from the banks of the straying river. The
turned earth, which storks wandered on their jointed red legs,
abutted expanses of wheat stubble, orchards of orange and pomegranate trees, ordered lines of walnut trees and olive groves.

The view recalled the same alluring patchwork – 'the whole plain in highest state of cultivation, abounding with rich pasturage, cornfields, vineyards, olives and fig trees' – that Reverend Arundell had admired in earlier times. The valley had produced, after all, the famed 'Smyrna' figs and 'Sultana' raisins that the British, the Edwardians particularly, had consumed by the shipload 'to titivate fog-dulled appetites'. One visitor early in the twentieth century marvelled at bottomlands that 'have been cultivated from the beginning of history, and yet are so fertile as to make one question the possibility of their exhaustion'; the cornucopia that the bearded god Meander held aloft on the statues and coins appeared set to overflow through all time.

Except that the enriching silt had for the best part of twenty years not been nourishing the valley but accumulating uselessly at the foot of upstream dams. The water the Turks otherwise appeared to revere was, besides, largely missing. And the Meander smelt. At one bend, where there rose a rubbish heap, it smelt particularly bad. A shawled woman with holed gloves was picking through a smouldering strew of plastic bottles and cartons, tyres, shoes, tins, stained cardboard and bloated bin bags that spilt rot, viscera-like, from their split flanks. The smiling image of a nappy-swathed baby beamed from a scrap of polythene packaging; like the tourism map, whose legend did not include riverside rubbish heaps or the impoverished people who picked over them, the infant seemed oblivious to its surroundings.

Opposite where I knew the ruins of Antiocheia to stand, set back as they were some distance from the south bank, I kept a close eye on the Meander's shallows. I was hoping the low water might at least have exposed a river-bed remnant of some sort,

perhaps an old pier footing or some other protrusion, to mark
the site of the six-arched bridge that had featured on the coins
of Roman Antiocheia. I found nothing; which, as the bridge had
been down for a very long time – certainly since 1147 – should
not have surprised me.

The bridge at Antiocheia, as its place on the coins acknowledged, had been a significant crossing for centuries; it was where
the ancient valley road had switched riverbanks. Unlike the
modern highway, which now kept north of the river as far as
Sarayköy, crossing beside the newly built outlet store, the old
road had taken to the south bank here, at Antiocheia, before
continuing east to Laodicea.

It was by this same road that the diverted forces of the Second
Crusade under the King of France were in 1147 obliged to travel
if they were then to make south for the Mediterranean port of
Adalia (modern Antalya) en route to the Holy Land. But the
Meander bridge at Antiocheia had been destroyed, perhaps
precisely to frustrate the Crusaders' advance, or it may have
been reduced in the devastation to which the Meander Valley
was generally subject, and which positively engulfed the region
during the twelfth century.

Half a century had passed since an appeal for assistance by
the Byzantine emperor had first brought the 'base and bastard
Turks' to Western notice. By the 1090s the Turks were threatening Byzantine territory to a greater degree than the Arabs
had ever done; their capture of Jerusalem from the Arabs had
further galvanised the Christian West. The result, the First
Crusade, had in the last years of the eleventh century achieved
such glorious successes as to confirm the Christians' assumption
that they could depend upon divine favour should they ever
again need to take up the cross against the Eastern infidels. By
roundly defeating the Turks at the bastion city of Dorylaeum

and elsewhere, pushing them back into the Anatolian hinterland, the armies of the First Crusade had not only secured the land route to Jerusalem but also fulfilled the sanctified mission of restoring the holy city to Christian rule. They had even established a whole series of Latin statelets – Outremer, or Beyond the Sea – across the wider region.

The fall in 1144 of one such possession on Anatolia's Syrian border, Edessa, had alerted the West that Islam was once more on the rise. It was time to reconfirm Christianity's pre-eminence in the East by serving God's wrath on the Turks, an altogether more formidable and alien race of Muslims than the Arabs. The summer of 1147 saw Western forces, boosted not only by the papal imprimatur but by the personal leadership of two European sovereigns, gather under the banners of Louis VII of France and Conrad III of Germany.

The German Army was the first to leave the European mustering grounds. It led the advance to Constantinople where Byzantine observers – contemptuous of these knights' wayward religious ways but fearful of their impressive fighting abilities – put the army's size beyond computation. And this without reckoning on the French columns, which were to reach Constantinople by the same trampled road a month later. It was a formidable force, one whose strategists were unlikely to have heard of a Byzantine backcountry town called Antiocheia; certainly, they had no reason to suppose in even their most pessimistic calculations that the place was ever to figure in their advance across Anatolia.

For the once-great road up the Meander Valley, which led past little Antiocheia, had long since lost out to more northerly routes. These passed through Constantinople, the world's greatest city, so that the great highway to the Holy Land, choice of traders, pilgrims and soldiers alike, only touched the Meander at its source deep in the interior. This 'straight and level' road, which ran through Nicaea, Dorylaeum, Apamea and Iconion, was crucially the route the knights of the First Crusade had taken. Many of those who now took the cross under Louis and Conrad divined in the direct nature of their itinerary, a broadly straight line to the south-east, something of the unswerving purpose of that first crusading generation. They saw that exemplary venture as nothing less than a sanctified template for their own enterprise, in all manner of ways but above all in terms of their designated route to the Holy Land. In such a spirit Conrad, first to lead his armies across the Bosphorus into Asia, set out down that same straight road in October 1147. It was not long after, however, that he and his men were comprehensively routed by the Turks a short distance from the site of the great Crusader victory won fifty years earlier at Dorylaeum.

So much, then, for God's wrath at the Turks or for the certain bestowal of divine favour; a presumption many Christians might also have questioned when He had allowed Edessa to fall a few years earlier. The same God who had seen to things half a century earlier had now left the Crusaders to prove their own mettle against a demonstrably strengthened enemy, and amid the first falls of snow and increasingly acute shortages of food.

So the Crusaders' south-easterly route began, like a headed sailing ship, to stray south; advisers proposed that Louis's armies and the remnant of Conrad's ravaged force should abandon the straight road and instead make for the Byzantine-held city of Philadelphia. They would thereby avoid the worst of the mountains and, though they would not publicly concede the fact, skirt what effectively amounted to Turkish territory. The diversion acknowledged the power shift that had taken place in Anatolia since the time of the First Crusade. It tacitly recognised the hinterland presence of the Turks whom the Crusaders wished to avoid, if only to save their energies for the slaughter they meant to serve upon them in dispatch of their sacred obligation to restore Christianity's increasingly shaky hold on the Holy Land.

The Crusaders, all said, were having a tougher time of it than the gilded accounts of the First Crusade had led them to expect. Hampered by the pilgrims, nobles' households, motley camp followers and other non-combatants under their supposed protection, sapped by the Germans' recent defeat and exhausted by the distance they had already travelled, they were now to turn aside and so bear the additional weight of moral compromise. The road to salvation was long and was, it now seemed, not even straight.

Indeed, they were soon to find themselves further consigned to Anatolia's 'crooked and treacherous byways'. Word now reached the Crusader camp that the proposed diversion to the south might also have its drawbacks: Conrad, chastened by the near starvation suffered by his broken forces on the retreat from Dorylaeum, advised Louis and his barons that they could expect similar provisioning difficulties on the Philadelphia road. The best option was to make for the south-west, fully at right angles to their intended course, and follow the coast road to Smyrna and Ephesus. From there, revictualled and rested, they could then take the ancient road up the Meander Valley to Byzantine-held Laodicea before heading south for the Mediterranean and so complete their journey by sea.

The holy blitzkrieg was fast losing, in short, all sense of direction. The expedition, badly blunted, rambled through provincial Anatolia. Louis and his entourage spent several farcical days press-ganging upland rustics into directing them back to the path they had mislaid. Their progress along the coast was particularly sorry, with the king's chaplain, Odo of

Deuil, chronicling how they encountered 'nearly every day steep, stony mountains and the deep channels of mountain torrents, which were difficult to cross even when dry and if filled with snow or rain possessed swift currents which neither horse nor infantry could swim through'. Conrad was ailing by the time he reached Ephesus; he did not need any encouragement when an imperial envoy arrived to inform him that palatial quarters had been readied for his convalescence at Constantinople. It was left to Louis to lead the advance up the Meander Valley.

So the Crusaders worked their way up the wintry plain. On their approach to Antiocheia the Turkish resistance, which had been shadowing them since Ephesus, materialised in force: bowmen on the heights, infantry across the valley and the rest, in Odo's words, 'massed on the other bank of the river to prevent us crossing'. For two days the Crusader forces advanced up the north bank in protective formation. Losses were modest but progress was slow, and the continued harassment convinced Louis that they must find a way to cross the Meander: a river, it is to be remembered, which a bridge no longer spanned, which no regulators had reduced and which, as Odo reported, 'ordinarily was deep and wide, but at that time was swollen with water from other streams'.

The stage was set for the engagement that was to ensue by the banks of the Meander on the morning of New Year's Day 1148. The battle was not to merit a name, though this did not prevent the leading Byzantine historian of the age, Niketas Choniates, from making it nothing less than the central episode in his account of the Second Crusade. The historian may have given the battle such prominence because he considered himself a local – he was, as his name indicates, from nearby Chonae – or because he had as a child seen for himself gory evidence of the sheer extent of the conflict that had taken place just seven years before his birth. It may also have been that Choniates recognised the battle as the one event in the whole sorry venture worthy of Christian commemoration; the moment when God came to the belated rescue of the Crusaders and, it might be said, of Niketas Choniates' otherwise untriumphant account of it.

So the first dawn of the new year broke, Choniates wrote, to reveal the opposing armies arrayed in battle order along either bank. He told how the king had reviewed his troops and roused them by denouncing the barbarian 'enemies of the cross of Christ' in whose blood his men had promised to wash themselves, taking vengeance on a people whose brothers had defiled the Saviour's tomb with their feet.

The problem was getting at these Turks; in the way lay a river whose 'rushing waters formed whirlpools, making it completely impassable'. The king's proposal was brazen. 'Massed in full battle array and couching our lances,' he declared, 'let us zealously rush in and charge on horseback through the river's current; and I am fully confident that the waters shall be stayed, draw back, and the direction of their course reversed as happened of old when the Jordan River was crossed by Israel on foot.'

These words stirred the Crusaders to action; somehow the knights and their weighted horses successfully forded the torrent to storm the far bank. They soon did for the Turks who were 'cut to pieces in diverse ways and fell on one another like ears of corn; and then, like grapes pressed in wine vats, their lifeblood was squeezed by the lance-bearing knights . . . others arrayed nearby were wounded with dagger thrusts and were plunged into ruin as the bronze spilled out of their bowels. The bodies of the fallen Turks completely covered the plains, the ravines overflowed with their blood . . . To this day,' Choniates concluded, 'the mounds of bones are so many and so high that they stand like lofty hillocks bearing witness to the hosts who fell there.'

Odo of Deuil, privy to the same events, was of the standard view that a divine hand had been at work. 'I do know,' he wrote, 'that in such straits such an easy and brilliant victory would not have occurred except by the power of God, nor would the rain of iron from the opposing army have fallen without causing death or wounds.' It was said, he reported, that some people had seen 'at the ford a certain white-clad knight' who had supposedly 'struck the first blows in the battle'. God had sided with them, that is, as He had abandoned the pagans of Pergamum to the Muslims and as His archangel had guarded the church at Colossae against inundation.

This was a selective reading of recent events, of course, one which ignored such reverses as the defeat of the Germans at Dorylaeum and the fall of Edessa; the Christian forces might have known better than to rely upon divine favouritism. For the Deity, as they were obliged to acknowledge, soon withdrew His support for them. Barely a week after their victory by the Meander the same Crusaders suffered a terrible mauling in the mountains above Laodicea, Louis barely escaping with his life. The Turks so dogged the expedition's progress to Adalia that the Crusaders were reduced to feeding off the corpses of fallen horses. A few men, mostly officers, finally made it to the Holy Land, but only to discover that the various Christian factions assembled there could not agree a common plan. The venture ended in humiliation. If the Second Crusade proved anything, it was that the Turks were firmly established across much of the Holy Land and Anatolia, and the differences between Western and Eastern Christians were such that they could not begin to settle them.

This particular instalment of the holy mission had in fact been compromised from the very beginning. Long before the knights' discovery that they were to be denied the favourable campaigning conditions that the men of the First Crusade had enjoyed half a century earlier – an on-side God to guarantee a steady stream of victories, and a straight road – these men had also learned that they must do without anything in the way of steadfast allies. For on their arrival at Constantinople they were informed that the Byzantines, for all their diplomatic protest-ations of goodwill, had recently made a treaty with the Turks to guard their flank in case of conflict with the Crusaders. The emperor might have extended hospitality to his ailing German counterpart, but most Byzantines viewed the Crusaders not as their co-religionists but as nothing less than 'a cloud of enemies, a dreadful and death-dealing pestilence'.

Nor did the Western Crusaders think any better of the Byzantines. Odo of Deuil compared them to the worst kind of tourist touts, offering rip-off exchange rates, letting down baskets from the safety of high walls to collect payments for goods they then refused to deliver, and in some cases mixing the barley they sold to the Crusaders with fatal quantities of lime. He listed their other treacherous failings: the Byzantines of Antiocheia had offered sanctuary to those Turks who had managed to flee the riverside carnage while the Byzantine commander of Laodicea had actually led a detachment of Crusaders into a Turkish ambush. Some of the Turkish forces that harassed the Crusaders were even under the leadership of Greeks. Any sense of common Christian purpose appeared to be beyond the churches of the Byzantine East and Latin West, officially sundered for a century, whose congregations had come to regard each other with outright hostility.

The truth was that Anatolia had already begun to turn Turk. The same Byzantines whose forebears had appealed for Western help against the accursed Turks just fifty years earlier now seemed more inclined to seek accommodations with their new neighbours from the east. Some Byzantines and Turks had begun to explore ways in which they might coexist. It was a social phenomenon that some chroniclers regarded as inevitable along the empire's contested margins, and which others saw as the understandable reaction of a populace who had long been regarded as a lumpen source of tax and of expendable soldiery, and had been generally maltreated by the authorities. The loyalty of these disenchanted Byzantines was negotiable, as some commentators noted. The islanders of Lake Beyşehir, just west of Iconion, 'by mingling with the Turks, not only strengthened their mutual bonds of friendship but also maintained strong commercial ties', and in time came to look upon the Byzantine authorities as their enemies. The populations of Christian settlements near Antiocheia, captured and deported by the sultan's forces at the end of the twelfth century, took a similar view; they were so generously 'apportioned fertile land for cultivation', provided with 'grain and seed for the growing of crops', and so lightly taxed following their arrival at the Turkish-held town of Philomelion that 'many who had not fallen into the Turks' hands but who had heard of what the Turk had done for their kinsmen and countrymen' followed their lead into Turkish territory.

This is not to say that an entirely amenable process of assimilation – that of Christian Byzantines into Muslim Turks – was under way by the time of the Crusades; there were plenty of instances of slaughter, abduction and the sack of cities, as we shall see, and even in the twentieth century the descendants of the same Byzantines and Turks would still be warring by the banks of the Meander River. Through the early centuries of Turkish dominion many Byzantines were forcibly converted; it was a condition, for example, among the young Christian men whom the Turkish authorities favoured for imperial service. Others converted to curry favour, to avoid persecution or to dodge premium taxes.

Perhaps, however, the chief influence on the Byzantine masses was the sense that the experience of their forebears had bred in them: that the time had come, as it did in Anatolia, to submit to the latest transformation. This plastic people whose predecessors had once been Arzawan, then Hittite, Phrygian, Persian, Greek and Roman, were no longer to be Byzantine but Turk. They were to change their language and bow before different gods, and so they were to survive by once more forgetting their former selves.

The bridge I finally reached was not far from the town of Kuyucak (alt. 133 metres). Beyond dusty orange groves a riverside *kahve*, a makeshift café, stood in a shaded garden. The place was deserted except for a grey-haired man drinking beer, a habit he had acquired during the thirty years he had spent in Holland. Europe had been good to Çetin. He had returned home a few years before to farm. The local orchards were his, but this year's harvest was sure to be disastrous.

'The water,' he exclaimed, his voice thick with disgust. 'When I was a child we drank straight from the river. The river brimmed with fish. There was water even through the driest summers. There's now so little, and so much filth from the factories, that I can't even use it on the orchards. My harvest will be wiped out this year.'

The stream that crept past the *kahve* was brown. The educated Çetin listed the factory effluents he knew it to contain: copper and lead, chromium and nitrates from the textile factories at Sarayköy and Denizli, and chlorides and sulphides from the leather and tanning factories at Uşak.

'They would never allow such a thing in Holland,' said Çetin, plainly disgusted.

The water was certainly filthy. But at least there was more of it; probably even enough, what with my sore feet, to float a canoe on.

CHAPTER SEVENTEEN

The man from the State Water Works – thigh-high in waders, sock-deep in water – was so absorbed in his work that he never noticed the approach of my canoe. He was measuring the Meander's flow below the bridge near the city of Nazilli (alt. 94 metres). In his hand he held a high-tech meter – matt black, scalloped grip, digital display – which evidently made for grim reading; like an infirmary nurse clearing a thermometer, the disbelieving man shook the meter before he plunged it back into the patient.

'Way too slow,' he muttered and cast a disapproving eye upon the river as if it were to blame for its own condition. This so rankled, given what his own organisation had done to the river, that I thought to surprise the man by paddling up to his patently unnecessary waders with an opinion of my own.

'Way too low as well,' I declared, promptly grounding.

At my words the man spun round. 'Where were you going?' he blurted. I clambered from the canoe, not for the first time that morning, and made a point of telling him how the plan *had* been to reach the sea. But by a river which, it now seemed, was unlikely to complete its own passage there.

The wonder was how those upstream obstacles – the endless loops, fallen willows and sudden bouts of current – could ever have tried my patience. I now recognised them as the river's vital signs. The same could not be said of these incessant groundings; any river that failed even to maintain the half-filled bath it took to float my canoe was not worthy of the name. The Meander, poached beyond enduring, was nearing an early end. As the man with the gadget was now discovering for himself.

That morning I had collected my stowed canoe from Feslek, brought it by *dolmuş* to the riverside *kahve* and reassembled it in the shade of Çetin's ailing orange groves. There was nobody about to see me push off and collide with what I took to be a rogue submerged sandbank only yards from the *kahve*. Further groundings followed in such quick succession, however, that I was soon down to my last hope: that I might learn to read the river anew, or what remained of it, and so dodge the riffled patches where the water was stretched so thin as to tear, just as I had once got good at negotiating tight gaps among the willows.

The hope was a forlorn one. If I learned anything that morning, it was the extent to which my trousers should be submerged – mid-shin – before I might successfully get back into the canoe, and I had relaunched repeatedly by the time the Nazilli bridge came into view. In the process I had transferred a lot of river water and mud into the canoe. The smeared clods, broken open between my feet, gleamed with veins that seemed to run with mercury.

Those factors – the mud, the effective lack of a river and now the first signs of chemical corruption – almost persuaded me to call it a day. I might have hauled out at the bridge, jabbed a finger at the hapless man from the State Water Works, upbraided his organisation, the river's supposed guardian, for having delivered it up to the power companies, to the irrigators and to the industrialists, and excoriated him for the dead turtles, and the brazen signs that enjoined the public to keep the water clean even as the same organisation turned a blind eye to the toxic effluent pouring out of the factories. The man was not solely to blame, however, and the river was not quite dead, so

I pushed on, but inadvisably, because it was not long before the river became very filthy indeed.

With every advance, whether by stroke or step, the mud worsened, the churned water billowing clouds the colour of charcoal. The stuff that now splattered the canoe, my clothes and gear, had a foul, anoxic smell. That same morning I had passed some wading fishermen, stripped to the undershorts to net for gasping carp in the shrunken shaded pools beneath the bank-side willows. By the afternoon, however, the same potbellied mudlarks had either come to their belated senses or expired in the mephitic mire, for I passed no more groups of them. Like the birds, the fish and the turtles, they were gone, and with them went the last faint vestiges of the Meander's pastoral allure. Beneath a flat sky the river now looped like a bowel, carrying its foul load, and me, towards evacuation.

It was then that I saw the culvert, and I shuddered; a treacly black substance was creeping onto the river. Initially the viscid filth formed a regular fringe along the bank. In no time, however, it had begun fingering out into the river, its malign ribbons drifting apart beneath the cut of the canoe bow. The spidery, grease-flecked branches dispersed until the entire river ran black, and a sour smell rose from the water. The smell, that said, was not the one I feared. Besides, the colour was wrong. That realisation lifted my spirits, but only until it struck me that I, who had recently walked by fields of thyme, and climbed a gorge in a confetti of yellow butterflies, and passed roadside urns of sweet shaded water and donkey-mounted villagers swathed in turbans, saddlebags holstered with collected firewood, was now consoled, apparently, to figure the filth that lapped at my canoe could not at least be shit. It was time to get off this river, at once and possibly for good, before it finally died, and I risked doing the same. At the foot of the next bridge I drove the canoe ashore and dragged it among some oleanders, stopping only to grab my splattered rucksack.

For once, however, the river offered no easy exit. It was a moment before I worked out the dread significance of the fact that the Meander's banks had not been trampled to the usual slopes: the waters Çetin once drank had turned so foul that even the local livestock knew better than to slake their summer thirsts here. Parched cows were not so foolish as to go where I had been, and it appalled me that I had spent the best part of a precious day wading through filth. I began to question the worth of the entire project and was soon seized with a swelling sense of desperation that I must at all costs get off the river. I threw myself, mumbling incoherently, at the bank of dried mud and scrambled headlong through the thick stand of reeds at the top. To the brittle clatter of snapping foliage, and with a sigh of relief, I heaved myself onto the plain.

It was a beautiful sight; the plain was bathed in a lemon light and gnats danced in spinning columns. Beyond the bridge the road ran north to a town at the foot of mauve hills, the last of the sun flaring against the distant windows. I followed the road through strawberry fields. The muezzin sounded, fading into the noise of traffic. I crossed the highway and the adjacent railway line, passed freight sheds and made my way into Sultanhisar. I climbed a sloping street lined with shabby apartment blocks, the balconies stacked high with wooden fruit cartons. A sign warned off pedlars and travelling salesmen, but the town had not pronounced in relation to filth-lacquered foreigners. I might have gone unregistered if it had not been for the muzzles of the pavement strays, which lifted to quiver at my passing. Even the taxi drivers in their pressed shirts, chatting across yellow bonnets in the town square, pointedly ignored me, as if my condition discounted the possibility that

I might constitute a fare or that they would welcome me as one. The fountain in the square bore a plaque decorated with arabesques and an inscription: *All Living Things Were Created With Water*.

It was then I noticed how the road from the square wound up to something unexpected: a hotel, with flagpoles and flower beds, marking it out as precisely the apparition that had repeatedly teased me along the upland road to Yenice. This one did not dissolve, however, and so offered a real prospect of the comfort I had not enjoyed since my arrival in Turkey. The hotel had also attracted the only other foreigners I had seen since Pamukkale, even if the elderly Koreans then disembarking from their luxury tour coach appeared to take the place for granted. Their indifference was all the encouragement I needed to consider mine the priority claim, though I would have to hurry to press it. The wild and malodorous figure that shambled into view, shedding bits of reed and caked mud, so unsettled an elderly lady at the steps of the coach that she turned for the safety of her seat, pushing against those who were trying to follow her. In the cartoon confusion I nipped through the hotel entrance where the receptionist, visibly startled, promptly dispatched a porter to escort me from the foyer before the Koreans got there, though that was not how she put it. The man would show me straight to my room, she explained, thinking that I might prefer to book in once I had had the chance to freshen up.

Later that evening I was emptying out my rucksack to ready it for a much-needed turn of its own beneath the shower. Feeling deep in a side pocket I found something hard, which I did not immediately recognise. It was the glass jar, its contents pure as the river's waters were now corrupted, which I had filled back at the Meander's source at Pınarbaşı. I remembered how my journey had started, where I had hoped it would lead, and determined then to reach the sea even if the Meander would not carry me there.

In the morning I was crossing the narrow lane at Nysa, the ancient site in the hills above Sultanhisar, when a yellow taxi drew up beside me.

'May you be clean!' the driver exclaimed. He evidently recognised the foreign tramp who had paused by the fountain in the town square the previous evening. Aydın Greatspring, short of teeth but blessed by a generous smile, threw open the passenger door.

'Welcome,' he said. 'Why not come see their village?' Aydın indicated the two old men in the back seats, their chins silvered with stubble, and with an onward sweep of his arm also took in the hills where the village of Kavaklı was to be found. The prospect was enticing; Nysa, the cultured city where Strabo had once studied, could wait. The old men were exchanging grievances.

'No money in the soil any more,' moaned one.

'Except for the middlemen in the cities,' said the other.

'The ones who don't get their hands dirty,' the first added contemptuously.

'Can't get a fair price for anything,' the other one added, throwing up his hands. 'Not for apricots or strawberries.'

'Nor for cherries.'

'Walnuts.'

'Not plums.'

'Pomegranates. Bah!'

'Not for peaches.'

Neither man seemed willing to let the other have the last word. I feared they must continue to work their way through the list of locally grown products, which I knew to be famously extensive, until one of them signed off with a final grouse.

'And now' – he sighed – 'not even a *dolmuş* to town.' Aydın Greatspring, presently benefiting from the recent closure of the village's minibus service, directed a placatory shrug at the rear mirror. The road corkscrewed upwards. In the fields were chokes of bramble and pomegranate trees stippled with delicate orange flowers. Box-shaped timber beehives, blue like faded boats, lined winding pathways and higher up, below a ridge, stands of cypress trees showed black against the sky. With a brutal twist the road climbed to a final bluff, terminating in a tiny square shaded by the brindled boughs of overhanging plane trees. Aydın set about helping the old men with their shopping bags. I looked around, and at once saw why the *dolmuş* no longer ran to Kavaklı. Rusted padlocks hung from the door of the mayor's office and the village store. The tea house had also closed, though nobody had taken it upon themselves to extinguish the possibility that it might yet reopen, for the space I palmed in the window grime revealed chairs and cloth-covered tables neatly in place. There were ashtrays and pots of sugar, even spilt decks of cards, the whole feathered with a shroud of dust.

The mosque was yet to go the way of the tea house. It was a fine, eighteenth-century building, with a stucco exterior in which the timber door and windows were bordered with stencilled motifs in black, blue and rusty brown – domes, potted flowers, trails of chevrons – and sacred exhortations in both Arabic and Latin scripts. I pushed through the door to find myself beneath a timber mezzanine, with rough-cut hayloft steps but railed like a galleon stern, and painted in the same turquoise gloss as the door and windows. Everything was in its place; the imam's gowns, ivory and black, and two fezes, turbaned in white calico to leave vermilion tonsures, hung on neat hooks from the side

of the painted *mimber*, or pulpit, which rose to the wall like a
set of aircraft steps. Across the carpets, worn but recently beaten,
sunlight fell in fierce stripes. The remaining villagers evidently
devoted their dwindling energy to the maintenance of the
mosque; the village's young were long gone, I guessed, perhaps
to Sultanhisar but more likely to Denizli or Aydın, even Izmir
or Istanbul, leaving only the aged and their observances behind.

It was only on leaving the mosque that I noticed the sign –
comparatively recent, and more slickly produced than the usual
home-made contrivances – whose arrow pointed to the *Museum
House of Yörük Ali Efe*. Aydın had not yet returned from delivering his elderly passengers' shopping, so I decided to take a
look. A boulder-strewn track rose through the silent village, past
sagging roofs and walls that had collapsed into stands of dank,
snake-infested weeds. There was no indication of the plaque's
arrow coming to land, but I knew I had found its target the
moment the corner house came into view. In a village teetering
on abandonment, Kavaklı's unlikely attraction was conspicuously restored, if not with any great sensitivity to the regional
vernacular. The place had emerged from its makeover with a
roofed and gated porch, hacienda-style, and with the walls of
both the garden and house crazy-paved in a job lot of industrial
marble. The first-floor terrace was enclosed by an ornate filigree
railing, with exterior red-brick hearths finished in a shiny
varnish, which only added to the persuasive expat villa aesthetic.
The ground-floor rooms were empty but for the house martins,
which flitted by the margins of my vision. Nobody was in attend-
ance; and on the subject of Yörük Ali or his house there was
not a single written word. So I sat in the walled garden, by a
fig tree coming into leaf, and considered the one-time occupant's
name. Which told me that a nomad called Ali had once lived
in this house.

Nomads were not supposed, of course, to live in houses; Anatolia's roving pastoralists, the Yörüks – or Turcomans, to give them their earlier designation – traditionally lived not within permanent walls, like those who settled beside tended plots of land, but in round tents 'made of interlaced rushes, and pointed roofs formed with bent withies'. Certainly, they had done so when the Selçuk Turks first forced Anatolia's eastern door, as Manuel Comnenus, the Byzantine Emperor, had one day had occasion to see for himself.

It was 1146, a year before the armies of the Second Crusade were to arrive. The possibility that the Western armies might sack the Byzantine lands rather than pursue their stated aim of consolidating the Christians' hold over the Holy Land had not yet occurred to the Emperor; it would be some months before he thought to guard his flank by arriving at terms with his traditional Turkish enemies.

In the meantime he had been pursuing a vigorous campaign against the Turks in the region around Iconion, or Konya, as the Selçuks knew the city where they had established their sultanate's capital in 1097. Taking a rest from the fighting, he broke off to fall back on lands that had been restored to Byzantine control during the divinely ordained successes of the First Crusade. On the plains around the headwaters of the Meander, the Emperor went out to hunt as Persia's kings and satraps had done 1,500 years before. There he spied from his horse 'movement far off in the undergrowth'. Scouts reported 'many tents assembled there, and the movements in the grove were the horses of those in the tents, grazing on grass with unbridled mouths'. This was a band of Turcomans – Turks of a nomadic, tribal and stubbornly independent cast – whom the indignant Byzantine forces drove from their tents and put to flight.

The Byzantines no doubt notched up the minor skirmish as

a victory. The truth, however, was that the few wounds they inflicted, the tents they no doubt torched and the horses they rustled, could not begin to mitigate the slaughter visited upon their forces by the Turks at the great battles that had taken place both before and after this brief engagement by the sources of the Meander: at Manzikert, eastern Anatolia, in 1071 where the Byzantines and their substantial levies, ignominiously overrun, had left their emperor to fall captive to the sultan; and at Myriocephalon near Dinar in 1176 where the field was piled high with scalped Byzantine corpses. Myriocephalon lies about 1,000 kilometres to the west of Manzikert; the location of the two battles would appear to constitute an excellent means of metering the rate – roughly a kilometre a month – at which the Byzantines ceded Anatolia to the rampaging Turks over the twelfth century.

The calamitous defeats at Manzikert and Myriocephalon certainly weakened the Byzantine military machine, obliged the Byzantines to abandon strategic military outposts and fatally undermined imperial self-belief. They were not decisive, however, in determining the fate of Anatolia; what actually lost the emperors their land, and by a contrastingly erosive process, were the Turcoman incursions such as the one Manuel witnessed on the same plain where Apollo had once bested Marsyas. The Turcomans, whom Manuel thought to have put to flight, had merely slipped out of range to await the passing of the imperial force. In the meantime they raided settlements, trampled crops and poisoned water sources, all the time reducing the land until it was unable to sustain the settled Byzantines even as it provided all the grass that the Turcomans required of it. It was a strategy that the Byzantines, their orchards and fields levelled, their pigs slaughtered and cattle carried off, were ultimately unable to resist.

The difference between these trespassers and the Saracen Arabs, raiders of earlier centuries, was that they did not eventually go; they were not a merely temporary scourge that would be absorbed into Anatolia's bitter memory. For in their easterly wake these nomads had left little by way of attachments; only the trail of their Turkic language and the fading circles of dust where their encampments had once stood. With nowhere to return to, they had brought not only the tents that were their walls and carpets 'without nap, and in broad stripes and figures', but also their women and children, their livestock and their few other possessions. They were hardy, mobile and lived in the saddle, where the men learned to fire their bows, the women to wean their infants.

These wild Turcomans, who functioned opportunistically beyond the advance positions of the conventional forces under the sultan's command, their interests chancing to be aligned, were soon spilling into Anatolia in vast numbers. Drawn to the grasslands and the vulnerable settlements of the infidels, they camped in the ruins of abandoned settlements whose names and classical heritages meant nothing to them, like Dorylaeum, where an estimated 2,000 tents were reported in the late twelfth century. In 1190 there were reckoned to be some 100,000 Turcomans ranging between the Meander's headwaters and Konya. By the following century they had established such a presence that the region around Chonae, Turkish Honaz, was commonly known as the Plain of the Turcomans. Before the advance of these people, 'numerous as locusts' in the phrase of an appalled Niketas Choniates, the Byzantine villagers retreated to the safety of the towns, the townsfolk to the cities. Walls were raised around the remaining settlements. Beyond the weakening fist of Byzantine resistance, and the ponderous counter-thrusts of its forces, the Turcomans roamed at will. The Byzantines, according to a thirteenth-century commentator, 'thus fear the Turkmens so that they do not dare to go out from their cities or castles if they do not take with them a horse. . . . For they assert that the Turkmens will kill him straight away . . .'

By reducing these lands to little more than pastures dotted by the occasional beleaguered bastion, these nomadic irregulars played a leading role in breaking the Byzantine hold on Anatolia, a fact the Selçuk authorities were quick to acknowledge, even admire. The same authorities, busy establishing their sultanate at Konya, also knew that a yawning gulf now existed between their transitional culture and that of the Turcomans; the traditional Turcoman contempt for sedentary peoples and systems of administration increasingly threatened the ordered society the Selçuks sought to build. For in the course of the Turks' migration the nomadic instinct so evident among the die-hard Turcomans had otherwise been abraded by civilising contact with the settled, comparatively sophisticated and increasingly appealing cultures – notably of the Persian Sassanids and the Byzantines – which they had encountered along the way. A chief consequence of the migratory process was that many Turks no longer counted themselves steppe itinerants by the time they reached Anatolia; to many of them the Turcomans were a throwback to their wild and untutored past. Some partially transformed by adapting to the semi-nomadic practices for which Anatolia was especially suited, moving between established winter bases and the high summer pastures, or *yayla*, where grazing was abundant, temperatures were cool and the debilitating malarial mosquitoes were absent. Others went yet further, adopting home, hearth and regulation to participate in a society that was in some respects modelled on the one they had overrun; for this reason the Selçuk Turks, betraying their own astonishment at the distance they had come and what they had achieved when they got there, chose to know their new sultanate as Rum, or Rome, much as the Byzantines had known the land. It was around this same time,

however, that the Western chroniclers, in a striking acknowledgement of their own take on the new order, began referring to
Anatolia not as Romania but Turchia or Turkomania.

With the passing of time, the settled Selçuks saw less to
admire in their wild Turcoman cousins and more to fear from
these unruly and lawless mobs. As early as the eleventh century,
when Turcoman feats of arms remained fresh in the mind, one
chronicler noted how there had 'arisen a certain amount of
aversion to the Turkmens'. For the Selçuks were learning that
living the settled life meant protecting themselves from the
unregulated nomads they had themselves once been. They were
obliged to erect defences around their homes, their towns and
especially their *hans*, or caravanserais, where travellers and
traders might take refuge at night.

The ill feeling was to deepen. The Turcomans now ranged
across those formerly Byzantine territories that had since come
under Selçuk control. They supplemented what livings they
gleaned from their herds by preying on isolated homesteads or
travellers of any colour or caste. They mounted raids against
Christians and Muslims alike.

So Anatolian nomadism, which had once glittered with martial
allure, fell headlong into brigand disrepute. Those valiant tribal
auxiliaries who had spearheaded the advance into the Turks' new
homeland came to be regarded as common bandits. For all their
ostensible criminalisation, the Turcomans flourished; the Turkish
authorities found them no easier to control than the Byzantines
had. In fact, they were still flourishing in the eighteenth century
when Richard Pococke and Richard Chandler ran into them in
the Lycus Valley, and gave no better account of the Turcomans
than the Byzantines had some six hundred years earlier. 'These
Turcomen,' wrote Richard Pococke, 'when they attack people,
strike from the woods, and travellers are wounded or murdered

without seeing any enemy.' Richard Chandler told of a band of
Turcomans beyond the Meander who 'had very lately plundered
some caravans, and cut off the heads of the people who opposed
them'.

By the time of Pococke's and Chandler's travels, of course,
the Ottomans had long eclipsed the Selçuks. This tribal dynasty,
which had come to power in Anatolia during the fourteenth
century, had finally extinguished the Byzantines with the
capture of Constantinople in 1453. It had then brought much
of Arabia, Africa and Europe under its imperial sway, famously
advancing to the gates of Vienna. The Ottomans never managed,
however, to control these unruly *montagnards* in their neglected
Anatolian backyard. The authorities were largely to blame; an
empire addicted to expansion, and to the relentless production
of fighting men, had no choice but to ingrain soldiering so
deep in its populace that many conscripts discovered upon
demobilisation how little remained of the pliant, productive
peasants they had once been. The Ottomans had somehow
reverse-engineered these young men, turning them back into
fair approximations of the steppe itinerants who had characterised their race at the outset. They joined the upland gangs
of Turcomans and made untaxed livings as brigands. They fell
upon passing caravans and couriers, pilgrim groups and those
villages that lay outside their local support base. They inter-
cepted and fleeced detachments of Ottoman soldiers whom
they sent packing in their drawers. And from the eighteenth
century, when they were increasingly known as Yörüks, they
also preyed upon the medicine chests and purses of the foreign
travellers who were often found hunting out hidden treasure
in the same ruins where these nomad gangs traditionally made
their camps.

The surprise, which Pococke and Chandler must surely have

shared, was discovering that one of these notorious freebooters was to be accorded the honoured rank of *efe*, or leader, and to get a museum in his name.

Aydın dropped me back at Nysa before hurrying on to pick up a fare. I walked among column bases where the red gossamer petals of thin-stemmed poppies flapped raggedly in a soft breeze. Meadow grass lay freshly cut among the wild olives. Triangular shards of tile lay scattered on the ground. In the ravine that ran through the little city tortoises grazed on shaded weeds and purple sheaths thrust obscene from wide-mouthed arum lilies. A group of French visitors, silver-haired, elegant and shod in blue deck shoes, wandered through the site. The group followed their Turkish guide's commentary, but loosely, repeatedly interrupting him to hold exclusive dialogues, working up the guide's plain facts into gilded insights into Greco-Roman life, which they batted among themselves.

Nysa had been named, *soit que quelqu'un s'intéresse*, after a Seleucid queen. It was under the Romans, however, that the city had enjoyed its heyday. A renowned centre of scholarship, Nysa attracted an impressive roster of orators, philosophers and rhetoricians. Strabo had himself studied here under the distinguished rhetorician Aristodemus. The guide showed his charges the remains of the second-century library, with niches set in the tottering walls where scrolls were stored. Then he led them to the fine theatre so they might look out across the patchwork of the Meander plain, all geometric lines except for its wandering, colon-black seam.

The library and the theatre spoke of a secure and flourishing culture; something with which the French group, given their age, station and nationality, felt a natural kinship. I might myself have lingered on Nysa's life of ease and intellectual enquiry, of lectures and theatrical spectacle, if the point I had reached in Anatolia's narrative had not left the city's golden age behind by roughly 1,000 years. The rhetoricians and philosophers were long gone. Nysa's library had come to serve, it may be assumed, as a store for emergency supplies or munitions; its upper floors had perhaps been dismantled by the Byzantine residents to provide extra tiers in the raising of the city walls. I had arrived, in short, at the final moments in the life of Nysa, as I had that morning witnessed a Turkish hill village deep in its own decline. I thought of Kavaklı's padlocks, and of the accumulating concerns and scribbled calculations that had eventually led the proprietors of the village's tea house and store to leave their doors closed one morning, a final neighbour's death or departure confirming that their own time to leave had come.

By the twelfth century the people of Nysa found themselves at the heart of the bloody struggle for control of Anatolia. By the 1170s the Turks' territorial ambitions stretched to the Aegean. The sultan dispatched an army of some 20,000 men with orders to lay waste the Meander Valley and not to return unless they brought with them 'sea-water, sand, and an oar'. The Meander Valley came to serve as the front line in the conflict. All along the valley cities like Miletus and Priene, Nysa and Tralles repeatedly changed hands, the retreating forces destroying much of what they were forced to abandon. Homes and harvests were torched to prevent them falling into enemy hands. The advancing forces consumed or destroyed what little remained.

It is known that a Turkish clan chief called Menteşe sacked Nysa in 1282. No details survive, but an account of the sack Menteşe's forces shortly afterwards inflicted upon neighbouring Tralles may serve in the case of Nysa. Tralles, destroyed in an earlier sacking, had recently been rebuilt by order of the Emperor Andronicus. By dispatching his own son along with 36,000 colonists, the Emperor meant to create an imposing bulwark against the enemy; here the Byzantines would comprehensively block the Turks' advance.

The new city, accounted 'one of the most considerable places by the Meander', had barely been completed before Menteşe's forces closed in. It soon became apparent that the city suffered from a fatal strategic weakness: it had no water reservoirs and 'it seemed impossible to dig sufficiently deep' wells. It was not long before the Turks had cut off the supply from the river and also blocked the city's links with the surrounding fields. Within the walls the citizens soon grew thirsty; they were reduced to drinking the blood of their horses. The Turks starved Tralles into a submission its citizens repeatedly offered but which Menteşe was not minded to accept. When the Turks finally gained entry, the city was levelled and the slaughter was extensive. Some 20,000 survivors were carted off into an enslavement 'so harsh that they rejoiced for those who had been slain'. It may be supposed that Menteşe's mood had not been much better at Nysa.

That evening there was a wedding party in one of the hill villages above Kavaklı. A niece of Aydın's was to marry the following day. From the lane that led to the house of the bride's family I saw into shadowy corners where shawled matrons squatted over wood fires, stirring the steam from tureens of lamb stew and vats of milk pudding. Men in shirtsleeves handed over discreet dowry envelopes before helping themselves to the contents of the silver-painted plastic trays – cigarettes or boiled sweets – which circulated among the cloth-covered tables the family had set up outside their house. The men sat beneath the mulberry trees and drank lemonade or tea while whispering politics or speaking of plans to visit the *yayla* where their Yörük forebears had passed the summers until well into the twentieth century. The villagers took pride in the semi-nomadic ways of their grandparents long after they themselves had been transformed into taxi drivers, hotel workers or metering men of the State Water Works. Aydın told me he planned to take his family to the mountains that same weekend, by yellow taxi, and I was reminded of the Yörüks I had glimpsed in the mountains above Antalya a decade earlier. I had been hiking along a path on a spring afternoon when a flock of strong-smelling goats shouldered by. There followed a string of haltered camels laden with blankets, straw pallets, jerrycans, blackened kettles, axes and buckets, then the few sun-darkened figures who padded through the pine trees before the dust of the goats enveloped them, and I knew the sight was sliding into the past before my eyes; a journey made countless times, every spring, had barely a decade left to run.

The bride was dancing where the land lay flat, between the old village goalposts, in a circle of fairy lights. In a green dress and a white headscarf she danced to the rhythms of Turkish pop, alone except for the disc jockey who matched her every move from behind his bank of flickering equipment. The bride's married friends, wearing red scarves, sat on white plastic chairs all around the dance floor.

'When I married in the 1980s,' Aydın shouted over the music, 'we danced to the local village orchestra.' His words, a lament for lost traditions, seemed to express private astonishment that his youth had also got away.

The bride left the dance floor and was led to a plastic chair where a man in a grey suit appeared out of the darkness to join her. It was the groom. The couple glanced at each other before they turned, bashful, to watch the bride's friends who had replaced her on the dance floor. The friends danced in a curiously truncated way, their movements traditional above the midriff but strikingly modern below the waist, as if the scarves that guarded their heads against undue influences could do nothing to stop them getting in through the feet.

The music grew louder, and more young women, girls and grandmothers streamed through the dark trees beyond the goalposts to gather at the dance. The dancers moved faster, blurring into red flashes. As women at the back of the crowd passed chairs over the heads of those in front, and nudged hunched or elderly relatives through to better seats, so the advancing front row of the audience appeared visibly to age, losing its looks and its teeth until bride and groom were crowded by crones, and the shrinking circle in which the women danced was edged by futures in which child-rearing, fieldwork and the stirring of stew tureens were to dominate.

The music reached a peak. Pigeons rose as one from their nearby roost, flocked above the dance floor and crossed the moonlit sky in search of a silent tree, and Aydın's phone rang with another job.

CHAPTER EIGHTEEN

It turned out that Yörük Ali Efe had a second museum in his honour, and with opening hours and ticket prices clearly displayed, although nobody was opening up or taking for tickets when I visited. Only the custodian's snores could be heard beyond the museum gates long after he was supposed to have unlocked them.

The museum was at Yenipazar. The *dolmuş* I caught in the morning speared south to the bridge where I had stowed my canoe among the bushes before continuing straight on across the wide valley. There were straight lines, in fact, all over the sun-struck flats; a bordered patchwork of angular orchards, strawberry fields, tomato plots, hay meadows, maize stands and fallows often seamed with reed-choked drainage ditches.

The Meander Valley's natural lines, that said, had always been contrastingly fluid ones; not only the winding river but the sinuous indents all along the outer edges of the flood plain whose remarkable extent, fully eight kilometres across, was evidence of the exceptional inundations the river had brought through its history. This explained why the watchman's hut by the Feslek regulator was the only bank-side building I had passed since the textile factory at Sarayköy. It accounted for the long walks leading from the river to settlements like Sultanhisar, settlements historic experience had taught to keep to the plain's edge, their trousers rolled, in a manner of speaking, against the winter

floods. With the recent installation of the dams and regulators
these floods appeared to have ceased, of course, though there
was little sign anybody here had noticed. The people of Yenipazar
had always known the bottomlands to be uninhabitable through
the winter months, turning to muddy morasses that extended a
full mile from the banks, and even now the only structures they
had dared to raise there were occasional polythene greenhouses.
So strictly did their homes, shops and minarets keep to the
valley's edge that the town resembled a little port, and the sea-
flat plain was scored by tyre wakes where tractors turned like
ferry boats beneath the plumes of their stubby smokestacks.

Yenipazar faced Sultanhisar directly across the valley. It
boasted no ancient cities, however, nor a hotel. There were no
coachloads of foreign visitors, no railway station, and no steady
flow of long-distance coaches and refrigerated trucks. All
through its history the main road had kept to the more populous
northern edge of this westerly stretch of the valley, with the
consequence that a palpable torpor greeted the *dolmuş* as it
pulled into Yenipazar that morning: a narrow lane, Yörük Ali
Efe Street, which broadened briefly to pass through town; the
flattened stacks of sticks, grasses and shredded plastic bags atop
the electricity poles where storks had raised their nests; an
unexplained life-size elephant islanded on a tiled, dry water
feature in the main square; and the yawning custodian who
eventually appeared at the museum gates, sheepish face bleared
by the tread of a cushion's unforgiving weave, to admit his
unexpected visitor.

The custodian led the way through gardens to a ticket booth
before directing me to a modest stucco house beneath a low-
slung tiled roof. The house was full of heirlooms and exhibits.
The walls were hung with sepia photographs of moustachioed
men whose fixed, even exaggerated stares evidenced a childish

wonder at the camera and an absolute attention to the instructions of its operator. Otherwise the men, arranged behind and
beside their seated seniors in the manner of school team
portraits, might have appeared fearsome in their military, if
makeshift, mix of Great War serge and dress coats, broad belts,
patent leather knee-high boots, fezes and turbans. Vitrine cases
contained other costume items whose derring-do romance had
not faded with their colours: bandoliers, and blue-whorled waistcoats, high-cut with tightly fitting sleeves, and black embroidered
leggings, culottes, cummerbunds adorned in silverwork, and
chainmail sashes. There were *yatağans*, or short scimitars, in
decorated brass sheaths, and bolt-action Mauser rifles, family
trees, identity cards, commendations, and campaign maps lacer-
ated by the thrusts and counter-thrusts of colour-coded arrows.

The man himself stood on a plinth among the tended lawns
and borders, a carbine slung across his shoulder, palm shielding
his searching gaze against the sun. Boards displayed folk poems
in his honour. Fresh flowers had been laid at the marble tomb
of this Yörük, who had clearly made something of himself.

Despite the odds. Ali, born at Kavaklı in 1895 to semi-
nomadic parents, could hardly be said to have enjoyed good
prospects. A brutish existence had long been the lot of the
common Anatolian. The nineteenth-century Ottoman elite had
appeared more interested in eyeing the displays of the latest
Parisian fashions along Constantinople's Grande Rue de Paris,
and in boasting of their showcase capital's early installation of
such technological novelties as lighting systems and an underground railway, than in relieving the living conditions of the
rural masses. Provincial rule remained as backward, unjust and
unaccountable as it had ever been. The people were poor. They
remained pitifully educated, disease-prone and largely illiterate.
A visit from authority could only mean it was once more time

to find the tithes due to the local *ağa*, to contribute to the hard-pressed coffers of the Imperial Treasury, or to serve in the sultan's armies.

The Turks, accounting themselves a warrior people, had traditionally tended to view military service with equanimity, even pride. *Jihad*, or Holy War, figured large in Turkish fighting tradition. Many Turks not only took their very name, Mehmet, from Islam's warrior prophet himself, but also saw their revered sultan in indisputably martial terms – the Sword of Islam. The imperial economy's traditional dependence on booty and tribute meant that the Turk learned to measure himself above all as a soldier. In the earlier Ottoman centuries, when the empire swept away all before it and the proceeds were so prodigious as to trickle down to even the humblest conscript, Turks were proud to serve.

By the time Yörük Ali reached adulthood, however, the Ottoman Empire was not so much acquiring new territories as fighting for ones it meant to retake along its increasingly contested borders. Beset by the independence aspirations of subject peoples and by the expansionist ambitions of imperial neighbours, the Ottomans faced national breakouts and territorial smash-and-grabs on all sides. Between 1911 and 1918 the Ottomans were to wage wars in defence of almost every frontier: 1911–12 in Libya against the Italians; 1912–13 against a Balkan coalition including Greece, Bulgaria and Serbia; 1915–17 in the Caucasus against the Russians; 1915 against British, Anzac and French forces on the Gallipoli Peninsula; and 1916–18 against British-backed rebels in their Arabian and Palestinian territories.

In this phase of terminal contraction, as it would prove, the loyal heartlands increasingly served as the hard-pressed empire's only reliable recruiting grounds. Across Anatolia, where the conscription officers most regularly came calling, the authorities progressively extended the age of conscription so that by 1916 boys of just fifteen, and men as old as fifty-five, were being called up.

These conscripts suffered appalling privation. They were undernourished, poorly paid and ill equipped. They fought winter campaigns in lightweight summer uniforms and in some instances were obliged to wrap their feet in rags if they were not to go barefoot. They endured not only frostbite but typhoid, cholera and dysentery. Disease and climatic extremes, not to mention battle wounds, caused the deaths of hundreds of thousands of Ottoman conscripts. The greatest loss to the Ottoman Army, however, was from another cause entirely; in the course of the Great War an estimated half a million men deserted. Among them was one young man from Kavaklı, a village near Sultanhisar on the northern slopes of the Meander Valley.

Little is known of Yörük Ali's desertion from the Russian front – only that he eventually made his way home before taking to the mountains where even now the old Turcoman gangs persisted; in fact, the outlaws' ranks had lately been swelled by exceptional numbers of wartime deserters and other truants. The young man who fell in with one such gang must have known that he was running from a government bullet. Certainly, Yörük Ali had no reason to suppose he might one day gain an elevated rank and two museums, not to mention statues and streets, in his honour.

We have seen the fearful impression that Yörük Ali's Turcoman kinsmen had made on the likes of Pococke and Chandler a century and a half earlier – though this was perhaps the lamb's view of the wolf. For while such men had every reason to regard the Turcomans as cut-throats and robbers – the Turcomans in turn counting such affluent strangers as fair game – the truth was that their indiscriminate raiding instincts had gradually been tempered, at least to the point of distinguishing between their enemies and those deserving of protection.

A code, a rough but chivalric tradition based on hunting and raiding, on skills such as horsemanship and falconry, had come to govern these mountain outlaws whom Western Anatolians now knew for their admired warrior attributes as zeybeks. The zeybeks, organised in paramilitary hierarchies under the command of their *efes*, turned the fighting talents that had repeatedly served the empire, and gone unrewarded, on those who drew flagrant profit from it; the provincial governors and the grasping *ağas*, the prosperous merchants and middlemen and their high-value caravans, the detachments sent to hunt the outlaws down, the *haj* pilgrims making for Mecca, the couriers and conscription officers, as well as those affluent European antiquaries who happened to cross their paths. Among these was William Hamilton who described the zeybeks he came across in a roadside café near Sultanhisar, with their 'numerous pistols, dirks and yataghans', as 'the most ferocious-looking, daredevil, impudent set of fellows I ever saw'.

The local people saw the zeybeks, however, in a far better light. A century before the time of Yörük Ali, the zeybeks had begun to be viewed as popular champions, heroes of the proletariat resistance to the tyrannical demands of the authorities. These zeybeks came to be lionised among a rural populace who duly served as their constituency. The villagers, whom officialdom had exploited to the point of outright defiance, willingly gave the zeybeks their silence and secrecy, provisioned and provided them haven, and even answered their calls to insurrection. For their wild greenwood the zeybeks favoured the

mountains, the natural preserve of their nomadic heritage, especially where they abutted lowlands rich in settlements and trade
routes; nowhere than the cave-riddled heights fringing the
Meander Valley better suited the hit-and-run strategies of these
Anatolian Robin Hoods.

The romantic deeds in the 1820s of one such outlaw, Bald
Mehmet, were immortalised in the folk songs and ballads that
rang through the Meander Valley during Yörük Ali's boyhood.
Bald Mehmet, whose home town of Atça lay just six kilometres
east of Sultanhisar, nursed the usual social grievances but was
particularly incensed that his suit for a local *ağa*'s daughter
should have been so airily dismissed. Thwarted in love, Bald
Mehmet headed for the hills to return at the business end of
his own zeybek band. The region answered Bald Mehmet's
call to rebellion. The revolt rolled out on a wave of popular
support, and the local authorities were put to flight. Bald
Mehmet had barely made the *ağa*'s daughter his willing wife,
however, before he was gunned down by imperial forces in
1830.

The authorities in Atça have since made posthumous peace
with their legendary rebel by raising a statue in Bald Mehmet's
memory; in the case of Yörük Ali, however, no such rehabilitation
would be necessary. The state's bullet never felled him. A dramatic
transformation of his fortunes ensured that the brigand from
Kavaklı would be honoured by Atatürk himself, would be known
as '*Efe* above all *efes*' and live to enjoy a happy retirement in his
backwater home on the sleepy southern edge of the Meander
Valley.

What redeemed Yörük Ali was one final war. The difference
was that this one did not take place at the empire's distant edge
where the land meant little to its bloodied defenders; a foreign
army was advancing up the Meander Valley. The local Turks,

with home and hearth to protect, were quick to take up arms; this time they were not about to desert.

I walked west out of Yenipazar. The potholed lane followed the alluvial land's very edge, winding like a tideline into the smallest indents the plain had forced among the rocks. The route of the tarmac, which gave the impression of having found its way there as liquid, was clearly meant to avoid submersion beneath those winter floods that the State Water Works had since consigned to history.

What the State Water Works had also stopped, of course, was the rich layer of silt, a 'coat of manure', which the flood waters had seasonally deposited across the plain. On the hard dry flats the soil now lay old and unrenewed. What natural process had once done for the fruit groves and maize fields, making the Meander Valley Turkey's produce basket, was now being achieved by artificial assistance; by the likes of *Mataro F1: Gives High Yield in All Conditions*, and *Foliacon 22; Nothing Better for Calcium*, to judge by the company signs affixed to the telegraph posts. I had stopped to sneak a few succulent strawberries when a handwritten sign – *Attention; this plot sprayed 15/5* – did for my appetite and I walked on.

A breeze blew through a roadside screen of poplars, riffling the leaves into dappled patterns of translucence and shade. In the stork nests' undersides, scruffy as sprung mattresses, sparrows were busy making homes of their own. An expanse of low rocks, roughly upright but uncut, stood in a walled enclosure. They so recalled Breton menhirs or the *chevaux-de-frise* fortifications of an Iron Age fort that it was some time before I realised what I was actually looking at. It was a village cemetery although the headstones bore no inscriptions, never had – those who lay there no more knowing the form of their own names than their mourners did. It was a glimpse into the gloomy world that had persisted into Yörük Ali's boyhood; villages of superstitious and beleaguered illiterates who were never to recognise the resting places of their loved ones by the miraculous secret of script but must instead rely on some distinguishing mark or by the headstone's position in relation to a familiar olive tree. These were people denied the basic components of identity. They were born to labour and to be forgotten.

I had walked for some hours before I reached Alanlı. The village's sweat-stained farmers beckoned me over to join them beneath the shaded awning of the roadside tea house. I drank *gazoz*, or sweet soda, and the men asked where I had come from. I told them of my journey and of the black river stretch I had hauled through.

'That's effluent from the olive oil factory,' a man explained. 'The black sludge is what's left after they've pressed the olives.'

'But it goes straight into the river.'

'That's because they don't need it; they've removed the oil.'

'I meant: it's terrible for the state of the river.' The men knew not what to make of my ecological complaint.

'Your Queen was here,' said one of them, changing the subject. I nodded, having learned of Elizabeth II's recent state visit to Turkey from the headline – WE DID AWAY WITH OUR SULTAN; LONG LIVE THE QUEEN! – which I had seen in that morning's paper.

'But now she's gone home,' the man added approvingly, balancing the native courtesies with a proper degree of Republican ambivalence.

I walked on. The lane was still called Yörük Ali Street when I reached the small town of Dalama, with its dusty poplars and sack piles outside the seed merchants, and another statue of the man standing on a captioned plinth: *What Happiness*, it read, *To Drink from the Fountain of Dalama, the place chosen of all the Efes*

by Yörük Ali. Out in the countryside the mulberries were turning
pink. By the wheat fields the brick shells of abandoned houses
stood doorless, and nailed to the whitewashed walls of the empty
rooms and the timber verandas were wooden coat hooks, which
still showed the buffed sheen of dead men's collars. From the
roadside rose the green-wash shrines of wandering dervish saints,
makeshift tombs of stone and block cornered with ornamental
globes that worshippers had wrapped with floral headscarves, and
in such quantities that the hard stone could not be felt beneath
their layered depths. The wall of a cistern bore the painted memorial to a young conscript martyred while on national service during
the 1990s in the country's Kurdish south-east. By a lonely stretch
of road an old man had lain down, his crutch laid out beside him,

and I bent to check on him as I passed; his breathing was even, and in the hot afternoon a dreamer's smile showed among the lines on the man's face.

In the evening I reached a wide road, which severed the lane, heading north in a sudden rush of traffic. A *dolmuş* carried me across the Meander where I glimpsed silvered shallows. The far side of the plain glittered with lights. A sign told me that I had reached Aydın (alt. 67 metres); the name my taxi-driving friend in Sultanhisar shared with the city once known as Tralles.

The Ottomans, shattered by their involvement in the Great War and by the successive wars that had preceded it, surrendered to the Allies in October 1918. The following year delegations from the victorious nations met at Sèvres, Paris, to plot the defeated empire's dismemberment. The delegates thought not only to confirm the loss of remaining imperial territories in Arabia and elsewhere but also to apportion much of Anatolia among themselves. The Turks were set to lose vast swathes of their homeland – and chiefly to the same several Western races long before encountered in the Anatolian narrative.

It was the French, the conference hosts, who had enjoyed particular influence with the Turks in recent times; in the centuries since Louis VII's crusading armies had forced their bloody way up the Meander Valley en route to the Holy Land, relations had markedly improved. By 1918 theirs were the most privileged trading terms any country enjoyed with the empire. They were also the Ottomans' main creditors, which substantiated their claim for priority in the Anatolian province of Cilicia, one that was intended to secure extensive cotton interests there and also to buffer their hold on neighbouring Syria.

The Italians, busy playing colonial catch-up with their European rivals, were also prominent at Sèvres, where they made much of their ancient historical record in Anatolia. The parcel they claimed, the peninsula's entire south-west corner, was rich in the ruins of their Roman ancestors. Nor was the connection exclusively ancient, the Italians pointing to the fact that Anatolia's Orthodox Christians were even now known as Romans, or Rum in the Turkish; this was the small but tenacious minority whose forebears, resisting every pressure to turn Turk and convert to Islam, proudly traced their roots back to a Byzantine and thus Roman ancestry, even to the early Christian communities St Paul had fostered in the Lycus Valley. This cultural justification the Italians buttressed by presenting the territory they claimed as a natural extension of the immediately adjacent Dodecanese Islands, which their forces had won off the Ottomans in 1911. The region's coast was dotted with ports, moreover, whose names bore witness to Italy's continued commercial influence in the region. Among these was the bustling harbour of Scala Nuova, or Turkish Kuşadası; Italian interests in this Aegean port and its hinterland gave substance to their territorial claims, which extended north from the Mediterranean as far as the banks of the Meander River.

Here the Italians ran up against the rival claims of the Greek delegation who, asserting a yet more influential historic association, sought to establish their inalienable rights to the lands immediately north of the Meander, and even hoped to include the entire valley in their portion. The 'Roman' designation, as the Greek delegates were quick to remind their Italian counterparts, had always been imperial rather than ethnic in origin; the Rum people were quintessentially Hellenic and avowedly Greek Orthodox rather than Roman Catholic in their faith.

True, but it was also the case that these cussed Christian Rums, whose scattered communities amounted to a few million souls, had not been entirely immune to the Turkish centuries; many of them had lost their spoken Greek, though those who knew how to write had at least retained the alphabet of their ancestors. The bibles that America's nineteenth-century evangelists distributed among the Rums tended to be in Turkish but were rendered in Greek Cyrillic script. These were an acculturated people who largely rubbed along with their Muslim neighbours; they certainly had more in common with the Turks than with their Orthodox co-religionists in the Greek nation beyond the Aegean.

The Greek delegation at Sèvres could claim a more convincing kinship, however, with more recent arrivals in Anatolia; these were the Greeks who through the nineteenth century had left their impoverished Peloponnese and island homes, as their mercantile countrymen had done throughout history, to seek economic opportunity along the shores of western Anatolia. These settlers had never spoken any language but Greek and now did so with increasing fervour. Many were passionate champions of a culture, especially of its tongue and faith, which international sentiment encouraged them to cherish.

For from the eighteenth century Europe and America had been in thrall to all things Greek. Numerous books and pamphlets were published to enable the study of Greek grammar and rhetoric, philosophy, drama, literature and art. There was a spate of translations of Homer, notably by Alexander Pope, and numerous new editions of the Greek myths. Grand houses and civic buildings, gardens and cemeteries increasingly acquired pseudo-Grecian lines and motifs. Furniture, design, even hairstyling celebrated the Greek Revivalist movement.

No cause appeared more noble, therefore, than that of Greece's rebellion in 1821 against the Ottoman rule it had endured since the fifteenth century. Committees in London's influential Hellenist circles feverishly organised banquets and other fund-raising events for the valiant Greeks. Doctors and consignments of medicine were dispatched to treat Greek wounds. Poets and artists, lettered aristocrats, romantics and adventurers volunteered to fight alongside the Greeks; some, Lord Byron among them, lost their lives in a process that eventually led to the confirmation of Greek independence in 1832.

The Greeks were finally free, if only those of the newly constituted state; if a single ambition could be said to have emerged above all others in the heady upsurge of cultural rebirth and national destiny that attended Greek independence, it was the one known as the Great Idea – the re-Hellenising, even repossession, of the Anatolian lands which, from the time of Alexander the Great and through the Byzantine centuries, had been Greek in character. The time had come, many believed, for the Greeks to redeem the marchlands – as Apollo had once dealt with the barbarian Marsyas.

Many of these Greek settlers in Anatolia, inspired by the rhetoric of their priests, teachers and ideologues, took to the Great Idea with relish. The notion even began to find favour among those older Rum communities who had known nothing of Hellas, as liberated Greece was known, and had never thought of themselves as anything other than loyal Ottomans. One such Rum, distressed at being unable to communicate with a Greek visitor to his home town of Nazilli, was reported as having 'finally put his hand on his heart and said to the interpreter in Turkish; "Tell him that though my tongue is Turkish my heart is Greek."'

It was no surprise, then, that Anatolia's Greeks, a politically motivated and energetic minority, were quick to spot an opportunity when the negotiators at Sèvres in 1919 invited Turkey's residents to help them decide on the land's political fate.

Summoning the renowned rhetoric of their ancient forebears, the Greeks of the Meander Valley and beyond were soon dispatching persuasive petitions, often in cultured French, to Sèvres. The Bishop of Söke, the main town of the Meander Delta, described the district – 'where our race largely predominates' – as the 'cradle of philosophy and civilisation of EPHESUS, PRIENE, MILETUS, MAGNESIA AD MEANDRUM etc.' – and its Greek population as the 'vigilant guardians of the tombs of our ancestors'. 'The Aydın district,' according to another petition, 'not only contained very ancient Greek cities, that have produced famous artists and scholars, among which Anthemius of Tralles who built Sancta Sophia in Constantinople, but also preserved up to this day its ethnological character even after the . . . Ottoman Turkish invasion.'

Some petitions came from further afield. One Mr Papadopoulos, self-styled 'Delegate Plenipotentiary of Denizli District', declared how 'The District of Denizli . . . was always fundamentally Hellenic, as historical and geographical witnesses attest, the excavated historical sites, the surviving monuments, the research of experts . . . the inhabitants of the region were always Hellenes.' Papadopoulos reminded the delegates how the region's cities, Hierapolis, Laodicea and Colossae among them, had 'superbly cultivated Greek literature and science', and how 'Xerxes, Cyrus the Younger, Alexander the Great, Frederick Barbarossa and others' had passed through these towns, where various Byzantine dynasties 'had fought for Hellenism against the Seljuks, Tartars and Turks'.

If these latter claims were true, then it was also the case that the Byzantines had lost their fight for Hellenism. Five hundred years had since passed. Over that period Turks had come to be in the majority across the contested area: some ten Turks to every Greek in Denizli, and as many as a hundred to one in outlying areas of the same district such as Çal.

These were contradictory facts, however, which no Greek rhetorician was about to concede. It was by guile, after all, that Apollo had bested Marsyas.

CHAPTER NINETEEN

Through the nineteenth century it was increasingly recognised that the Meander Valley, abundant source of classical artefacts, was exceptionally productive in other respects. In 1914, when the carve-up of the Ottoman territories was already keenly anticipated, the region was high on the wish list of every contending power. 'Everybody wants Smyrna and the Meander Valley,' as a Greek diplomat baldly put it in a private dispatch.

The British, mindful of the valley's historic role, had thought it might even prove central to the furthering of their imperial ambitions. When a British company began to lay Turkey's first railway up the valley in 1856, some saw it as providing them with the beginnings of an overland route to British India, as 'the channel of communication between Europe and Asia, the great artery through which the pulses of Asiatic trade must throb for evermore', much as it had done in the time of Strabo. In the shorter term, however, the railway's backers expected healthy profits from the traffic, which the first phase of the line alone would surely generate; this was to run between Smyrna's Aegean quayside and 'the great entrepot of the internal trade of Asia Minor', as a commentator described the city of Aydın.

This anticipated traffic was pointedly not in passengers, however, but almost exclusively in goods; it was the valley's remarkable fertility which the Smyrna–Aydın Railway intended

to tap. A specially commissioned report, commending 'the alluvial nature of the soil', listed the valley's crops 'of all kinds from
the rarest to the coarsest qualities. Tobacco, the fig, the vine,
the olive, the poppy, the cotton plant and mulberry tree are all
indigenous products, whilst wheat, maize, barley, beans, flax,
hemp and a variety of pulse and oleaginous seeds are raised in
large quantities. Valonia, yellow-berries, wool, goats' hair, dye-
stuffs, drugs, skins, honey, wax and likewise abound.' The only
hindrance was the primitive condition of the region's Ottoman
infrastructure; by revolutionising the pre-industrial carriage of
the valley's largely perishable produce, the railway company's
backers meant to make a killing.

As for competition, the railway company need not concern
itself with the roads; they were no better off in the 1850s than
they had been in Strabo's time. On the better stretches, in good
weather, bullock carts could bump along, but the usual journey
between Aydın and Smyrna, by camel or mule, took four days.
It could cost more to deliver the produce to market than it was
worth. Aydın, though described as 'fertile to excess', was said
to be home to 'large bazaars filled to overflowing with produce
of all kinds that can find no market. Two years harvest of grain
and valonia are still stored there with no means at present of
finding transport to get it away.' When a consignment of the
region's famed raisins were finally dispatched, the considered
opinion was that the festering fruit 'should have been in
Marseilles or Liverpool six months ago'.

The deterioration in quality from such delays was slight,
however, compared to that 'caused, particularly in delicate products, by the frequent lading and unlading consequent upon the
nightly rest of the camels'. The produce, mostly carried in hair
sacks, was particularly vulnerable to being set down on wet
ground when the bottom 'six or seven inches' of the sacks'

contents could be 'entirely spoilt'. With the opening of the railway in 1866, the company was able to move covered cargoes from Aydın to Smyrna's quayside warehouses in just three hours. The economic argument was unanswerable; the railway was soon transforming the prospects of the valley's producers.

These producers were largely foreign; many were the same migrant Greeks whose numbers had been rising steeply from the moment the line's first sleeper was laid along the valley. These Greeks were characteristically quick to form an active, entrepreneurial, affluent and educated regional minority. They wasted no time in reinvesting profits in the purchase of agricultural holdings. They came to acquire many of the valley's commercial interests; the workshops, olive oil and soap factories, watermills and fisheries were often under Greek control. Some of them set up as traders and as inland agents of Smyrna's export agencies. They were prominent in the new railway, managing the company's freight interests and serving as station staff. Greek communities, complete with churches, hospitals, Greek-language schools and clubs, sprang up throughout the Meander Valley.

Of these communities the most impressive was at Aydın. By 1919, that 'great centre of transit trade, and a mart for the produce of the rich districts around' had spawned a flourishing Greek quarter. Home to some 12,000 shopkeepers, merchants and manufacturers, the quarter had 'its finely placed church, its well-equipped hospital, its school, its theatre, its cinema, its electric light, its flour mills, its factories for crushing olives and making soap'. Greeks had also become active in the city's bazaars and warehouses, in the tanneries and dyeing works, the cotton factories, 'silk-winderies', and machine-works. The Aydın Greeks had done well from the railway; they showed their appreciation by garlanding the train that carried the season's first fig consignments to Smyrna with sprigs of laurel and myrtle.

The local Turks felt differently; the commercial justification of the railway, as even its owners acknowledged, had never been to provide the locals with a passenger service. Instead, it over-whelmingly served foreigners' interests. With the line's every easterly extension – the railway was to reach Sarayköy in 1882, and Dinar in 1889, before continuing onwards past the source of the Meander around the turn of the century – the Turks had watched with increasing disquiet. In their view the railway had hastened the advance into their land of mainland Greeks, foreigners who had soon grown both prosperous and strident, while it did nothing for the Turks themselves. The line had ruined, moreover, the largely Turkish haulage industry, putting some 20,000 camels, 500 mules and their drivers out of work. The despised railway, a tool of the infidel interests that increas-ingly controlled the land, became a focus for Turkish resentment. The Turks feared it could only be a matter of time before Greek armies followed the Greek settlers up the line.

They did not have long to wait. Arguments soon embroiled the powers at Sèvres. The Italians pressed the Greeks to give up their claim to the Meander Valley in exchange for a job lot of Dodecanese Islands. The British favoured the Greek claim to the region; they thought of the Greeks as compliant allies in the furtherance of their imperial ambitions in Asia. The French increasingly resisted any settlement that deprived the Turks of the Meander Valley, in favour of either the Greeks or Italians, fearful that it would affect the Turks' ability to maintain interest payments to their French creditors.

The Italians, sensing an unfavourable wind, decided on unilateral action to press their claim; in early May 1919 they landed troop detachments, which occupied the Mediterranean ports of Bodrum, Marmaris, Fethiye and Antalya – the jewels, by happenstance, of modern Turkey's tourism industry – before moving north to the Meander Valley where they further occupied the towns of Söke and Kuşadası. This high-handed move incensed the British, who persuaded their allies to authorise a Greek landing at Smyrna on 15 May 1919. Within days there were Greek soldiers stationed along the Smyrna–Aydın railway.

On a concrete bleacher at Aydın's stadium I sat beside a man in a suit whose card identified him as a school inspector called Mr Flag. If Turks had a weakness for flags, more even than for business cards, it especially showed on 19 May. All over the city the national Star and Crescent was draped from public buildings and from the balconies of crumbling apartment blocks. The red-and-white standards flew across the stadium and trailed in the wake of the drilled military bands, which paraded among the smart scout troops and the schoolchildren. Some among the crowd were cloaked in their flags like the football fans who usually occupied the bleachers. Others waved the miniature flags printed on stick-stapled sheets of celluloid or on balloons they had bought from the dark-eyed hawkers who traipsed the bleachers, trailing the smell of woodsmoke behind them.

The stadium had known better times. The main stand carried, writ large, the word *Champions!*, though nobody in the uninformed crowd, not least Mr Flag, seemed sure when the members of the city's football team had last been in a position to call themselves such a thing. The exultant utterance that day appeared to have a wider, national resonance. For on 19 May 1919, four days after Greek forces had put ashore to make these lands their own, the Turks had first signalled their intention to resist. Barely had the Great War in the West ended upon a thrice-repeated number – the eleventh hour of the eleventh day of the eleventh month – than the Turks' preparation for yet another war began with a trio of nineteens.

The schoolchildren marched across the patchy turf. The boys were in purple, their smocks utilitarian as those of surgeons or death row inmates, while the lilac-clad girls waved their white kerchiefs aloft. Some paraded banners bearing messages of state agencies like the health authority, which discouraged smoking or commended the benefits of walking. 'To gain a tourist,' another declared grandiloquently, 'is to win the future.' This impressively choreographed display might have recalled Ceauşescu-era Bucharest or even Pyongyang if it had not been leavened by a more maverick presence – the men who had been given leave, it seemed, to wander the perimeter at their own pace. These men were got up in a clannish period look. Their baggy shorts, felt caps covered in colourful floral baubles, high boots, purple neck scarves and shoulder-slung rifles recalled the costumes I had seen in the sepia photographs at Yörük Ali's museum; they were dressed as fearsome zeybeks. These honorary outlaw militiamen advanced in no kind of order, drifting past the goalmouths and even dropping back beyond the view of their *efe* to field surreptitious calls on phones plucked from the depths of their waistcoats, much to the amusement of irreverent elements in the crowd.

'Hey, Zeybek,' somebody called out. 'Bet the signal's better here than in the mountains.'

Mr Flag, meanwhile, was seeking to win the promised future by practising his English on the tourist he had discovered sitting beside him. The school inspector ventured a series of questions, one about my surname, before processing my answers through the digital dictionary he carried.

'An amphibious mammal,' he declared unsteadily, pointing at me. 'With flippers.' My surname appeared as noteworthy to the tedious Mr Flag, and to the surrounding crowd, as his did to me.

I had been reflecting upon Turkish surnames that same morning. In the ceremonial solemnity of Aydın's central square, where the city honoured its past, I came across a memorial to the local men who had died on Turkey's Gallipoli Peninsula in 1915. The inscribed monument, of polished black marble, moved me, and not merely because of the slaughter – of some 90,000 Ottoman men – occasioned by the desperate defence of that crucial spur of land, key to Constantinople; the greater poignancy was that the Turks had then had no effective mechanism for distinguishing between many of their martyrs.

The memorial listed the men by their first and only names. Further identification supplied by their fathers' names often proved inconclusive; of the many Mehmets, for example, a good number were given identically as the son of Mehmet, while several more were similarly indistinguishable sons of Hüseyins, or of Mustafas or Alis. Even the literate bereaved could not always know which inscribed entry commemorated their own fallen Mehmet.

Mehmet had always been, of course, the most popular name among Turkish males; it was to be expected that Mehmetcik, or Little Mehmet, should have come to denote the Turkish soldier. The usage drew broad comparison, in the fond and admiring affection that it conveyed, with the British 'Tommy'; where it differed was in signifying Turkish soldiers both alive and dead, so that its meaning also encompassed the more exalted notion of the Unknown Soldier. The Turkish war graves of the Meander Valley and elsewhere were set with marble headstones, an engraved Star and Crescent and the attendant tulip blooms picked out in blood-red paint, but were otherwise marked only as the resting places of the 'Martyr Mehmetcik'. Unlike Western military practice – the war dead only accounted unknown after the failure of all administrative and forensic attempts to identify their remains – the fallen of late-Ottoman Turkey seemed more readily prised from an identity they had never fully acquired beyond the bourn of friends and families. Just as widespread illiteracy had meant nameless headstones in the villages, so it was often impossible to distinguish the men that these war graves and memorials commemorated. It sufficed, it seemed, to remember the war dead as unidentified instances of the heroic archetype.

That legendary repulse of the Allied onslaught at Gallipoli was closely associated, of course, with the day's commemorations at Aydın's football stadium and across Turkey. What connected them was one Colonel Mustafa Kemal; the same man who on 19 May 1919 put ashore in Anatolia to lead the resistance against the latest invasion had been largely credited with leading the Turks' earlier defence at Gallipoli.

Gallipoli was where Mustafa Kemal had first made his military reputation; his example there inspired extraordinary loyalty and sacrifice from the men under his command. In the carnage by the Dardanelles he acquired the aura of dogged defiance which was to rouse an exhausted, cowed and broken Anatolia to a final act of resistance four years later. The Turks, who even now were quick to account themselves a warrior people and who revered their war heroes above all others, had subsequently raised countless statues to Mustafa Kemal. In Aydın's main square he stands opposite the Gallipoli memorial where I found him among a thicket of floral wreaths, which pledged the allegiance of the city's political parties and military, its chambers of commerce, bar association, city council and many other organisations to the ideals of the man who was to become known as Atatürk.

I had seen Atatürk, of course, all along the Meander. From the leader's giant rusting outline above Dinar to his photograph over the door of the Fearless family farm, from busts in villages like Bahadınlar and framed portraits in the tea houses to the impress of his head on every coin in my pocket, I was witness to a uniquely enduring personality cult. No state had ever fostered the posthumous memory of their one-time leader so absolutely and for so long.

A singular conjunction accounted for it; the unique impression, that is, that this man's exceptional wartime achievements had made upon a people especially entrenched in martial tradition. Atatürk had saved the Turks from national annihilation at Gallipoli; and from 19 May 1919 he was to do so all over again. The vast and enduring regard that his people came to have for him would grant Atatürk unparalleled political latitude between the founding of the Turkish Republic in 1923 and his death in 1938. Unlike his modernising peers in Persia and Afghanistan, shah and king respectively, modern Turkey's saviour and founder was able to impose nothing less than social revolution upon his people and to enshrine that order in the national constitution. Atatürk's standing furnished him with the political wherewithal to achieve reforms – in terms of such social fundamentals as religion, language and dress – which weight of populist conservatism would otherwise have surely blocked.

The period iconography was a powerful reminder, of course, that Atatürk had in fact died before the outbreak of the Second World War. The vast banners unfurled on the walls of an adjacent school presented him in a pinstripe suit, with pointed collars, and parted hair in the Edwardian fashion. His statue was decked out, meanwhile, in full evening dress: morning suit, bow tie and wing collars, waistcoat, knobbed stick and top hat. In these outfits Atatürk had appeared at 1930s state banquets and embassy functions. Even so, to such rigs there now clung an impression not of the statesman so much as the dandy; something of the European aristocrat, even of the abdicated

monarch, a leisured itinerant dividing his time between hotels
with names like the Bristol or the Splendid, and the local baccarat
tables. The costumes that Atatürk had worn to signal the national
destiny had long fallen out of fashion and now looked as
outlandish to the citizens of Europe's political union as they
must always have appeared to the bemused Turks. The passing
of time had stranded Atatürk in a period fancy dress that spoke
of exclusive privileges that Europe's masters, having never
shared them with their own masses, were certainly not about to
disburse among the supplicant Turks.

Atatürk's image, that said, had not always been the ubiquitous
presence it is now. In fact, his face had been removed from the

country's banknotes and stamps in routine fashion shortly after his death. His restoration there more than a decade later was as a sop by a government anxious to reassure the secular military that the few Islamic freedoms the politicians had introduced – allowing, for example, the call to prayer to be made in the traditional Arabic – were not to be feared as harbingers of a wider assault on the great leader's legacy. By this ploy of its political opponents, then, the secularist establishment recognised that Atatürk's passing need not prevent his continued service as a highly visible exemplar. Atatürk, co-opted into the national iconography and essentially deified in the process, became the steering mechanism by which his ideological bearing might be maintained.

Now, however, that rudder appeared to have gone awry. Certainly, the guardians of Atatürk's legacy seemed hard pressed to preserve the secular order against an impressive Islamic electoral majority. In that respect the expressed will of the Turkish people and of Atatürk seemed increasingly at odds. The speeches that sounded through the loudspeakers at Aydın's stadium seemed intent on avoiding any mention of Atatürk's Western-style secularism, fearful, perhaps, of the lukewarm reception it might induce, but instead invoked attributes on which all Turks were heartily agreed; they spoke of the great warrior who had saved the nation, whose forces had saved Aydın itself, from both the European aggressors and the Ottoman authorities who had so cravenly connived in the proposed dismemberment of the Turkish territories.

'There are and have always been two Atatürks,' declared the provincial governor, a short man dressed in a grey suit. 'The one who saved us, and the one in our hearts and our futures too.' We stood for the national anthem. When its last notes played and the band fell silent, a sound was heard from across the city. It was the Arabic chants of the lunchtime call to prayer.

The bleachers began to empty. Mr Flag pocketed his digital dictionary and slipped from my side. I wandered through Aydın, recalling the 'trees, lofty domes and minarees of mosques inter-spersed' that had once greeted Richard Chandler, a place of 'innumerable tame turtle-doves, sitting in the branches of trees, on the walls, and roofs of houses, cooing unceasingly'. The city also impressed Charles Fellows. 'I have in England been at fairs and races, and have witnessed the commemoration days in Paris, and the masquerades and carnivals in Catania and Naples,' wrote Fellows, airing impressive travel credentials,

> but all fall short, in gay variety and general beauty of costume, of this Turkish market. The foliage of the plants and trees growing in the streets formed a pleasant relief to the dazzling whiteness of the veils, and the splendid colours of the embroidered trowsers, of the multitudes of women attending the market; light blue worked with silver was very commonly seen in the dresses of the peasants, and every turban had its bunch of roses or flowers . . . The passing of camels and loaded asses through the crowd called forth continually the warning voice of the driver. The women had their children tied on their backs, and these, with the gay colour of their dresses and their heads ornamented with coins, contributed their part to the general picturesque effect.

In this modern city of numbered streets there was not the least reminder, however, of the doves and embroidered trousers, the camel trains and the zeybeks' floral turbans. The streets were lined by apartment blocks painted in institutional shades. Lines of washing, children's tricycles, dead pot plants, rusting air-conditioning units, and the placarded details of lawyers', dentists' and gynaecologists' premises, showed among the flag-draped concrete of the balconies.

Then I found my way by chance into 1629 Street. Here, where an older city survived, the apartment blocks were yet to intrude. Behind elegant railings stood gardens shaded by orange trees, and in the arched vaults of a high-walled *han* men in thick glasses braced themselves over antique sewing machines, firing off stitch bursts like squinting *mitrailleurs*. It was fitting that the street should have been home to Aydın's Antiquarian – or *Lovers of Old Things* in the touching Turkish rendition – Society.

The society's chairman was called Mehmet Trueblueeyed. Framed portraits of Mehmet's predecessors in the post, all ties, jackets and prominent moustaches, hung from the walls of the office, a single small room, where any suggestion of cultured association had long been lost in the cram of collectables. The members' diverse interests and magpie tendencies had done for such pretensions, transforming the office into something altogether more animated; a hoard store of enthusiasms, the shelves lined with old radios, their speakers fronted with lacquered weaves, and moth-eaten items of zeybek costume, piles of 1950s magazines whose monochrome covers featured farmers standing proud beside their American tractors, and stacks of yellow-brown bricks.

The old bricks of his native city, it turned out, were the particular interest of Mehmet Trueblueeyed. He had collected more than a hundred of them. Across Aydın he picked through piles of rubble for prize examples; bricks free from cracks and chipped corners, and carrying the clear imprint of the maker's initial or name. In the continued demolition, then, of the city's old buildings Mehmet caught precious glimpses of their creation. These nostalgic keepsakes commemorated not only their makers but the historic buildings to which they had recently belonged, and every day Mehmet learned of new sites where he might grow his collection.

'The owners of these old houses don't think to live in them,' he said. 'They only value the plots the houses occupy. They are interested in profitable development, and over several storeys. Their problem is that the old houses are now protected by law. The solution is to leave them unoccupied and unrepaired, and wait for them to fall down. The houses of greatest historical value are the ones that stand empty; the neglect they suffer is deliberate.'

Mehmet led me to a few such houses. Some stood beside empty lots, which had been readied to receive apartment blocks. Deprived of their neighbours' support, the houses had begun to sag; chunks of their stucco façades, lavishly painted with columns and capitals, had fallen into the cleared lots where they turned to powder. One such villa had wide eaves patterned in a woodwork lattice, high arched windows and faded ochre walls richly worked with neoclassical cornices white as icing, with festooned borders, elegant lintels and with the same meander patterns that adorned the baths and temples of ancient cities. The house, hemmed in by a modern pavement, was also covered in black scrawls. The graffiti were illegible but seemed nevertheless to curse the lovely structure for a Greek hindrance, seeking only its collapse.

Mehmet led the way to the banks of a deep stream, where the city's tanneries had once turned out 'fine yellow morocco' leather. The present bridge was no more than a slab of reinforced concrete; as functional as the earlier crossing there had been graceful. For, largely obscured beneath the rust-stained underbelly of that flyover replacement, there still stood the high, keystoned arch of an Ottoman-period bridge. Beyond the stream we wandered past a school and among the pine trees of park-lands. We walked wide residential streets lined by 1950s homes and apartment blocks. There was no sign of the neoclassical detailing – the meanders and the vine festoons – I had seen elsewhere in the city. It was then that Mehmet pointed out two stone projections that flanked the concrete steps of an outdoor café. From these rounded bases, badly chipped and painted pink, the columned entrance of St George's Church had once risen. The pedestals were all that remained of Aydın's Greek quarter.

CHAPTER TWENTY

The historian Arnold Toynbee, on assignment for the *Manchester Guardian*, had occasion to visit Aydın in February 1921. Toynbee witnessed how 'ruins flanked the railway for miles as one came into Aidin' on the train from Smyrna. He also saw what had happened to the city's Greek quarter. 'The work was deliberately done,' he concluded. 'The buildings were not destroyed in the heat of battle but burnt one by one, and there is a sudden sharp boundary between the gutted Greek houses and the intact Turkish centre of the town. Here were twisted bedsteads, there safes with holes knocked in their sides, here a shred of clothing or a boot.'

This same city the Turks had also razed in 1282; they had then subjected Tralles' 20,000 surviving Christians to a captivity so intolerable that many were said to have envied their fellow dead. Toynbee's observations might then have been taken to confirm Turkish form, in Aydın especially, when it came to laying waste to the lives and homes of the local Greeks.

Toynbee's observations appeared consonant with the behaviour that appalled Westerners had expected of Turks ever since learning of their accursed existence around the time of the First Crusade. Pope Urban II, rallying knights to the Christian cause by fulminating against the heathen race, thereby set the papal seal on a millennium of anti-Turkish sentiment – one which, it should be admitted, centuries of all-out Ottoman expansionism only helped to inflame. With the Turks' every advance or incursion the defiant but fearful invective deepened across Europe. The people of Christendom denounced the Turks in their pamphlets and prayers as bloodthirsty ghouls no less inhuman than their Mongol and Tartar kin. Masses were held in the hope that their fiendish war machines might mire in the Hungarian mud. Plays and entertainments were peopled with turbaned bogeymen, and references to Turkish body parts were liberally scattered among their pages: the nose of the Turk, for example, which went into the cauldron in *Macbeth* – not so much, it seemed, for its potion efficacy as that the audience might savour the implied fact of its one-time severance. The Turk's Head, a popular name among many pubs and hostels, no doubt pandered to their patrons' same vengeful impulses.

Such attitudes were especially prevalent from the late eighteenth century; a loathing of Turks was the natural corollary of the widespread enthusiasm for all things Greek. The historian Thomas Smart Hughes dismissed Turks as 'cruel tyrants, bathed in the blood of their own Emperors upon every succession; a heap of vassals and slaves; a people that is without natural affection; without pity; without morality; without letters, arts, or sciences; in a word, a very reproach to human nature, and that has made the garden of the world a wilderness'. It was a view that resonated in 1919 when a British Foreign Office mandarin, firmly in stride with the avowed philhellenism of his prime minister, David Lloyd George, privately observed that 'No one but a congenital idiot could be pro-Turk.'

Except for those, perhaps, who had gone to the trouble of acquiring first-hand experience of Turks. When Charles Fellows set out for Anatolia in 1838, just fourteen years after Lord Byron died of marsh fever in the sacred Greek cause at Missolonghi, it was no surprise that he should have declared himself 'strongly biased in favour of the Greeks and equally prejudiced against the Turks'. In the course of his travels, however, as Fellows was at pains to acknowledge, 'this unfavourable idea of the Turkish character was gradually removed by a personal intimacy with the people'. 'To their manners, habits and character, equally as to their costume,' he wrote, 'I am become not only reconciled, but sincerely attached; for I have found truth, honesty and kindness, the most estimable and amiable qualities, in a people among whom I so little looked for them.'

So Turks, as I myself had since learned, could come as an agreeable surprise; and Anatolia's Greeks, if only because they enjoyed so elevated a standing, had regularly proved a disappointment. Reverend Arundell put it more strongly. 'It is impossible,' he declared, 'not to be disgusted with many prominent features of the modern Greek character . . . gratitude is not among their virtues.' Other travellers found them grasping, disingenuous, even devious. The Greeks were not always so good, nor the Turks so bad, as people liked to think. Neither race, that said, was to emerge with any credit from the events about to unfold at Aydın, which the Greek forces occupied on 27 May 1919.

The Allied Command had justified the landing twelve days earlier of 13,000 Greek troops at Smyrna on the grounds of maintaining law and order. It was a decision that incensed the Turks and a pretext they did not believe.

Nor, patently, did most Greeks. Not the newly landed soldiers who performed jubilant jigs around their stacks of equipment on the Smyrna quayside. Neither the Greek newspapers who were to invoke the great anabases, the eastward forays of Xenophon and Alexander, at every stage of the Greeks' subsequent advances up the river valleys east of Smyrna. Nor the citizens who waved Greek flags, rang church bells, and chanted the name of Prime Minister Venizelos, architect of Greece's

'Ionian' ambitions – and whose first name actually translated as 'Liberator'.

It was as liberators, certainly, that the soldiers had entered Aydın in the view of many of the city's Greeks. In elegant neoclassical homes celebratory dinners were held and glasses raised to the city's proud Hellenic heritage: Aydın had been home, after all, to St Anthemius, architect of Constantinople's Haghia Sophia basilica, the very font of Orthodox Christianity, and also to the Tralles Stone, the marble whose inscriptions had unlocked the mysteries of ancient Greek musical notation. The city's Greeks soon gave themselves over to public celebrations; there were 'continual processions with flags', as one English eyewitness noted, and 'portraits of Venizelos in all the houses, shops and cafes, their ridiculous patriotic songs, sung all day long by the street scum and the soldiers . . .'

Such triumphalism, merely tedious, soon descended into a more spiteful subjection. Some Aydın Greeks, increasingly secure in the strength of their position, did 'their level best to make themselves obnoxious, unpopular and hated by the Turks'. Turks were jostled and warned that the Greek forces could not be held responsible for the lives of those who would not replace their Ottoman fezes with Western-style hats. Prominent Turks, professors and lawyers among them, were arrested on suspicion of holding anti-Hellenic views.

As the Greek forces continued their advance, which the Allied authorities had not authorised beyond Aydın, so the hostilities and humiliations intensified. At Nazilli the houses of Muslims were attacked, men were beaten, women violated and muezzins abused while making the call to prayer. Sarayköy's Turks were forced to carry portraits of Venizelos beneath the triumphal arch that had been erected to welcome the Greek soldiers.

Tensions especially escalated from 19 June. That night the Greek forces, under instruction from the Allies, withdrew from their unauthorised advance positions. They left Nazilli under cover of darkness, 'suddenly evacuating a town without warning either the inhabitants or the Turkish forces', as a report was to censure them, 'and then pointing with satisfaction to the murdered inhabitants as a vindication of their statement that Greek domination is essential to the safety of Anatolia'.

The immediate provocation was what befell the thirty or so Turkish men who were forced to accompany the Greeks on their retreat. One, said to be unable to keep up with the column, was executed on the way. At the railway town of Köşk, possibly in response to the fire that some townspeople were said to have directed at the Greek soldiers, several of the captive Turks were killed and their bullet-ridden bodies left lying in the road.

It was evident, barely a month after the Greek landings at Smyrna, that the situation was increasingly uncontainable. The war-weary Turks, one observer judged, had largely been prepared to accept the Greek presence as long as it 'was well defined in limits and conducted in some measure of decency. Information so far received appears to show that neither of these conditions have been fulfilled.' The result had been to rouse 'Turks of all classes from [an] attitude of passive surliness to one of active hostility'. Insurrection was abroad. Greek misrule was intolerable, to the zeybeks especially.

It might have been assumed that rapid industrialisation – the modernised farms, the proliferating factories and the steady extension of the railway – had long since made colourful anachronisms of the Meander region's legendary brigands. That was certainly the impression gained from an 1873 guidebook's description of Aydın's 'very picturesque *meidan* with coffee-houses, where the zebecks may sometimes be seen enjoying themselves'; the old irregulars had been reduced to café habitués, it seemed, who earned their coin by hamming it up for the tourists.

In fact, the Greek landings had soon galvanised the zeybeks throughout the hinterland. The provocations along the Meander Valley, as an observer noted, served to endow them with a higher purpose. 'What was at one time but a normal . . . state of brigandage and highway robbery,' he explained, 'has now developed into a national movement aimed primarily against the Greek forces, but additionally against the constituted authority in the capital.' The zeybeks formed gangs, old adversaries now joining forces in common cause against the invaders and Constantinople's collaborationist Ottomans alike. Across the expanding area of occupation they postered the villages with calls to arms. Their men broke open the poorly guarded stores where the surrendered munitions of the Ottomans' disbanded regiments had been collected, and helped themselves to bullets and rifles. Then these patriots fell upon the invaders where they knew they would find them: along the hated railway.

The railway had played a central role in the Greek advance, carrying soldiers and supplies inland. By shadowing the nearby Meander River – the boundary between the Greek zone and the occupied area the rival Italians had lately established immediately to the south of the river – the railway soon came to serve, moreover, as the Greeks' southern front line. From the south side of the Meander, in the safety of the Italian zone, the incensed Turks watched the Greek forces make themselves at home along the railway. The Greek soldiers stored munitions in the yards, billeted troops in the train sheds and warehouses, and with the enthusiastic assistance of openly supportive Rum Greek staff turned the numerous stations into armed camps. The railway had effectively declared in support of the Greeks, which was no surprise to the zeybeks, who from the middle of June saw to it that the railway bore the brunt of their resistance.

The Turks dynamited bridges and cut telegraph wires. They ransacked station offices. They fired upon passing trains. They killed and abducted station staff. They skirmished with the Greek soldiers garrisoned along the line. They attacked Greek civilians in the station towns. Reprisal attacks ensued. Greek and Turkish villagers alike fled their homes; the Greeks at the station town of Karapınar, following the slaughter of eleven of their number, a child and an eighty-year-old woman among them, fled in their nightclothes for the comparative safety of Aydın. The fields and fig orchards stood deserted. The villages burned beneath black plumes. The old pattern was repeating; the Meander Valley was once more being wasted as West and East laid ancient claim to the region.

In this febrile atmosphere a young reservist, Lieutenant Ben Hodder, was tasked with maintaining some vestige of order. Hodder, the British control officer at Aydın, was returning from supervising repairs to a sabotaged bridge on Saturday 28 June when his special train was held up at Umurlu; the town had been back in Turkish hands since the Greeks, abandoning Nazilli, had nine days earlier withdrawn to within a few kilometres of Aydın. This railway town had since become a mustering station on the fringe of the occupation zone, and the platform there was crowded with armed and excitable fighting Turks: 250 regular soldiers, Hodder reckoned, along with about 1,000 zeybeks from a wider band whose total complement was estimated at 6,000 men. The regular forces, whose officers took their orders from the Allied authorities even if their true loyalties lay elsewhere, claimed only qualified control over the zeybeks; these belligerent and impassioned men meant to march on the Greeks. The zeybeks refused to allow Hodder's train to leave Umurlu until they had handed over an ultimatum, which the control officer was to deliver to Aydın's authorities. The Greek forces had three days' notice to quit Aydın; if they did so, the city's Christians would be protected. Otherwise, the zeybeks vowed to 'burn and pillage the whole town'. The ultimatum was signed by one Yörük Ali.

The brigand from Kavaklı, now twenty-four years old, had evidently distinguished himself since deserting from the Russian front some years earlier. He now headed a powerful alliance of zeybek bands whose stock among nationalist Turks, civilians and officials alike, had been transformed since the Greek landings at Smyrna. A photograph taken that June shows Yörük Ali in the company of considerable establishment figures. He appears seated in pride of place between an army officer in broad buckled belt, high collar and astrakhan-style *kalpak*, and a local politician in waistcoat and fez. Behind this nationalist triumvirate stands a sombre but resolute crowd of rifle-bearing zeybeks and straight-backed villagers, their collarless shirts buttoned to the neck in a makeshift gesture of disciplined formality; a broadly representative sample of the force tasked, given the substantive demobilisation of the regular army, with ousting the hated Greeks and their European sponsors. Theirs was a cause, of course, with historic echoes; as nomadic irregulars had first won the land for the Turks in the eleventh century, so these men were to regain it. Beginning with this young zeybek chief, slim, solemn, and clean-shaven beneath his high turban, whose signature confirmed that the Greeks must leave the city or expose themselves and Aydın's Christians to the consequences.

By the time Hodder's train reached Aydın that Saturday afternoon, however, events had outrun the ultimatum the control officer was to deliver on Yörük Ali's behalf; some 2,000 Greek soldiers and some rogue zeybek bands were already locked in fierce fighting to the south of the city. The gun battle continued through the night. By Sunday morning it was clear that the outnumbered Greeks were losing ground. They withdrew their field guns to the heights behind the city, where the ruins of ancient Tralles stood, before resuming their bombardment of the advancing zeybeks. Meanwhile their front-line soldiers took up holding positions in the city.

'Aidin was in a state of terror,' wrote Hodder. 'Every house was closed as bullets were flying in all directions.' The control officer made an attempt to reach the train station, where he thought to receive news, but was driven back by the crossfire. He sheltered inside his quarters while the battle raged on the city's streets. The Greek forces made a stand around the station, distributing arms among volunteer Greek civilians and setting up machine guns on the roofs of houses in the Jewish quarter. The Turks, who had moved up their field guns, now rained shells onto the city. One demolished the cupola of St Charalambos Church. Another hit a building alongside the French convent where Aydın's Christian population had begun to take refuge.

In the course of Sunday the Greek forces were steadily forced back. Acknowledging that they could not hold Aydın, some determined to destroy the areas belonging to the Muslim enemy. Retreating through the Turkish area, the Cuma quarter, they began to slosh gasoline against the walls of the houses, coffee houses, businesses and mosques. 'It was not long,' Hodder reported, 'before there was a conflagration in the Turkish quarter.' From the streets and rooftops the Greek soldiers shot down Turkish civilians as they escaped their flaming homes; they looted the houses the fire had not yet reached, assaulting or killing the occupants. The Greeks then fell back north of the railway line before retiring to the heights where their field guns were positioned. As the day drew on, word of the Greek retreat spread among the city's Christians who hurriedly followed in the footsteps of those who had already made for the French convent.

At dusk, when the first few zeybek scouts began ghosting onto Aydın's streets, Hodder received a message; the chief of the zeybeks, Yörük Ali himself, wished to meet the control officer. The two men convened in a sheltered garden near Hodder's quarters. Yörük Ali had with him six men; their picturesque costumes moved Hodder to describe the troop as 'braves'. These zeybeks stood guard while Hodder invited Yörük Ali, accompanied by a French-speaking secretary, into his offices. Refreshments and cigarettes were provided and the two men conversed, the aide-de-camp interpreting, and in that moment of civilised parleying it may perhaps have been possible to forget the slaughter and the burned houses. The other possibility was that the darkness had prevented Yörük Ali from realising the full extent of the carnage wrought throughout Aydın's Turkish quarter. At any rate, the zeybek chief even now seemed intent upon negotiating a settlement, requesting Hodder's help in delivering a further ultimatum: that if the Greek commander now evacuated the region entirely and did not return again, Yörük Ali would guarantee the safety of the local Christians. This ultimatum was witnessed by Hodder before a messenger carried it away. Hodder entreated Yörük Ali to keep his men in hand, hoping that he would not allow them to behave cruelly to the Christians.

'Hodder Efendi,' exclaimed the chief. 'I have not come here to war against innocent people, women and children, but we do not and will not have the Hellenes here, we will drive them out. They may come back and drive us out again, but we shall continue to fight for our country to the last man.'

Yörük Ali's speech was unequivocal, even dignified, but the dispatched ultimatum was to prove as redundant as his previous one. The old hatreds that had historically consumed the Meander Valley would once again have their way. Through Sunday evening a thickening stream of frightened Christians made their way to the French convent. By Monday morning some 4,000 people were crammed into the compound.

The main zeybek bands, wary of ambush, had awaited the dawn before entering the shell-strewn city. All night they had smelt the smoke and the sweet stench of the gasoline; they had heard the dogs and the keening. They now saw for themselves the empty fuel barrels, the broken possessions and the ripped clothes that were scattered throughout the blackened swathes of the Cuma quarter. Turkish women and children lay dead in the streets, arms outflung in flight, flies at their nostrils. A smouldering shell was all that remained of the mosque at Dükkanönu. The zeybeks saw what the Greek soldiers had done and they now directed their steps towards the Greek quarter. On the deserted streets nobody stood in their way. At their leisure they looted the houses whose raised stucco detailing – the neoclassical columns, garlands, rosettes, volutes and meanders – appeared like proud pronouncements of Aydın's new Hellenic age. The houses burned and the inhabitants hiding inside burned with them. The fleeing Greeks the zeybeks encountered on the streets were shot without regard for age or sex. Then the zeybeks collected at the gates of the French convent.

The French flag flew over the building; the convent might have offered effective protection, even for the ever-growing number of refugees. As it was, the uncontrolled fires that threatened to engulf the compound gave its occupants no choice but to seek refuge elsewhere. The zeybeks were waiting for them; as the first jibbering civilians spilled into the street shots rang out, killing twelve of them. Only then did a dispatch of regular

Turkish soldiers, who had managed to reach the city from their base beyond the Meander in the Italian zone, succeed in putting a stop to the firing. These disciplined troops were thinly spread, however, and there was little they could do to stop the zeybeks from stripping the Christians, the living and dead alike, of their purses and jewellery. The terrified crowd, shedding coats and shoes and valuables, eventually reached the relative safety of the nearby *konak*, the local government building. There the senior Turkish regular officer, Colonel Şefik, dutifully did what he could to feed and protect them.

The sheer number of zeybeks soon ensured, however, that they had control of the city. One eyewitness, an employee of the Ottoman Imperial Bank, described Tuesday as 'the most complete anarchy'. Aydın, he wrote, was entirely in the hands of the zeybeks who released the common prisoners and took it upon themselves to judge the city's notable Greeks on the basis of 'simple accusations, ancient grudges, the complaints of Muslims'. Some thirty persons, including Mrs Jean Philippides, Nico Avyeries, Dr Yorghanjioglou, the banker Mr Georgiades and the three brothers Papaconstantinou, were executed or led away to the mountains. Lieutenant Hodder, busy negotiating to evacuate trainloads of Christian refugees from the city, saw bodies everywhere: '11 women and 8 children and 3 men who had been cruelly done to death' in a ravine north of the city; 'a further lot of 13 women, 15 children and 22 men' in the city; and 'the remains of 8 children that had been burned in one house'. Both sides accused the other of rank obscenities: the bodies of some 200 raped Muslim girls were said to have been uncovered in vaults near the French convent, while it was alleged that the disembowelled remains of Greek children, entrails wrapped round their necks, had been discovered in the burned shell of St Charalambos Church.

Two days later, just as the Turkish regulars under Colonel
Şefık were beginning to re-establish a semblance of control,
news spread that a reinforced Greek column totalling some
10,000 soldiers was closing on the city. Colonel Şefık wasted no
time in urging all Turks, zeybeks, regulars and civilians alike,
to leave Aydın. By four o'clock that Thursday afternoon there
was 'a veritable stampede of Turks towards the Meander'; their
safety lay south of the river where the Italians, actively antag-
onistic towards the Greek occupation, were busy befriending
the nationalist cause by offering Turks safe haven and succour
beyond their protective screen. Among the last to leave the city
was Colonel Şefık who called in to say goodbye to Lieutenant
Hodder.

'I have done all in my power,' the Colonel declared, 'to safe-
guard the Christians and I hope the Greeks will behave likewise
towards the Turkish population. Today the Greeks are entering
Aydın and we are leaving the town, but we shall drive the troops
back and enter it again.' By eight o'clock the following morning
it was reckoned that just 105 out of some 25,000 Muslims
remained in the city. The Battle for Aydın was over. The city
had once more changed hands, as it had always changed hands.
It would do so again; though it would take more than three
years, the Turks would finally recapture Aydın, as Colonel Şefık
and Yörük Ali had vowed.

In the meantime, any shred of pretence that the Greeks'
presence in Anatolia was to maintain law and order was dispelled;
this was their attempt to confirm for once and for all, by force
of arms and with the tacit support of Great Britain, the historical truth that here truly was where the West extended, not
where the East began. From the banks of the Meander River
north to the shores of the Sea of Marmara, the roughly rectangular area occupied by the advancing Greeks soon descended

into barbarous war. Ben Hodder, witness to the hatreds that had flared in Aydın, would not have been surprised; the local Turks, he reported, had developed a 'fanatical hatred of the Greek; the war is now a religious one and it will be hard to appease and settle matters'.

So it proved; with every successive springtime advance of the Greek divisions, the old sectarian accommodations that had once prevailed between the land's Muslims and its Rum Christians were obliterated in a welter of slaughter and burning. The animosities were at their most bitter along the Meander Valley where the Turks, falling back before the well-equipped Greek forces, took their revenge upon Christian civilians. Most of Umurlu's Rum Greeks were killed and thrown down the town's wells. Other Christians, often barefoot and even naked, were driven into the interior. In the burning rubble of Nazilli Greeks and Turks were buried alive. The corpses of the slaughtered were left to be devoured by dogs. On the road between Nazilli and Kuyucak, a distance I had alternately dragged and paddled my canoe in the course of a short morning, an eyewitness counted fifty-three corpses. Bodies formed floating rafts on the Meander.

By the spring of 1921 the Greeks' eastward advance up the Meander Valley had carried them as far as Çivril; they were now within striking distance of their historic frontier by the Meander's headwaters. To the north the city of Eskişehir – classical Dorylaeum, where the armies of the First Crusade had famously defeated the Turks eight centuries earlier – also fell to Greek forces. They now closed on Gordium where Alexander had cut the knot before founding his empire in Asia. The newspapers in Athens found the weight of historical precedent irresistible; with the inevitable fall of the nationalists' capital at Ankara, it seemed nothing could stop the Greeks from achieving their Great Idea by making western Anatolia theirs once more.

Except that Turks in great numbers had deserted the towns and villages of the interior for the front. In time, moreover, these irregular hordes had been fashioned under Atatürk's leadership into a formidable fighting force. It helped, of course, that the anti-imperialists in Bolshevik Russia were now supporting the Turks' cause by delivering increasing quantities of munitions to the Black Sea ports that remained under nationalist control. Even so, the Turks' supply lines were long and threadbare, and it was often civilians who bore the shells and provisions on their own backs over the Anatolian mountains to the front. Grandmothers fashioned soldiers' tunics out of carpets or learned to hammer petrol tins into canteens; workshops that had once repaired stoves now turned out daggers and bayonets. In the course of August 1921 the Turks finally brought the exhausted and overstretched Greeks to a standstill on the hills south-east of Ankara.

The tide now turned; the French, who had themselves been fighting the Turks for control of Cilicia in southern Anatolia, sued for peace, not only freeing up the Turkish divisions they had been holding down there but also surrendering large stocks of arms and munitions in the process. Britain, quick to reappraise its own interests, declared its neutrality. The Greeks, stalemated and alone, soon found themselves as short of money as of morale. There was nothing for it but to dig in and hope to hold their positions against the inevitable offensive.

The Turks eventually attacked in August 1922. The Greek line, pulverised by artillery fire and sheer weight of enemy numbers, rapidly disintegrated. The Greeks fell back, as they had done three years earlier through the streets of Aydın, and as then they destroyed what they would not be able to keep for themselves. They seized women from the Turkish villages and killed the men who attempted to shield them. They doused villages with kerosene. They torched barns and mosques. Fields were burned, orchards hacked down, farming equipment smashed. Basic possessions like copper pots were destroyed. Korans were ripped to pieces before their owners' eyes. The villagers were left to glean 'handfuls of singed grains' from their smouldering fields.

The Turkish forces continued their rapid advance. They reached Aydın on 7 September 1922 where a Greek machine-gunner resisted from the minaret of the burned Selçuk mosque; it was said that Yörük Ali, who had now attained the rank of colonel, silenced the gunner with a single bullet. A Turkish flag soon flew from the minaret. The city had changed hands for the last time.

Later that month, the Turkish forces reached the terminus of the same hated railway that had carried the Greek forces into Anatolia. At the Smyrna quayside where the Greek forces had put ashore in 1919 they took their revenge on soldiers and civilians alike. In an orgy of slaughter the infidel city burned.

In the afternoon I made my own way back to the street that had somehow survived the sackings of Aydın – 1629 Street was peaceful. The tailors were drinking tea deep in their shadowed arches. An octagonal shrine stood in a walled enclosure amid a littering of headstones. A few of the houses that lined the street still bore the hand-shaped metal door knockers that I had also seen in the Aegean islands.

Among all this, and in the Turkish way, there stood a public toilet. The old attendant dozed beneath a handwritten sign, his wrinkled hand outstretched like a turnstile across the entrance and cupped in a striking resemblance to the door knockers. I placed a coin in his palm and pushed through.

'Wrong way,' the attendant murmured. I was making, however, not for the toilet but for the adjoining garden in order to access the impressive building that had caught my eye from the street; it was built from fine old bricks and topped by domes fuzzy with grasses grown from wind-borne seeds. The door to the building stood open.

Stepping inside, I found myself ankle-deep in fallen plaster. The air was oddly sweet. Dust billowed upwards, back-swirling through the light shafts that streamed past the rusted crossbars and down the deep vaults of the windows. A fountain pipe rose from a circular marble enclosure in the centre of the room. Recessed doorways, arch-shaped and stepped in the Selçuk style, led onwards to rounded chambers, with broad alcoves where marble partitions and the lips of floor basins showed above the depth of debris. The fallen plaster had exposed the brickwork in the dome where inset panels of glass striped the gloomy interior with angled bars of light. It was an Ottoman *hamam*, or bathhouse, of cathedral splendour. The effect was to transport me back to the city Charles Fellows had known; the steam hems hanging heavy over the marble slabs where camel drivers and fig farmers, murmuring at the soreness in their limbs, had once reclined to sweat the dust from their pores.

As my eyes adjusted to the half-light I began to notice that the building had not stood empty since its closure as a *hamam*. From the rotted hemp sacks that showed through the blanket of plaster hundreds of small cylindrical objects had spilled; they were corks. Nearby I now spied green bottles, their coarse glass strewn with air bubbles and flaws, which had been stacked in their hundreds against one wall; the lower tiers, gradually extruding beneath the weight of the heap, threatened the entire bank with collapse. Piles of old grape baskets had been reduced to raffia skeletons, wood cartons lay scattered and the walls of one domed chamber were lined with wooden barrels. The *hamam* had done time as a winery.

The vintners' office had occupied a wooden mezzanine at the top of some rickety steps. The wall calendar showed a still life of a fruit bowl overflowing, in the way of the valley itself, with oranges, grapes and cherries; it hung open at the page for December 1976. There was a road map on the wall, and shelves that had partially collapsed so that the dusty ledgers were piled in the rhomboid troughs. Bottle labels, parcelled in neat string ties, proclaimed contents 'Made from the Aegean's Excellent Grapes'; and a further set of labels was for one Mr Bluedanube's 'Excellent and Delicious' cherry jam. I felt sentimental for the

passing of the vintners and of Mr Bluedanube's jam makers; it saddened me that the *hamam* should have closed, the winery too, and that a malodorous toilet was all that now occupied the site.

I heard noises. A gang of men trooped through the door.

'You must have arrived by the toilet,' observed Osman, the man at their head. Osman was a scrap dealer; he wondered what interest I could have in the place. I liked old places, I explained; it was the atmosphere they exuded.

Osman shrugged. 'Then you should meet the man out at the new mall,' he said. 'We've been supplying him with lots of this junk. Today it's barrels we're delivering.' I wondered what a new mall could want with old wine barrels.

'Search me,' said Osman. 'But once we've loaded the pickup, you're welcome to find out for yourself.' So I joined Osman on his delivery run. We drove through the city, stopping at a corner stall for water. Osman drank deep. 'The stuff of life,' he gasped. Then he pitched the drained plastic bottle out of the window.

From Aydın's southern edge we headed out along the same road I had travelled up the previous evening. In the fading light I had not then noticed the collection of new buildings where we now drew up. Out on the plain, apparently confident in the efficacy of the dams and the regulators, a kind of island mall had risen; a new world of fashion stores, a hotel with flagpoles, an agricultural dealership fronted by a line of machines called rock pickers, and the Café Marin, where Osman's barrels were destined.

The mall had established itself as Aydın's prestige social destination. Black cars, expensive marques, had shoaled along the tarmac apron. From beneath parasols in the garden of the Café Marin leisured locals in bright T-shirts, their tables littered with car keys, cigarette packets, phones and sunglasses, surveyed the empty plain beyond the line of rock pickers. From self-serve plastic trays they ate 'meal choices', which fairly resembled the photographs hanging by chains above the serving counter. The uniforms of the serving staff complemented the fast-food format, one that the management had cut with a refining gallery aesthetic. Minimalist chrome chairs were scattered around, and prices for the framed prints that hung from the walls were to be sought at the various screen-topped terminals where assistants decked out in curatorial black occasionally appeared. Not yet content with this curiously textured ambience, the management had begun littering the place with artefacts in the manner of a museum. I had barely begun to take in the various displays, of old-fashioned brooms and raffia baskets, grape presses and antique typewriters, before I realised where they had all come from.

'I guess nobody had been inside that *hamam* for the best part of thirty years,' the café's proprietor, Ali Ironhand, told me. 'We were amazed what we found there. I think these old pieces look good here.'

Osman and his men had begun to unload the wine barrels. I asked Ali what he knew of the Meander. He told me how as a young man, working in the cotton fields, he had often swum in the river. He had even taken boats downstream to shoot duck around the town of Söke. That was a long time ago and he had not been to the river for years. He guessed there could not be enough water for my boat. I thought I would see for myself.

As I walked down the road towards the river bridge I noticed the message marked out large in an arrangement of white stones across the hillside within the fenced military area to the south of the valley. *The Greatest Achievement*, it read, *is the Nation's Security*. Martial hyperbole went down well with the Turks. Behind the inflated words I heard, however, a truth the river's bitter history had only confirmed. The yearning that I felt for Aydın's vanished worlds of doves, domed *hamams* and elegant villas, the nostalgia that had prompted the Café Marin's heritage artefacts and Mehmet Trueblueeyed's collection of bricks, could not disguise the fact that Turkey's past had been an overwhelmingly pitiless one. For as little as a long lifetime ago the river I was following had been a no-man's land, a boundary between implacable hatreds. Was it of any account, then, that they had not yet learned to respect the river if the land was at peace, if the bodies of the slain no longer littered the roads and choked the river?

Beneath the bridge the water showed stagnant among the Meander's braided sandbanks. For once, though, it did not matter that it would be some time before I could relaunch the canoe.

CHAPTER TWENTY-ONE

T he Turks had won, and a glorious war had earned Atatürk not only the national leadership but also the freedom to rebuild the country much as he saw fit; along the lines, ironically, of those beaten or bested nations that so recently had meant to dismember it.

The transformation was to begin, less than two months after the Turks' recapture of Aydın's cindered ruins, with the abolition of the Ottoman monarchy, the sultanate. The state was proclaimed a Republic, Western and secular, in 1923. The Caliphate, office of the Supreme Head of all Muslims, and the sole position the deposed sultan continued to occupy, was abolished the following year; the Caliph and his family were expelled for ever from the borders of the newly constituted nation. The religious courts were closed down. Ingrained Ottoman practices such as polygamy and the husband's right to divorce his wife, or any number of them, merely by repudiation were outlawed; a Western-style civil code was introduced. The bureaucrats were commanded to abandon their Ottoman frock-coats and fezes for lounge suits and brimmed hats, and the public were increasingly shamed into following the official example; the wearing of veils and the segregation of the sexes was actively discouraged. The Arabic script was replaced by the Latin alphabet. Friday, holy day of the Muslim week, was ousted by the Western weekend; the Islamic calendar, reckoned from the Prophet's flight out of Mecca, was replaced by one that instead

began with the birth of Jesus Christ. In barely a decade it was
done. It must have seemed unaccountable to many Turks, of
course, that they were being forced to adopt the same infidel
ways of the Christians whom the new nation had so recently
expelled.

Many Rum Christians had needed no such prompting; they
fled Anatolia before the rout of the Greek forces, conscious of
the climactic bout of bloodletting it was sure to unleash. The
first to reach Anatolia's ports, otherwise the richest or luckiest,
managed to buy or beg safe passage on ships or fishing boats.
Even as they watched their homeland recede, however, they
could see the columns of footsore civilians and creaking buffalo
carts that were already engulfing the quaysides they had lately
left; the exodus of over one million Rum Christians had begun.
The earliest of them soon reached the safety of nearby Greek
islands like Samos, or cities such as Athens or Salonika, where
they were billeted in public buildings, in ruins, in warehouses,
in old moored freighters, even in damp caves. Later waves of
arrivals fended for themselves as best they could by throwing
together tents or low hutments in the camps that sprang up at
the fringes of the cities. Many of the arriving refugees had been
plundered of their few remaining valuables. This destitute
majority, in which children and the elderly figured large, was
particularly prone to hunger and illness. In the cramped and
filthy camps smallpox, typhus and dysentery ran riot; in the
summer months malaria further ravaged those who had not
found proper shelter.

Many of these Rum refugees sustained themselves in the
belief that a political settlement would eventually allow them to
return to their homes and pick up their former lives. By 1923
it was clear, however, that there would be no going back to
Anatolia. At Lausanne, Switzerland, the Greek and Turkish

authorities agreed on an exchange of minority populations; those Rum Christians who had fled Turkey were to be permanently settled in Greece while the estimated 180,000 who remained in Anatolian regions largely remote from the war, like Cappadocia, were also to leave.

This further exodus, which gathered pace from the end of 1923, soon overwhelmed the processing capacities of Greece's port authorities. The packed coasters and steamers had no choice but to wait their turn at the quaysides; in the meantime the onboard living conditions became indescribably squalid. One observer witnessed the arrival at Salonika of a refugee ship in the winter of 1923:

They were packed like sardines on the deck, a squirming writhing mass of human misery. They had been at sea for four days. There had not been space to permit them to lie down to sleep; there had been no food to eat; there was not access to any toilet facilities . . . They came ashore in rags, hungry, sick, covered with vermin, hollow-eyed, exuding the horrible odour of human filth – bowed with despair.

Six months after being forced from their homes many others had not even cleared the transit camps that had sprung up by the Turkish ports. The horrors continued through 1924. All around the Aegean whole communities, stinking, sick and starving, huddled around campfires. Western sentiment blamed the Turks. *The Times* described the wretched refugees as the victims of the Turks' 'fanatical Nationalism, which is merely a manifestation under new forms of their traditional intolerance'; it was said that the Turks were now doing to the Greeks what the Turks and the Kurds of eastern Anatolia had done to the

Armenians in 1915. The land's Christians were treated much 'as Asiatic conquerors dealt with the conquered in the times of the Old Testament. They interned or destroyed the men of military age; they took the marriageable women to their harems.' Turkey, it was alleged, was hell bent on extirpating a Christian presence whose roots could be traced to the Lycus Valley communities St Paul had first fostered at Colossae, Laodicea and Hierapolis almost 2,000 years before.

At Lausanne it was also established, of course, that many Muslims faced expulsion as well; these were the Turkish peoples of Greece who were to make the same journey now being forced upon Anatolia's Christians but in reverse. The numbers were unequal, with some 400,000 Muslims affected by the exchange, though this did not justify the sheer lack of Western interest in their plight. One commentator 'wondered whether it was real- ised that the Moslems had suffered only a few degrees less than had the Christian subjects of the Porte. In the . . . so-called exchange of human beings, as if they were goods and chattels, the wretched Musulmans . . . were being dumped on the devas- tated coast of Asia Minor, to take up, as best they could, the holdings of the departed Christians.'

The wider historical truth, which the pro-Greek powers had consistently ignored, was that this influx of Muslims into Turkey was just the latest in a long series of mass arrivals there. For centuries Turkey had been receiving refugees rather than making them. From the 1820s until 1913 Anatolia opened its door to an almost unbroken flood of Muslim refugees from the Balkans, southern Russia and the Caucasus. Those lands, an arc-shaped swathe wrapped around the northern shores of the Black Sea, were progressively lost to the Ottomans in the series of defeats they suffered to Imperial Russia as well as to newly independent Greece and Bulgaria. With every victory these states set about zealously Christianising lands that had formerly been home to mixed populations under the Ottomans.

The victims, inevitably, were the resident Muslims: the Tartars of Crimea, the Circassians of the Caucasus and the various exotically named populations – the Koniari, the Vallahades, the Pomaks – of Greece and Bulgaria. The intention, to reduce or remove the Muslim presence, was sometimes achieved by administrative pressure, with extortionate taxation proving persuasive, or by sustained campaigns of harassment. In other cases, however, Muslim villages were plundered of their cattle and equipment, and the residents were ordered to leave. As the ceaseless catalogue of wars raged, villages were often destroyed and their residents massacred; there were instances of Muslim women being repeatedly raped before they were herded into barns piled high with harvest straw and immolated. Mosques were turned into latrines. Cavalry units fell upon the columns of refugees and the survivors carried nothing with them out of their lands other than festering sabre wounds. In the course of a process barely acknowledged in the West, where the atrocities perpetrated by the Ottomans alone appeared to be worthy of condemnation, an estimated five million Muslims were driven from their homes; the survivors among the expelled largely found refuge among their co-religionists in Turkey.

The Ottomans, by contrast, had continued to tolerate their own minorities for much of the nineteenth century; they had even permitted, as we have seen, fresh waves of Greeks migrants to settle and prosper in areas like the Meander Valley. The discrepancy between the population sizes involved in the exchange, which the West cited to justify the concentration of its resources in aiding the Christian arrivals in Greece, should instead have been taken as indicative of a telling nineteenth-century truth; Christians evidently found life in Anatolia more tolerable than Muslims did in the Christian lands. The West had it that Turkish barbarism played a leading role in endorsing ethnic cleansing by the nation's participation at Lausanne, and that the Turks' brutal slaughter in 1915 of the Armenians constituted the original genocide of the industrial age. In fact, the 'monstrously wicked' solution that Turkey agreed to in 1923 was nothing more than a formalised version of the one it had for a century or more watched its Orthodox Christian enemies inflict upon the Muslims of those benighted lands beyond the Black Sea.

With the first call to prayer I walked out of Aydın. The city was half-lit. On the empty streets I now noticed the number of businesses and properties – a freight company, an apartment block, a money-changing booth, an electricity supplier and a café – that called themselves *Menderes*. Given the state of the river, however, these seemed like empty acknowledgements, and for once I was not tempted back to the high dry banks. Instead I let the rail tracks I had first followed from the Meander's source, a daily presence since Sarayköy, guide me out of the waking city. I followed the roadside railway past the lorries fuming at the traffic lights, past the sign that forbade horse-drawn carts from joining the nearby motorway to Izmir, past the track-side warehouses of the farming syndicates and out into the fig orchards.

At the town of Erbeyli a man was painting the railway station's waiting room with long pink licks of his wide brush; another had wedged a parasol, spokes protruding from the faded and ripped fabric, into the cracked platform and raised a precarious stack of strawberry punnets beneath it, and when I pointed to a lower tier he laughed and held up two fingers, but in encouragement rather than insult, lowering one the moment I indicated that a single punnet would do; and a third man, watering the flower baskets that hung along the platform, invited me with a companionable grunt to wash my strawberries beneath his hose. The man asked about my vehicle, and upon discovering that I did not have one he turned out his pockets to signify the pennilessness that we had in common. We shared the strawberries. Then, rinsing my hands beneath the hose, I wandered down the platform to investigate a curious obelisk that rose beside the road.

The slender memorial was dated 21 June 1919 – precisely a week before the fighting for Aydın began – when rising tensions had triggered a skirmish between Erbeyli's Turks and the occupying Greeks. *Lest We Forget the Heroes Who in Firing the First Bullets Against the Enemy Gave Their Lives to the Motherland*, the memorial declared. The grand rhetoric gave way to more homespun sentiments, however, when it came to the roll-call; for this time the heroes were not merely listed as the sons of fathers in the traditional way but rather were named for the attributes, however humble or informal, that best distinguished them. Among Erbeyli's dead were Durmuş from Izmir and Hafiz from Isparta; the barber Sadık and the porter Mehmet; Mustafa the son of Osman the shoemaker, and Ahmet the sheep farmer's son; the carter's son Ahmet and Hasan the son of the lame Abdullah; Bald Ibrahim's son Ahmet, the Cretan carter Hasan and Hasan the son of the islander Ali.

It was a memorial I might easily have missed and with it the moment that I had been anticipating, I now realised, all through my journey: evidence of ordinary Anatolians asserting rights to identities, however modest, of their own. If my journey had taught me anything about the history of these people, it was that they had been accounted an anonymous, uncouth and secondary herd for millennia. Ever since the time of the ancient Greeks they had been dismissed as common barbarians compelled to bow before successive conquerors and their gods, and to fight their distant wars. They had then been left impoverished, uneducated and unrecognised in their flea-ridden hovels. In honouring their sacrifice the memorial at Erbeyli acknowledged them, at last, in something like the fullness of their individual selves – where they were from and what they did, even fleshing them out with the inherited traits they might have developed, like baldness, or the features they might have accidentally acquired, like lameness, if their own lives had only been long enough. Anatolia's peasantry, its porters, carters and the rest, had for centuries been condemned as 'Turks', even as stupid 'Turk-heads', by those who ruled over them. But now the disgraced Ottomans were gone, along with the Rum Christians, and it was as Turks that a newly proud people took belated possession of a land, however shattered, which should have always been their own.

Nowhere did that pride flare more memorably than in the Turks' response to one of the last of the great Westernising reforms; the surnames that they were required to find for themselves, in the manner of the expelled Rums, in 1934. They might have been expected to make conventional selections, based on the likes of their father's first name, or the family's profession or provenance, as the memorial at Erbeyli only appeared to anticipate. But during the eighteen months they were given to decide, many followed rather the lead of Mustafa Kemal, their beloved President, whose own choice – Atatürk, Father of Turks – confirmed the widespread hunch that splendid brio was the form when it came to the Turkish version. For his close acquaintances, especially favourite generals, Atatürk took pleasure in proposing the names of the battles they had won or the mountain ridges their men had heroically defended during the war; for others he suggested such inflated surnames as Sublime, or Spiritual Companion.

So his people went for Trueturk, Bravelion, Greywolf, Whitestar and Overthrower-of-Mountains, and, in the case of the forebears of those I had encountered along my own journey: Darkeye, Truehero, Fearless, Skirmisher, Blessed, Greatspring, Flag, Trueblueeyed, Bluedanube and Ironhand. The choice proved easier for others, especially those who were already confirmed in their two-part names, like Yörük Ali, who simply transposed them to become Ali Yörük; so that on the occasions that bureaucracy required, no doubt with all due deference, a surname of the revered freedom fighter, Nomad Ali went as Ali Nomad.

And now the offspring of modern Turkey's first generation, their aged children and their grandchildren, travelled the road westwards where I walked. All morning they and their own young passed me in speeding lorries and trundling tractors, and in *dolmuşes* hung with football pennants, which drew up with a jolt to pitch them into the dusty verge by the shabby towns of the wide valley; grey-haired men in their worn suits and women with their baskets of aubergines, who stepped over gutters littered with the discarded shells of watermelons and the puddles of sump oil, and walked past the car repair shops and machine works, the grimy glass-fronted kebab houses, and the occasional offices of provincial doctors, dentists and lawyers where every premise bore the proud surname of its Turkish owner.

The road was hard, the sun high and a woman put up dust as she appeared out of the fig orchards. I noticed her earrings and curly hair before it occurred to me that the woman wore no headscarf, which was unusual out in the countryside. As she crossed the tracks towards me I was pushed to remember when a woman had last gone out of her way to make my acquaintance; the one, I reckoned, who had stopped me in the uplands village near Bahadınlar to tell me of her children who were now making prosperous lives for themselves in Switzerland. Rarely did the sexes stray from their appointed spaces in rural Turkey, I had learned, unless they were sufficiently young or old that it did not signify. Or unless it was themselves that they sold, in whatever place provided a degree of privacy, like the depths of the trackside fig orchards where the woman with one word now invited me. I had backed away from her graphic proposition, making for the quiet of the river, when it occurred to me that I was leaving the railway for the last time.

The railway and the valley had run together since Sarayköy. Now they were diverging, the one veering north towards İzmir's quaysides, the other trending south on its final mazy leg to the delta. The odd thing, it now struck me, was that I had not seen a single passing train since the beginning of my journey, and I remembered something Mehmet Trueblueeyed had said; that only the poorest people were prepared to endure the long waits that Turkish train travel entailed. The railway had not stopped paying, it seemed, for its collaborationist past. Certainly, the infidel line had long since lost out to the roads, with their constant flow of *dolmuşes*, and to the new motorway, and all the efforts that had lately gone into the neat station platforms, with their freshly painted waiting rooms and flower baskets, and all the labour of line gangs like the one I had seen that first day near the source could do no more to save the railway, I now feared, than the whips the drivers had uselessly raised that their camel trains might compete with the advance down the track of the newly laid sleepers 150 years before.

I walked through a very long day and was within a few miles of Söke, stumbling in the darkness, when a *dolmuş* stopped for me. The nondescript cotton town (alt. 27 metres) was quiet but for the rumble of closing shop grilles and the clang of gas canisters being unloaded off truck beds. The one hotel, the Ephesus Palace, appeared to date from the agricultural boom the town had enjoyed in the 1950s. The receptionist had since retreated into his little glass office and turned his back towards the television, posting a handwritten sign that forbade guests from entering his sanctuary, as if to barricade himself against a weight of grievances, however reasonable, and the pot plants had gone from the stair-side alcoves where cigarette butts gathered, and a little pink bin, with a black trim where its plastic liner showed, stood guard outside my door.

I was sore and exhausted, and had gone out in search of something to eat when I spied a window whose grille was yet to fall; it was a tackle shop, with a display of rods, nets, hooks – and an orange life jacket. I took encouragement from that jacket; as a reminder that the sea must be near, like a whiff of wind-blown salt, it would have been a welcome sight even if it had not been for the image of a paddling canoeist above the word TURKEY printed large across the chest. At up-country tea houses and regulators the account I had so often given of myself, as a sea-bound canoeist, had been greeted with such silent incomprehension that I had long yearned for the least acknowledgement; so I was happy when it finally came, even if it was from a buoyancy aid.

The town of Söke, which Italian forces had occupied for much of the Independence War, had fared somewhat better than Aydın; the Greek quarter had largely survived, even if its name – Kemalpaşa Evleri, or General Kemal's Houses – was a pointed reminder that the place now belonged to Atatürk's Turkey. An erratic wind was gusting as I wandered among the elegant merchant houses, some still bearing their Greek inscriptions and late nineteenth-century dates, where I spotted the same extensive motifs – the flowers, rosettes, festoons and the hand-shaped door knockers – I had seen at Aydın.

The most common pattern in evidence, however, was the meander. In Söke's old quarter it all but ran amok. There were meanders in the exterior plaster, in the rusted brackets beneath the rotting wooden balconies and in the filigree ironwork above the doors; through windows I saw how they also ran round interior plaster cornices and how they bordered staircases and doorways.

In its Söke setting, in short, the motif seemed insistent; what I had taken to be merely decorative now appeared to endow the houses where they were inscribed with the overt affiliations, even the political aspirations, of their owners. I speculated that the meander, for all the shifting significances that had attached to it over the ages, had by the beginning of the nineteenth century become, at least in the region, a tacit embodiment of nothing less than the Great Idea; the assertion of a territorial claim that would eventually lead to occupation. It had acted, I guessed, as the badge of a prosperous and influential minority whose loyalty lay with the Hellenic invaders. In their turn the Turks might even have regarded the meander with something of the same unease that the swastika – and the two motifs, I had noticed, were commonly entangled – had signified to those in the path of Nazi Germany's blitzkrieg. It was a thought, that said, that I had never heard expressed. On a whim I waylaid a passing Turk, a man carrying a radiator, and asked what the patterning meant to him. With the shrug of one, however, who had a life to be getting on with, the man patted his radiator and continued down the lane.

It was a warm morning and I was content to buy a sesame bread ring, or *simit*, and chew upon it as I rested my sore feet in the Warriors' and Martyrs' Park. Children played about their mothers, and elderly men, comfortably canted on the benches, raised wrinkled eyes to the sunshine and ran prayer beads through their fingers. One, whose name was Yusuf Grape, came to sit beside me. Yusuf, who was seventy-seven, took pleasure in telling how he had once worked precisely where we now sat when the four chimneys of Söke's liquorice factory, since demolished, had dominated the country town's skyline. Liquorice, yet another of the Meander Valley's many crops, was a thickly rooted weed, which prospered in the deep silt soils. It had once grown wild, across the untended lands and in the fields alike, and the factory owners had prospered on exports to America and Europe where liquorice was used in confectionery and medicine, and to flavour tobacco and cigarette papers, and thoughts of the opium trade of the valley's uplands reminded me that the Meander region had always served narcotic pleasures.

Yusuf had spent much of his working life in the liquorice

business. 'Every spring, when the ground was wet,' he explained, 'my brothers and I used to go down into the delta, around villages like Atburgazı and Güllübahçe, and dig up the spidery liquorice roots thick as a child's wrist. We had some half-dozen camels we used to load – 100 kilos on each flank. In those days you could see mountains of the root piled by the pathways. We sold the liquorice at the factory gates. Later, when I was in my thirties, I worked in the factory, boiling the dried roots time and again until they formed a thick syrup, which hardened into a black paste. We sent the liquorice to Izmir, and from there it went overseas.'

I wondered why the factory had closed.

'Things got difficult from the 1950s,' explained Yusuf. 'That was when the tractors first came, and with their deep ploughs they tore up the liquorice roots. Then they began to sow the big cotton fields, and we liquorice diggers and the holes we made were no longer welcome. The owners shut down the factory in 1969, and the Western managers left, and all us workers, some thirty men, lost our jobs.'

Yusuf's elegy explained why no liquorice digger commanded the plinth in Söke's square; a shawled young woman, a Soviet-style heroine of the cotton fields, instead stood beside a wicker basket that overflowed with her pickings. I left the town by the main road and soon arrived at a new mall, complete with Starbucks and McDonald's, which might have finally confirmed the end of traditional inland Turkey if it had not been for an adjacent sign offering Sacrificial Lambs for sale. I worked my way back to the river where there were ruined farm buildings, their ceilings lathed with sagging reeds, and in the midst of a big field inch-high with red-stemmed cotton seedlings a farmer stood tiny in his torn waistcoat.

'Filthy water,' he said despairingly – and not enough of it, so the season's cotton harvest was sure to be miserable, the pickings meagre as the previous year when the crop had been barely a fifth of the usual yield. The fields were shadowless except where storks passed high overhead, and by the riverbank old metal ferry rafts had been flipped onto their low gunwales to rust away. Lines of eucalypts, planted in the 1960s to help drain the malarial marshlands, shaded me along the river until the ruins of a Byzantine bastion rose from the far bank, and at last I knew myself to be close; for here, at ancient Myus, my journey would once have ended.

Once, that is, being back in the fifth century BC when the sight of 200 warships riding at anchor might have greeted me on my arrival at the seaport. Five centuries later I would have yet had a way to go, however, when the same place was only reached by heading 'inland for three miles in rowing boats'; and further still a century later yet when Myus, beset by the gnats that swarmed from the encroaching marsh, stood largely abandoned. The Meander, a sophist wrote, 'had taken the sea from the navigator, and given it to the husband-man to be divided into fields; that furrows were seen in the place of waves, and kids sporting in the room of dolphins; and that instead of hearing the hoarse mariner, you were delighted with the sweet echo of the pastoral pipe'. What stretched ahead, in short, were the delta lands that the river's alluvial deposits had reclaimed since the beginning of recorded time.

At the village of Sarıkemer an old stone bridge spanned the river; its arched underside was riddled with holes where the sloughed skins of snakes hung, creating a hollow rattle in the breeze. The river remained as low as ever, and only in the memories of the old villager I met at the tea house was the water abundant. Hüseyin Crane, whose surname celebrated the great birds that had once visited the delta villages in profuse numbers, recalled the winter days when he had operated the Meander ferry between the villages of Atburgazı and Balat; when the receding waters stranded vast numbers of fish across the April flats, and the *dalyans*, the fish traps, had harvested prodigious quantities of eels and grey mullet; and when men like the Grape brothers came with the spring to dig for the damp liquorice, and made a mess of the fields and the irrigation canals where they rooted for the deep weed like the filthy pigs the Rum people had once kept in their villages.

I thanked Hüseyin Crane for the tea and passed out of Sarıkemer, and to my left I could soon make out the watery expanse of Bafa Lake. A few fields separated river and lake. Then the two began to close and when I judged they were at their closest, with not a football pitch between them, I left the river and walked down to the lake. All around the mountains flared pink, taking their evening colour, it seemed, from the flamingos that stood shadowed in the shallows until something put them up, and they took off down the wide waterway, a swished gauze, and were gone from view.

I walked beyond the crusted mud where the water lay and bent before raising a dipped finger to my lips; the water was warm like blood and – preserving a memory from the time of those ancient warships, when the lake had been a gulf of the Aegean – there was also salt in it.

CHAPTER TWENTY-TWO

In the morning I retrieved my canoe and returned to the lake, dragging the assembled craft down to the water. When I looked back, I saw that the canoe's rubber underside had left a broad smear, wiping my tracks from the soft grey mudflats. After the succession of exhausting valley walks that had brought me here – from Feslek, from Yenipazar, from Aydın, from Söke – I was glad to see my footprints go.

I was back on the water, though not on the river, and so might have been accused of wandering off course; but I was not about to be censured, not on the Meander, for doing so. The river had always mingled, at any rate, with the waters that I now paddled. Once, of course, its sweet outflow had mixed freely with the salt waters of the Latmian Gulf, as the Aegean inlet was then known. What was striking was how the river's physical separation from that gulf, by the actions some 2,000 years ago of its very own silts, had not prevented a continued association; the regular spilling of the river's winter flood waters into the lake, raising the levels there by fully a metre or more, meant that the two had shared seasonal reunions ever since – the last twenty years pointedly excepted.

The waters were clear under the sun and I paddled east up the old inlet, through the shore-side reed stands, until the lake lay wide open within its hem of hazed mountains. The heights that rose from the northern shores, wooded with olives and scrub oak, were strewn with house-high boulders,

all suggestively smooth, even spherical, as if countless tides
had rolled them there; there were mysteries in the high folds
of that mountain – holy Latmus to the ancients – which had
been 'a grand resort of fanciful devotees, and secluded
hermits, a nursery of saints, another Athos' from the seventh
century.

A good wind had gathered at my back. It pitched me across
the shimmering lake until there rose out of it an island, wooded
but whitened, the olives, bays, figs and tamarisks serving as the
shit-splattered roosts of countless waterbirds. The cormorants
held their ground at my approach but the egrets and herons
put up in their hundreds, and from their raucous wheels overhead they cast me in a strobe-like dapple of wing shadows. Over
the weed-rimmed base of a fluted column, which protruded
from the shallows, I looped my painter and went ashore.

The old bastion walls had been reduced in many places; above
the dusted brambles their unevenly exposed courses were

occupied by lines of cormorants, black as the notes of a tumbling musical score. In the wall rubble I could make out column drums, and broken bits of pediment and frieze from an edifice of the Hellenistic era. I thought how these mountain-ringed, moated Byzantines had with the stones of their forebears once raised here their own innermost defences, no doubt hoping that the Turks or Saracens or Persians, or whichever Eastern peoples were then taking their turn to maraud the land, would content themselves with the region's more accessible settlements. The sun was high now and the flow tide of its glare had submerged almost all the island, and the few resident goats jostled for space in the last remaining banks of shade. They were reluctant to concede ground when I claimed their shelter for my picnic site, and soon they were back, stumbling boldly about me, hot and rank, as I broke into my olives, cheese and bread.

Later, when the wind strengthened, the lake increasingly resembled the sea it had once been. I drove on, struggling to keep the canoe from shipping the waves that broke at the bow, and it struck me that I might have done more than admire – like buy – the orange life jacket I had seen at Söke. I did not doubt, however, that I could safely beach the canoe even if the waves did cause it to founder. In the heat the water looked positively inviting. At that moment it occurred to me that I was enjoying myself. I wondered how it was I had only now noticed that the worrying – about handling the canoe, dogs, maps, the sinister significance of watermills, fallen willows, dams and regulators, sleeping arrangements, crossing points, river levels and trowels – had largely ceased. I was doodling along, as I had always meant to, and I felt fine.

The canoe, bucking and flexing, fell down the big waves that the sea wind, the *meltem*, pushed up the lake through the afternoon. I passed another fortified island, broken walls toppling from the rocks, where a terracotta cross showed between the paired narrow window arches of a basilica, and an intact ring of grey crenellations crowned a nearby promontory. I came into the lee of the long bay at the head of the lake where the mountain slopes withdrew, and there were low-lying fields, and a shoreline curious with apparently miniaturised ruins; one-room cottages of whitewashed block, with single chimneys cornering the tiled pitches of the roofs, cracked patios shaded by tumble-down vines, and bleached window shutters hanging askew from their hinges.

The lake's main inhabited settlement lay well beyond the abandoned cottages. Directly opposite the ruins of yet another fortified island, this one flying a Turkish flag, was a bone-white strand where I ran the canoe ashore among blue fishing caiques, the high prows piled with rank-smelling nets, and wandered up the lane, past the turpentine trees and a sign to the Selene Restaurant, into Kapıkırı.

From the profusion of downed columns and shattered platforms, tottering arches and ashlar tiers, it was clear that the villagers of Kapıkırı had themselves followed the Byzantine example in settling among the ruins of earlier civilisations; but whereas the visible evidence was that the Byzantines had forever been in retreat, forced back to the last stands they made behind the walls of their offshore Alamos, finding safety as sparse as the shade today's goats sought on those same islands, the current occupants now squatted secure. They occupied the heart of Hellenistic Heraclea, and while that one-time city's own impressive walls, complete with gates, parapets and towers, suggested that life back then can barely have been safer than the latter-day Byzantines were to find it fifteen centuries later, today's Turks appeared to have no use for them other than to confine their cattle. All through the present-day village the doors of their rough homes stood open. The old dangers had evidently receded; perhaps the greatest threat to the current community was from a national museum service in thrall to the tidying tendency, which might one day seek to remove the modern settlers from the ancient city, as it had done at many of Turkey's other historical sites.

For now, however, Heraclea's uncurated stones had been left to the villagers of Kapıkırı. The column drums served as their garden tables, the agora doubled as their football pitch and an old man at his door stopped to press an arthritic heel against a length of fallen column, having learned over the years that its fluted rim was just the thing to assist him in easing off his rubber boots. The villagers' casual customisation of the old city, alive to the historical continuities that museums thought to arrest, was evocative.

The tourists certainly thought so; they had been visiting the village for some years now. I took a cabin in a *pansiyon*, home to the Blueeyed family, which occupied a bluff above the strand. In the gardens I drank beer as the farmers returned from the fields, their donkeys piled high with fodder or firewood, and the herons made for their island roosts. The light slipped by degrees until all was charcoal – the birds and the smooth ashlar of the temple walls, the stilled water and the rounded boulders and the five peaks of Latmus – except for the wash of moonlight; the moon, of course, for the myth of Endymion, which some had set among the spilled secretions of Pamukkale's travertines, was first and for ever associated with Mount Latmus. I remembered the beautiful shepherd, and the moon goddess who had machinated to make him hers, and the divine stupor into which she had cast him high on this mountain, and I guessed it had probably begun with the nocturnal fantasies of some lonely shepherd who could sleep neither for the brilliance of the moon nor for the longing within; and my main thought was that such shepherds had less to fear than the women reduced to selling sex in the fig orchards along the Aydın road.

The advice, that said, was that I should not wander the mountain on my own; according to the locals, who knew it for its distinct peaks as Beşparmak, or Five Fingers, it was easy to be lost among the viewless boulders and rifts. So Mehmet Blueeyed led me in a chill dawn through gates roughly wickered from bleached brittle sticks and over olive groves and meadows of poppies, crocuses and orchids. The air was sweet with the scent of the pinkish Chaste Tree, a verbena named for its supposed bromide-like qualities, and I wondered whether it was the local celibates, seeking preservation against the abandonment that had befallen Endymion, and doubting their power to resist, who had themselves cultivated the shrub in such profusion. But these were fanciful thoughts, and among the wrecked fortifications and rib arches of the acorn-eating ascetics' sanctuary at Yediler, Monastery of the Seven Brothers, there grew only grasses and pink rock roses. One hermit's cave, a weather-hollowed boulder, was ceilinged with a frescoed Crucifixion; a naked Christ, ribcage raised in torment, racked against a sky cobalt with divine insult.

Then Mehmet led me to a cave of older paintings. They were of a time before Messiahs, angels and expiation, about 8,000 years old, and were rendered wholly in rust reds and mustard yellows. The paintings, of rudimentary stick figures, animals, ideograms and handprints, were thick with the fascination of their makers; with the dawning realisation, perhaps, that their handwork might express meaning. Here was what the painters saw, even what they meant, but perhaps before they had the words to articulate those meanings and most certainly before they had developed the written wherewithal to record them.

The invitation was to comprehend, then, what they had

intended by their painted representations; the animals they plainly had rendered for the nourishment their flesh afforded and for the warmth of the skins, and their own hands they honoured as the miraculous tools of human will. Which left the less immediately explicable patterns that they had made. Much of their work consisted of repeated geometrical motifs. In a moment of purest pleasure I recognised the pattern that ran up and down, up and down the walls of the cave; it was the squared-off wave, the meander pattern in its purest form. Only the day before I had glimpsed what the meander may have come to mean – an assertion of cultural, even territorial domination – in its play on the walls of Söke's Greek quarter. Here, on earlier walls, I had the faint but insistent sense that it had once conveyed a more universal meaning; the painters' experience that every-thing went around, days, seasons, lives, the things that threatened and that gave strength, and everything came back, and so the red-dyed stick beneath their fingers ran not straight but turned and turned again, through the generations, until they left their caves and words came to them and writing too, and the people emerged into the half-lit history with which this narrative began.

We headed back through the scrub oak and the boulders, making for Kapıkırı's landmark minaret, and Mehmet spoke of the village. The villagers counted between them some ten surnames; theirs was a close community, originally of Yörük stock, though I had seen their poorly watered mountains and guessed that the Beşparmak range neither rose nor extended sufficiently to sustain the alpine meadows essential to seasonal nomadism.

'Our forebears never spent their summers in the mountains like typical Yörüks,' Mehmet conceded. 'These days we go to the mountains in the winter to harvest the olives. A few goatherds do summer up there and some of us go up to hunt wild boar, but that's about it.'

I asked about the boars and Mehmet explained that a good number of the younger villagers regularly ate the meat, though the imam was not to know. Mehmet thought the flesh delicious; an admission I would never have heard in Dinar. I felt the old orthodoxies lose their grip as the coast drew close; in this respect at least I had travelled out of one world and into another.

Mehmet's elder brother, Muammer, was preparing dinner when I got back to the Blueeyeds' *pansiyon*. It was bass, straight off the fishing boats, and so in a final crucial detail – its fish – the windy, wavy, salty lake was confirmed as an inland sea.

'In the winter the fish, the bass and the grey mullet, leave the Aegean for the river and reach the lake by the fishery canal,' Muammer explained. 'Though we do get some freshwater types, like carp, as well.'

I'd seen fish surfacing around my canoe, I told Muammer, as I passed by the little ruined cottages.

'You mean the old summer village,' said Muammer. It had once been the habit of the village, he explained, to abandon Kapıkırı through the summer for the lake shore; in the absence of suitable mountains the water and cooling breeze there had served instead. So the people of Kapıkırı had been nomads, but adapted ones, whose seasonal migration had amounted to a walk of no more than fifteen minutes.

Muammer fondly remembered the summer village and the improvements they had made there over the years: the tiles they laid on the roofs, the reed-lathed ceilings and the cupboards, the mosque they built and the grocery shop, and even the little tea houses where the grandparents liked to sit, watching the children learn to swim. There were games of football and after-noon naps, fishing lines wound around little fingers, and light work tending the aubergines, black-eyed peas and onions, and the lemon groves, and all through the long summer the village camped in contentment; in every regard, in fact, their summers were long holidays by the sea.

From the canoe, however, I had seen the abandonment that had overtaken the settlement; the place had gone to wrack, the rough plaster peeling off the block walls around the hearths, the tiles teetering on the roofs, the broken shutters and the invading reeds, and I remembered all the ruins I had witnessed along the Meander: the ancient cities and temples, the Byzantine monasteries, the abandoned upland villages beneath their tottering minarets, the brick shells of the buildings around the town of Dalama, and now the summer village at Kapıkırı. I had the inescapable sense that the ruination was not simply the result of the wars that had ravaged this land but was somehow endemic to the place. It was difficult to imagine why the villagers should otherwise have abandoned a way of life that struck me as idyllic. Muammer smiled and excused himself, for he had guests to attend to, and I then knew what he would have said if he had not been too gracious to do so: *People like you began to arrive*.

So Western tourists had discovered places like Kapıkırı. The villagers now had *pansiyons* and restaurants to run. The men had hikes to lead and boat trips to organise; the women were busy cooking bass and making beaded scarves, which they touted from plastic bowls on the agora where they also raised pyramids of honey jars. The people of Kapıkırı found that they no longer had time to spend at the summer village. It was the Westerners who lay by the beach and the Turks who served them.

CHAPTER TWENTY-THREE

On a hot morning I rejoined the river where I had left it some days earlier and walked its wandering banks across the delta grasslands. In the heavy air I heard regular rasping sounds, which appeared to come from a cluster of riverside trees; the Turkish flag flapping among the mulberry crowns might have been planted precisely to mark their source.

The flag actually flew over the old *dalyan* or fishery. Beyond a broad loop the river unbraided into a fray of caged and netted channels, which I crossed by a concrete bridge and found myself in a shaded yard. On every side stood decrepit buildings whose former functions were announced by varnished signs fastened above peeling jambs. The curious noises came from the middle of the yard where a solitary man, Adem Thunderbolt, was scything at the high grass around a gilt bust of Atatürk and its adjacent flagpole.

The fishery controlled the narrow channel between the lake and river where the sea shoals migrated, when water levels allowed, to their winter spawning grounds on the lake. Adem paid for the fishing rights, but the fee was nominal.

'Oh, I get a few grey mullet between September and March,' he said. 'The odd good-sized one, even as much as five kilos. The rest of the year I grow a little cotton and wheat, keep the place tidy. I was born here, after all.'

It had not always been like this; the factory sheds, offices, canteens, machine rooms and living quarters, the channels, the Atatürk bust and the flagpole, the boats and the rotted nets were all evidence of the bustling concession that had once employed an extensive workforce, Adem's father included. By an expressive gesture, miming a sack of coin he repeatedly weighed on an open palm, the forty-two-year-old remembered the prodigious catches he had witnessed at the *dalyan* in his boyhood. I myself knew of the formerly productive fishery from the travellers, Lord Patrick Kinross and Freya Stark among them, who had visited the *dalyan* in the 1950s.

At that time the fishery maintained the usual exceptional standards of Turkish hospitality – Kinross, Atatürk's biographer-to-be, described luncheons of salted eels and grey mullet, 'a profusion of pears and apricots', plentiful rakı, and peasants who sprinkled water on the ground beneath the guests' feet 'to lay the dust' – even as the staff saw to the daily business of the place: the packing of the fish roe, or *tarama*, for the island tavernas of nearby Samos, the freezing or curing of the mullet, and the readying of the eels for export to Holland and Germany. The formidable Freya Stark, who spent three days at the *dalyan* during the winter floods of 1952, wrote how the daily catch was such that 'twenty camels, each with a box on either side of it', were required to carry it away to market. Now, however, there was only the Thunderbolt family who dared to hope that each winter might throw up a few good-sized mullet.

The reasons for the fishery's fifty-year decline were wearyingly familiar; excessive fishing and irrigation, the polluting of the waters by fertilisers and by industrial run-off, had all been compellingly cited. In recent years large numbers of dead fish had repeatedly washed up on the shores of Bafa Lake. Some blamed the phenol-rich effluent from the oil presses in the olive groves around Bafa Town; others suspected the deaths were due to a lack of oxygen in waters starved of circulation, to the point of stagnation, by the influential representations of the downstream cotton growers who meant to protect the river, their irrigation source, by restricting the inflow of fresh water into the lake and the amount of saline water permitted to leave it.

Kinross and Stark were witness, then, to the historical moment when industrialisation began to degrade the Meander Valley, though at the time a more positive transformation appeared to be under way. Halil Özbaşı, then the fishery's affluent concessionaire, told Freya Stark that the rich summer grasslands of the delta were visibly dotted with the traditional camps of the Yörüks and their grazing herds during 1952. Özbaşı added, however, that he did not expect to see the distinctive black-wool tents there again. 'Next year there will be no Yürüks,' he predicted; 'it will all be under cultivation.' The nomadic herdsmen, like the liquorice diggers, were being driven from the fertile delta. New bridges would soon put the ferrymen and their traditional triangular rafts out of business. Some 40,000 tractors, largely paid for by American aid, were flooding into Turkey; 2,000 of them, according to Özbaşı, in the Meander Delta alone where their powerful ploughs would soon erase the crescent-shaped depressions from the relict channels of the former river braids, the faint dust circles left by the Yörüks' tents, and the liquorice diggers' pits alike. New farms were being built. Dams, power stations, harbours and metalled roads were under construction. Malarial marshes were drained and thirsty eucalypts planted to aid the process. Millionaires were being made in Söke, and even the peasants were enjoying a modest prosperity. The government, according to Kinross, had brought the country people 'new canalization, fertilizers to enrich new fields no longer flooded with silt, tractors to cultivate them, loans to develop them, usually in terms of cotton subsidies for the price of their crops'. A 'Menderes regime for the Menderes Valley', as the term went, had been established; for it was a local man with a local surname,

Meander, who had been Turkey's prime minister since gaining power in 1950.

The home farm of the Menderes family stood near the valley village of Çakırbeyli which I had visited some days earlier while in Aydın. Çakırbeyli was a neat, shaded place arranged around a spring of noted sweetness; the marble fountain was inscribed with the name of Adnan Menderes. It stood in the centre of the Adnan Menderes Park and Family Tea Gardens; a prominent framed portrait of the man – urbane, intelligent, clean-shaven, brilliantined black hair, spruce in his suit and tie – had been hung above the rose-scented gardens to confirm the devotional impression. Numerous institutions, most notably the university

at Aydın and the airport at Izmir, commemorated the name of
Adnan Menderes; statues had been raised in his memory.

The head of the village, who bought me tea, was also keen
to honour the man. 'What they did to him,' declared Mehmet
Iron, 'was an outrage against democracy.'

Adnan Menderes was born in 1899 into a prominent land-
owning family. He came to the political fore during the 1940s
when, in the aftermath of Atatürk's death, the national establishment began to allow a tentative transition from dictatorial
rule to multi-party democracy. The consequence, unexpected
in its immediacy, was that Menderes' Democratic Party crushed
Atatürk's ruling Republican Party in Turkey's first free elections.

It was as if, with the century's arrival at its halfway point,
Turkish society could wait no longer to make the next step in
its development; the one-party elite installed by Atatürk – urban,
intellectual, professional, bureaucratic, military – was rudely
unseated by the powerful alliance the Democrats had succeeded
in arraying against it. Menderes, who championed free enterprise over state control, counted among his constituents the
increasingly influential business class of industrialists and
managers. His family background meant he was also able to
attract the support of the landowners and the wider rural vote
they were able to deliver. Menderes, with his acute understanding of the Turkish peasantry, was quick to buttress their
support by paying court to that innate rural conservatism, not
least in terms of faith – 'the entire frame of everybody's existence' – which the Westernising state over the previous three
decades had so determinedly quashed. Many of the country
mosques were reopened. The call to prayer was once more
permitted to be made in the traditional Arabic. Religious schools
opened. Islamic periodicals were published.

As the popularity of the regime faltered through the 1950s

– it was running record trade deficits and manifesting an increasingly authoritarian streak – Menderes was to identify himself ever more closely with Islamic sentiment. His government was duly accused of conniving at the flouting of secular law in the hinterland where turbans had begun to reappear, not least on the heads of imams who performed polygamous marriage ceremonies and commonly reminded their congregations that those who withheld their vote from Menderes thereby declared themselves infidels. An imam forbade people from having their teeth filled, fillings being a sinful innovation unknown in the time of the Prophet. People were threatened for smoking in the streets during Ramadan, and it was said that one father would not permit his dying daughter to take medicine during the Fast.

The state increasingly feared that Atatürk's legacy was in danger of wholesale betrayal. The Democrats might have filled Turkey with modern machinery, but they had largely paid for it on unsustainable lines of credit and at once had exposed the national mind to the forces of reaction, thereby undoing much of the educational progress credited to Atatürk. All of which Menderes might have got away with, not least because his rural support remained solid, if he had not also incensed precisely those people who could act against him: the military.

We have seen how Turks had historically held soldiering to be the noblest of callings. High standards were expected of the Turkish officer; the reward was the regard, even the sanctity, that he commanded. Through the 1950s, however, Turkey's armed forces experienced a dramatic erosion of their traditional prestige. The job had never been a lucrative one, but as the cost of living soared – prices at the end of the 1950s were more than ten times what they had been at the beginning of the decade – the very same military men who had served so heroically in the Independence War were effectively paupered. Politicians and entrepreneurs grew rich while retired generals were forced to take teaching jobs. Landlords with burgeoning property port-folios did not trouble to show military officers around the plusher apartments, assuming the rent to be beyond them. Mothers advised their daughters against military matches which would once have been considered highly prestigious. Militarism, guardian of the constitution, had lost out to materialism. The army duly decided that the national adventure in democracy had gone far enough. In 1960, the government of Adnan Menderes was overthrown by a military coup.

That day at the fishery happened to be the anniversary of the intervention, 27 May, a coincidence that no doubt crystal-lised the parallels between 1960 and the political situation at the time of my journey; a disgruntled military class was once again acting against a democratically elected government by accusing it of violating Atatürk's secular constitution through pandering to the Islamic constituency. There appeared to be a broad difference, of course, though it effectively came down to style; where they had once used tanks and soldiers the military were now relying upon a blatantly biddable judiciary to close down the ruling party and ban its leaders from politics. Turks knew that the land's highest court was to rule on the case later that summer and many feared the outcome. Any closure of *Ak* would cause public outrage, but if the case against the governing party was dismissed, then it was possible that a thwarted mili-tary might be provoked into more direct intervention. Nobody was about to forget the army's form in this regard, nor the fate that had befallen Turkey's first democratically elected prime minister, Adnan Menderes, whom they had hanged along with two of his leading ministers in 1961.

*

The last regulator lay a few hundred metres below the fishery. The difference with this one, however, was that the river beyond it was full of water. I assembled my canoe with practised ease beneath the wide road bridge where cattle took the shade.

The river's recovery appeared miraculous; the explanation, in fact, lay not in the supernatural but in nature, as it had always done. A close look revealed no current whatsoever. Physical law dictated that the waters flowed through the low-lying delta, effectively a sump, only when the upstream river brought to bear the brimful force of its falling weight to flush out the lower reaches, something the dams, regulators and irrigation schemes had combined comprehensively to prevent. With only puddles at its back, and all out of incline, the Meander had done its running.

The greater marvel of the water, deep through these final flatlands, was its sudden clarity; the river bubbled and flashed with fish, and at last the inelegant turtles were back. They basked in the sun, the wavelets nudging their black shells where they protruded beyond the compacted platforms of rotted canes at the foot of the reed stands. Out on the open reaches of the river, where a stiff sea wind raised the waves to little hackles, progress was slow. I kept to the shaded shelter of the high reeds, reaching between the curving banks where the fallen seed husks dusted the still water. In one cleared break lay a dinghy piled high with nets, the floss-like filament weighted by a pair of slender-bladed oars, while an old carpet lay draped across the seat at the square stern; it was the first working boat I had seen on the river since my arrival at the fish farm at Gökgöl – on my very first day in the canoe.

A first glimpse of ruins – nothing more than a low ridge of rubble that a few rising courses, once walls, at least did something to substantiate – prompted me to put ashore; from my beginnings at Dinar I had now reached the city, once the greatest in all the Greek world, at the other end of the Meander. Only as I closed on the ridge did more of Miletus come into view; these were prestigious civic additions of the Roman period – a colonnaded agora, the intact platforms of temples, a monumental baths complex – which had initially been beyond my view precisely because of their low-lying position. Where they stood, below the elevated promontory site of the earlier Ionian city, the sea had formerly lapped.

In the centuries immediately prior to the time of Christ, however, those waters had grown increasingly shallow; they had then thickened into alluvial flats, as they had already done to choking effect at other delta cities like Myus and Priene. It was as if the standard concerns of the modern port city had been reversed; as the citizens of Venice now laboured to raise defences against the sea's advance, so the Milesians had once built to keep pace with its retreat. If Miletus was to preserve its port status, the mainstay of its wealth, the city was obliged to retain its waterfront, which it did from the fifth century BC by progressively relocating to the plain. It was hard, however, to keep pace with the silt, which advanced some twenty feet every year, as it would continue to do until the 1950s, and by the second century BC the port's approaches were peppered with hazardous shallows. The waters around Miletus were turning to mud and extensive dredging was required if the city's harbour was not to go the way of Myus, abandoned in its malarial marsh.

It was a natural process, but to a port it was natural as death, and the sophist who had rhapsodised over the landscape's transformation – the harsh calls of the mariner giving way to the melodious notes of the shepherd's pipe – must have had interests in agriculture rather than in trade or shipping. Otherwise he might have taken a less pastoral line in describing how it was that 'the great maritime city of the archaic period, mistress of the Aegean and birthplace of science and philosophy', found herself knee-deep in the Meander's evacuated soils. As Vesuvius had buried Pompeii beneath its ash, so the river had shat the great port unto death.

I made my way through the tamarisks and grazing sheep to the shallow depression that had once been the city's harbour, reflecting as I went that many of those already encountered on my journey, individuals and peoples alike, had also been at Miletus: Freya Stark and Patrick Kinross, of course, and a century before them the treasure hunters who had removed the city's prize antiquities to Berlin, and in their time early antiquaries such as Chandler and Pococke; the Turks who built their mosque from the Romans' stones in the fifteenth century, as the Byzantines had built their castle above the theatre before them; St Paul, who summoned the neighbouring Ephesians to Miletus to hear his goodbyes before he continued towards Jerusalem where he was to face arrest, denunciation and eventual deportation to martyrdom in Rome; Alexander, who subdued Miletus before continuing on a journey that would lead him to Celaenae, Gordium and the conquest of all Asia; Xerxes' Persian forces on their retreat from Salamis in 479 BC; and fifteen years earlier the Persians of King Darius whose more successful battle fleets in 494 BC had defeated the forces of the Ionian Revolt off the island shores of Lade, now a hillock in the delta plain, before razing the rebels' promontory capital.

For Miletus's heyday, however, I was required to spool back to the city that stood here roughly a century before Darius punished its insurrection with that vengeful sack. In the sixth century BC this terminus of the Meander Valley trade route, hub of an extensive network of colonies, and producer of its own highly prized speciality vines and wools, was accounted the first city of the Aegean world. Posterity was to remember Miletus, however, not for its commercial prosperity but for more durable achievements in the artistic and intellectual spheres – and largely for a citizen called Thales.

Thales appears to have lived between about 620 BC and 550 BC. None of his writings survive; what we know of this geometrician, astronomer and philosopher derives from the posthumous acknowledgements his example was to elicit from such illustrious successors as Herodotus and latterly Aristotle. Many of the stories associated with Thales certainly seem constructed from the usual recycled spoil of legend, with no footing in reliable fact, which is not to say that the central achievement widely attributed to this shadowy ancient should simply be dismissed. Thales is commonly celebrated as the source of rational inquiry; he is credited with first positing the revolutionary notion that natural process rather than divine action might be behind the shaping of phenomena. Thales' reflections on the nature and substance of matter challenged an old order which, ignorant as to inquiry's value in bettering the world, had never thought to look for causes beyond the arbitrary waving of the deity's wand.

For a man known only vicariously, such grand claims may appear grossly inflated. It may be that he is more compellingly evidenced, however, not in the subsequent commendations of Herodotus and his like but rather in the very fact of the exceptional crop of geniuses whom Thales' example appears to have inspired in the decades after his death: the historian of Halicarnassus himself, of course, Herodotus, who told it as men told him; Hippocrates of Kos, first to believe that diseases might have natural rather than divine causes; Heraclitus of Ephesus,

who surmised that the universe was defined by change and
opposition; the original mathematician Pythagoras of Samos; and
Hippodamus, himself of Miletus, credited with originating the
city grid and urban planning in general. It happens, as the map
reveals, that the home cities of these scientists and philosophers,
proto-rationalists all, are oriented in a compellingly compact
seaward circle around Miletus; they serve to place Thales at the
eye – and so make him the very cause – of the singular ripple
that spread to revolutionise the intellectual outlook of the region
in the immediate aftermath of his death. By his example Thales
delivered mankind, in the words of Freya Stark, 'into the world
of Athens and Augustine and Dante and Stratford and Rome';
all cities and men, ironically, from those western lands beyond
the sea that would one day be known as Europe.

The Thales legends tout a composite portrait in which a
broad wisdom is prominent. The distinguished man of Miletus
is canny and worldly, if not also prone to the stock distractions
and pitfalls common to genius. His main virtue may be said,
however, to be an absolute faith in the value of observation; a
unarguable starting point in the pursuit of reason. Herodotus
wrote roughly a century after Thales' death how the venerated
Milesian had been the first to predict a solar eclipse. A century
later still Aristotle made less, however, of that celestial *coup de
théâtre* and more of Thales' conclusions as to the comparatively
stealthy processes at work beneath his feet. For in seeking to
know the basic nature of matter Thales came to believe that it
all derived from a single substance, which was water.

The ancient Babylonians had long established wetness at the
heart of their own cosmogony. Where, however, they imagined
the universe had begun when the great divinity, perhaps with a
nudge from its magic wand, had stirred some inert primordial
sludge into life, Thales sensed that the miracle was inherent in

water itself. Moisture self-evidently gave life to seeds. Water was brimful with life.

These were general perceptions, even if they were remarkable for the sixth century BC, but it may be suggested that the transforming catalyst was the particular setting in which they took place. For at Miletus, exceptionally if not uniquely, Thales was privy to an extraordinary phenomenon – one we now recognise as alluviation – whereby water appeared to metamorphose into earth itself. In its season and from inland came the brown swirl that resolved with every passing year into drying earth. This inconvenient alchemy was evident in the grumblings of grounded ships' captains, and in the way old men spoke of lifetimes observing the shores thicken around the gulf and its islands. Thales saw how water turned to mud and thence to earth, and the very land solidified out of the water on which it floated.

The Meander's alluvial spews were eventually to engulf great Miletus, but not before their inexorable workings had set a man of the city on his intellectual course, his thoughts flawed but free, so that men first raised science above their idols. Miletus, we may even speculate, was not so much lost as sacrificed for the lasting benefit of humanity; the very process that did for the city showed one of its citizens where our minds might go and what they might truly do. As gravity began in an apple orchard, so reason itself was born by the Meander's silting mouth.

Halil Özbaşı was wrong about the Yörüks. I found a last family of them by the stones of the old harbour, like those first wild Turcomans who had pitched their tents in the war-racked ruins of Dorylaeum. They were a ragged couple, dark with the sun, who busied themselves with gathering up the shorn fleeces of their flock and piling them on a brown tarpaulin slicked with lanolin. Their son, twelve years old, straddled a prone sheep.

He had tripped it by the marble lion, once a proud mark of the harbour entrance but now sunk so low in the silt that only its eroded mane protruded. The boy worked with an old pair of iron shears, deftly squeezing the sprung blades so that the fleece fell away intact, and at the last he ran the shears, lovingly, along the sheep's brow. Then he threw the tool aside and stood, and the sheep rose from its fallen fleece and stumbled free, and the boy wiped his own brow and looked about him. A flock of bee-eaters, yellow and red, passed low overhead.

I made my way to the great baths complex, which the Empress Faustina had commissioned in the first century. Beneath high walls the baths were open to the blue sky. In the frigidarium, where bathers had once plunged into the cold waters of a low square pool, I came at last across the god of the river. For here at the head of the pool a bearded, muscular Meander reclined, naked but for the sheet slung loosely at his navel. I might have acknowledged the deity whose river I had followed from the source if a nearby sign had not declared him an impostor; it was a concrete cast of the statue that had once stood here. So I turned away and walked out to the road.

CHAPTER TWENTY-FOUR

That evening a *dolmuş* delivered me to Didim. The town, some fifteen kilometres south of Miletus, had grown up around the ancient temple of Didyma. This name replaced Yeronda, a corruption of the Greek word for temple, as the almost exclusively Christian population had known the place. The ruins of elegant Rum houses, classical and compact beneath the sagging loads of their tiled hip roofs, still lined the edges of the temple enclosure.

The Turks had generally kept their distance from the place they called infidel Yoran. From 1922, however, they were free to make the town their own. In recent years they had transformed it into a sprawling tourist resort. The consequence was that it once more attracted a largely infidel population, albeit one condemned to occupy rather less appealing homes than those of their Christian predecessors. Turkish developers, rushing to beat the breaking crest of Europe's holiday property boom, had raised a miserable thicket of concrete apartment blocks across the town. Many of these blocks stood empty in their fresh plots, the windows plastered with discounted prices and telephone numbers, and the first stains already showing up the poverty of the workmanship. On a few balconies bicycles and barbecue sets had appeared, and the replica T-shirts of English football teams flew from the washing lines. The streets brimmed with estate agents, hotels and tourist restaurants.

Around the archaeological site the developers had been kept

at bay. By the temple I pushed my way through the gate of a simple *pansiyon* where an old man was dozing on a patio beneath an awning of vine-clad corrugated iron. Ahmet Heart waved me in the direction of his son, Mahmut, who showed me upstairs to my room.

'Basic,' Mahmut conceded gravely. 'But I dare say you'll enjoy the view.' From the window I looked over a vast stepped platform where a walled edifice was set within a peristyle of broad columns; much of this stone thicket, 120 columns in all, had been reduced to truncated stubs though a surviving trio, intact unto their scrolled capitals, a pair even bearing a section of architrave, conjured the structure in all its original splendour.

Didyma was among the greatest temples of the ancient world. From roughly the eighth century BC until the Byzantines officially established Christianity in the fourth century visitors came here in search of answers. They sought divine counsel from the god of prophecy. The familiar old martinet of the upper Meander, he who had flayed Marsyas for his presumption and bent the hapless Lairbenes to his will, had turned up again. Along these shores, however, he controlled rather by the power of oracular utterance. Apollo's coastal business was in analysing risk; with nineteen major oracular outlets along Anatolia's Aegean shores and with another ten in Greece, his was a lucrative and influential franchise.

The Anatolians were the horoscope readers of their day, a weakness Apollo had long since learned to exploit. A consequence of his success was that he no longer deigned to serve the humbler sorts, leaving them to rely instead upon the value-brand utterances of the street-corner opportunists – their divinations based on dice throws or the inspection of the entrails of chickens lately surprised by, and prised from, the wheel rims of passing carts – when it came to deciding, for example, whether the time had come to sell the family cow. Prestigious Apollonian institutions like Didyma targeted weightier pockets and the concerns that came with them.

The oracle at Didyma, whose priesthood claimed descent from an honoured favourite of Apollo's, stood within an extensive precinct where the temple, the various ceremonial buildings and the initiates' quarters were arranged among sacred laurel groves. Didyma's lavish scale served to remind its clients that they must pay top whack to keep the oracles on side; generous retainer payments would not only guarantee clients preferential access to advice but might even advantageously influence the very futures on which the oracles pronounced.

The oracle boasted a varied client list, not least the nearby city of Miletus, which was linked with Didyma by a paved, colonnaded and statue-lined Sacred Way. The Milesians no doubt considered themselves the oracle's preferred sponsors, though that special relationship was not exclusive; it certainly did not prevent Apollo's agents from mining a wider seam of high-grade clients. Prominent among these was Croesus, proverbially wealthy king of neighbouring Lydia, whose exceptional largesse further contributed to Didyma's swollen coffers.

Oracles like Didyma were considered, even so, to have earned every last coin of their considerable wealth, not least because the issues on which they were commonly consulted – on affairs of state or of international geopolitics – were often so complex as to tax even the supposedly omniscient Apollo. The oracular science, as even clients appeared to acknowledge, was not always exact, and Croesus commonly hedged his position by retaining the services of a range of oracles.

The Lydian king certainly needed all the help he could get. It was Croesus's fate that he should have been beset by the political, diplomatic and strategic burdens of kingship at a time of particular foment; not for him the intellectual musings that his close contemporary, Thales of Miletus, was free to entertain. Croesus found himself confronted, in fact, with the defining dilemma of the age: what was he to do about the Persian power rising to threaten him in the east? After an exhaustive selection process the Lydian king went to the oracle that by general consent outranked even Didyma – Greek Delphi – to ask whether he should deploy his Lydian armies against the Persians. Delphi's apparently encouraging advice was that Croesus would thereby destroy a great empire; the empire that the king duly destroyed in a series of engagements during 546 BC famously turned out to be his own.

By that fateful decision Anatolia was first exposed to the foreign subjection it would endure for millennia; it was also, of course, a personal disaster for Croesus, who felt let down, stiffed even, by a deity who was supposed to be on the payroll. Delphic Apollo's flagrant disingenuousness hardly seemed like a fair return for the patronage Croesus had lavished upon the Greek oracle. In the welter of recriminations Delphi was repeatedly obliged to remind its client where ultimate responsibility always lay. For all these attempts to absolve itself of blame, Delphi's reputation did not appear to escape unscathed; certainly, the next embassy of note steered clear of the oracle for its advice and went instead to the one at Didyma. The issue in this case was a particularly knotty one, which had arisen, it happened, out of events leading directly from Croesus's defeat at the hands of the Persians.

With the fall of Lydia, Croesus's Persian conquerors immediately set about establishing their new authority over the conquered lands. Focused as they were on territorial objectives in the distant East, however, the Persians mistakenly apportioned key administrative posts to Lydians who were not yet ready, as they soon proved, to be ruled by Persians. Chief among the promoted natives was one Pactyas who, entrusted with crating up and delivering the brimful Lydian treasury into Persian hands, instead began distributing its contents among the mercenary army that he promptly raised to restore Croesus's Lydian empire.

All might have been well, of course, if only the patriotic Pactyas had been able to win over an effective coalition of what he naïvely supposed to be like-minded neighbours, not least in Ionia, to join his insurrection against the Persians. The problem was that many of the coastal city states, alive to the precariousness of their predicaments, had already sought terms with the new power, and though they had mostly been rebuffed, very few of them could be persuaded to declare against the all-conquering Easterners. In no time Pactyas found himself faced by the advance of a Persian army intent this time on fixing Lydia more firmly into place, and liquidating the ringleaders in the process. The failed rebel fled north to the Aegean port of Cyme where he was promptly followed by Persian envoys demanding his surrender.

It was the people of Cyme who now dispatched their embassy not to Delphi, freshly discredited by the fallout following the loss of their account with Croesus, but to Didyma. How, they asked Apollo, should they respond to this moral dilemma? Should the city violate the fugitive's sanctuary rights by abandoning Pactyas to the Persians? Or should it rather honour them and thereby risk the wrath of precisely the power with whom it had recently sought an accommodation? Apollo's oracle at Didyma replied that the Lydian fugitive should be surrendered.

The answer was refreshingly unequivocal; it came even so as such a surprise, sanctuary being an inviolable right, that some in Cyme thought the oracle's words must be falsely reported. A second embassy, led by a Cymean citizen called Aristodicus, returned to Didyma to confirm for themselves the oracle's answer. On receipt of the same response, and in defiance of protocol, Aristodicus casually wandered off among Didyma's sacred laurel trees to remove the baby chicks he found nesting there. Over much cheeping and the gasps of scandalised priests a booming voice demanded to know how the impious Aristodicus dared to interfere with creatures within the confines of the divine sanctuary. Aristodicus airily replied that since Apollo was so ready to protect those in his care, it might be asked how he could command the citizens of Cyme to give up the man in theirs.

It was a good retort; even the exalted gods, it seemed, could find themselves in predicaments like the Cymeans. In fact, Apollo's position was especially compromised since Didyma's coffers, stuffed with Croesus's gold, naturally obliged the oracle to declare in support of the Lydian patriot who meant to restore Croesus; the problem was that Didyma had also run up a substantial tab with Miletus, and Miletus had already reached a settlement with the Persians, which it would not suffer the local oracle to jeopardise.

It was left to the Cymeans to figure for themselves that they might just have sufficient steerage to slip between both civic dishonour and Persian offence – by the tried expedient of passing the buck. The citizens shipped Pactyas off to the island of Mytilene until the fugitive's position became as uncomfortable there, when they removed him to nearby Chios. The Chians had been already sweetened, however, by land rights the Persians dangled before them. The Chians took it upon themselves to drag the rebel Lydian from sanctuary in a local temple and to deliver him up. We may only imagine how the Persians dealt with the wretched Pactyas; it is recorded that they certainly showed no mercy to the few cities that had called it wrong by backing his failed revolt. The Persians sacked the towns of Priene and Magnesia, and enslaved their citizens. They then pillaged the plain of the lower Meander.

The incident revealed the seamy web of loyalties and obligations in which even Apollo could be snared. It perhaps even hinted at a secret from the god's deep past. In the Greek tradition Apollo was born in the sanctified light of Delos in the Cyclades. In fact, the god's true origins were not Greek but Anatolian and in ages past, as Aplu and Apaliunas, Apollo had served such Bronze Age Anatolians as the Arzawans and Hittites. He had form, moreover, when it came to taking the Eastern side; Homer had cast the god in the *Iliad* as the enemy of the Greeks, divine sponsor of the Trojans. Even Apollo could find himself in the classic Anatolian bind; here on the world's cusp the question, as ever, was where one belonged and where one's loyalties lay.

'My people were Muslims from Macedonia,' Ahmet Heart explained. 'They came from a village near the port of Kavala.'

We sat among the potted geraniums and the ancient temple stones on the patio of Ahmet's *pansiyon*. In his old age Ahmet had turned slight. His speech was gummy, his beard grizzled and his blue eyes were rheumy. His trousers hung slack from his braces and he wore a thick shirt against a chill I did not feel. He had been here for a long time.

'They were tobacco farmers from a coastal village called Kuçkar. The first thing they knew of the exchanges was when the Christian refugees from Anatolia started arriving in the area during 1923. These arrivals were poor and ill. They had nothing. My people gave some of them jobs. They wondered why these refugees had been sent to them; they gradually realised that these were the people who would take their houses once they were forced to leave. So it came about the new arrivals in turn told the locals of the lives that they could expect in Turkey.'

The prospects were appalling. Much of western Anatolia had been destroyed in the course of the Greek forces' retreat to Smyrna. Infant mortality rates stood at 80 per cent. Food supplies were pitifully short. Tuberculosis, malaria and dysentery were endemic. The local Turks had already taken possession of any surviving buildings; the Muslim arrivals from Greece were often reduced to settling in wreckage. They made their homes in derelict German-built train carriages abandoned in station sidings. A witness in Smyrna saw them 'at every step lodged in excavations, in the cellars of burned houses, under temporary roofs made of pieces of sheet iron supported on stones'. Nine hundred refugees were in one instance dispatched to new lives in Söke; within a year 250 of them were dead.

The people of Kuçkar were braced for a hellish future when they surrendered their papers at the gangplank of a Turkish ship that steamed out of Kavala one day in 1924. But they were to be lucky. On their arrival at the little port of Mavişehir they found that camels had been supplied to transport them and their possessions to the nearby town where their new lives were to begin. The town happened to lie, moreover, beyond the scorched line of the Greek forces' retreat. The Turks for their part had certainly looted and desecrated this Rum settlement where 'torn account books lay scattered about among fragments of bottles and debris of all sorts' in the shops and taverns, and 'everything was smashed, torn, trampled upon' in the school. The houses were 'littered with wrecked boxes, ripped-up mattresses, broken floors', with 'cupboards, sofas, shelves and broken petroleum lamps; children's toys, sewing machines, gramophone records and household utensils'. In the churchyard trunks lay empty, the lids ripped away and the locks pilfered.

The church itself had been reduced to 'heaps of boards, seats, ornaments, ikons, crosses, lamps, lecterns, all in pieces and thrown about anyhow'.

But the refugees, who had feared the worst, saw that much could be put right. The new arrivals were even able to select for themselves houses in which 'a good deal of the furniture was still in position'. One couple, newly married, chose to make their home hard by the huge piles of temple stones and columns in the middle of the town and set about making Turks of themselves. The following year their son was born in the house where he was to live all of his life. They called him Ahmet. The same Ahmet, born in the third year of the Turkish Republic, raised a bony finger and pointed to the wall where a framed photograph showed a view, beyond vineyards and country lanes, of a little town before a blue Macedonian sea.

'I won't get to Kuçkar now,' said Ahmet. 'But it may be that my son will.' He gestured that he wished to sleep. As we parted, I was overcome by a powerful valedictory sense. It was as if the old man had finally led me out of Anatolia's colourful but brutal past to emerge into a peaceful if prosaic present. The trade seemed like a good one. I left Ahmet dozing in the shade and, stepping out into the bright sun of summer, I blended with the hatted tourists as they made their way among the courts and colonnades of the great temple.

In the morning I returned to Miletus. The site was deserted and the eucalypts hung motionless in the still air. Outside the half-built museum stood the arrayed marbles – carved lions, friezes, capitals – which were to be exhibited there. Among them the original Meander reclined in magnificent ease beside a watchman's ancient motorbike. I thought of the distance I had come and thanked the river god for keeping me safe. Laying my hand on the statue's shoulder, warm in the returning sun, I particularly thought of the kindness and courtesy I had experienced among these barbarians. At no point had anybody threatened me or barred my progress; they had only wished that I might drink tea with them or take up their offer of a lift. They had befriended me, bought me meals and put me up, and generally treated me to exceptional hospitality. I now wondered if I was the beneficiary of a historical debt – if it was precisely the same kindness that their arriving forebears had once received that they in turn showed to strangers like me. Whatever the answer, Anatolia had turned out to be my ark, as it had also been theirs.

It felt odd, even so, all this kindness in a blood-soaked land. The hope was that the warring was finally done and all the people I had met would live out their lives in a peace the Meander Valley had rarely known. It might be that these Turks would never know where they belonged in the wider world, would never quite choose between Europe and Asia, but would learn instead that they were cursed and blessed to live between them. It certainly seemed that the Turks had freed themselves from the threat of invasion, which left them to work out the considerable contradictions that existed among and even within themselves. There were worse things, certainly, than peace and the politics, however fraught, which preserved it.

I walked past the old stones and came down to the river for the last time. I clambered into the canoe and pushed off. Swallows swooped to pluck the water's stiff surface and my strokes sounded clear in the silence. The land lay low now; across the salt flats flamingos stood on bamboo-thin legs among the clumps of samphire. An early sports fisherman was chewing on sunflower seeds beside his planted rod.

'Where have you come from?' he greeted me. And when I told him the man's eyes flared.

'By God, that's something!' he exclaimed. 'Not far now!'

The widening river now appeared to merge with the vast blue sky. From either bank there rose the reed walls and roofs of motley shacks, and water dripped from the frayed tethers of the fishing boats. In the soft sunshine weathered men mended their nets beneath the vertical plumes of cigarettes, raising lazy hands to me.

I could now see the scored line where the first wave broke at the river mouth. Beyond it rose the low outline of the Aegean islet that Greeks and Turks alike knew as Donkey Island. Out on a final sand spit a washed-up traffic sign, an injunction against overtaking, had been planted in the sand. As I paddled onto the Aegean, at the end of 500 horizontal kilometres and one vertical one, my canoe shied at the unfamiliar notion of the long swell and I gave its battered gunwale a reassuring pat of gratitude. Then I pulled out the little tablet jar, sniffed at its garlic-scented memories, raised it above my head and poured the source water into the salt.

I turned to face the way I had come. All up the long valley of the Meander the morning sun was hazing the mountains. The flamingos lifted in a line. As I paddled past the reed shacks the Turks invited me to join them for tea.

EPILOGUE

A few days later Turkey's constitutional court cancelled the amendment that would have opened the way for women to wear headscarves in public offices. It subsequently ruled that the *Ak* Party had violated the secular principle enshrined within the constitution.

A month later still the same court convened to decide on what was to be done with *Ak*. Of the eleven judges six voted to close down the party; a majority, but where a qualified majority – seven out of eleven – was required. *Ak* received a substantial fine but was permitted to continue in office. Many Turks were relieved by an outcome which averted a judicial coup while fostering the convenient impression that the old secularists continued to retain something of their former authority; many considered the result so fortuitous, in fact, that they suspected it had not been arrived at by chance. In the meantime the investigations into *Ergenekon*, that shadowy cadre of secular activists, continued.

The year had not run its course before the people of the Meander Valley noticed something unusual; the winter rains were heavier than many of them had known. These rains persisted. Rivulets poured off the drenched heights above Pınarbaşı to swell the springs along the foot of Samsun Dağı. They brimmed down the ditches of Dinar. Beneath black skies the lakes at Gökgöl and Işıklı rose to their brims, and spuming torrents clattered through the dam gates where Mehmet, concealing his hair loss beneath a woollen cap, had pushed my canoe out onto the stagnant shallows. By Kavak the river had burst its banks, and the farmstead and orchards of the Fearless family were flooded out. The waters lapped at the fringes of the Skirmishers' farm and thundered past the old watermills below Aşağı Seyit. All along the deep gorge at the base of Çökelez Mountain they boiled, and passed below the temple of Apollo Lairbenos to pour into the lonely lake of the waterskiing blonde. Onwards they swirled into the newly built dam at Çindere.

This empty dam, a welcome sump, was able to absorb vast quantities of water. It could do nothing, however, about the rains that had fallen quite as heavily along the lower valley. In spiralling slicks the water slid through the regulator gates at Feslek. By Kuyucak it had breasted the banks and poured out across all the wide plain. It inundated the old bridge at Sarıkemer and spilled into Bafa Lake, raising the waters there by several metres. At the *dalyan* Adem Thunderbolt, hopeful for mullet, found himself knee-deep in water. At Miletus there was so much water, all stirred with silt, that it was as if the sea had returned and all was back as it had been before this story began.

CHRONOLOGY AND CAST

A regional timeline, with explanatory notes on historical and mythical participants.

6000 BC: The Neolithic cave paintings found on Beşparmak (Mount Latmus) have been dated roughly to this period.

2700 BC: Rise of the Minoan Civilisation in Crete. Emergence of ancient Anatolian fertility deity, **Cybele**, the forerunner of **Artemis of the Ephesians** and characterised by pendulous and multiple dugs.

2000 BC: Rise of a civilisation, tentatively identified as Arzawa, in western Anatolia.

1800 BC: Emergence of the Hittites in Central Anatolia.

1700 BC: Sack of the Arzawan palace at Beycesultan.

1300 BC: Wars between Trojans and Greeks. Emergence of Olympian/Anatolian deities including **Apollo**, god of music and prophecy; **Marsyas**, satyr and virtuoso pipe player; and **Endymion**, a beautiful shepherd of Mount Latmus seduced by the moon goddess.

1000 BC: Gradual colonisation of Anatolia's shores, especially the mid-Aegean – Ionia – by mainland Greeks.

800 BC: Rise of Phrygian Empire in central Anatolia under the legendary **Midas**, who was given asses' ears by Apollo as a

punishment for championing the pipe playing of Marsyas, and further chastised for his foolish greed when the gods granted him the golden touch. Midas is supposedly related to the mythical **Lityerses**, a Meander Valley deity notorious for killing his harvesters.

600 BC: Miletus celebrated as commercial and cultural centre of the Aegean world, and home to residents such as the scientist, philosopher and proto-rationalist **Thales**.

580 BC: Apogee of the Lydian Empire under **King Croesus**, byword for inordinate wealth.

546 BC: Defeat of Croesus by the Persians after the Lydian King misinterprets the advice of the Delphic Oracle. The beginning of Persian rule in Anatolia.

(?)545 BC: Attempt by **Pactyas**, a Lydian, to lead a revolt against Persian rule. On his flight to Cyme the citizens of that Aegean port ask the oracle at Didyma whether to honour the Lydian's request for protection.

499 BC: The Ionian Revolt against Persian rule.

494 BC: End of Ionian Revolt and the sack of Miletus.

c.490 BC: Birth in Halicarnassus of **Herodotus**, so-called Father of History.

481 BC: Persian invasion force under **King Xerxes** at Celaenae, and his meeting there with **Pythius**, a Lydian, who thinks to curry favour with the King by offering him his entire fortune.

480 BC: Xerxes crosses the Hellespont into Greece. Heroic Spartan defence at Thermopylae. Defeat of Persian fleet at Salamis.

479 BC: Further Persian defeats at Plataea and Mycale.

460 BC: Persian defeat at the Battle of Eurymedon.

401 BC: The anabasis, or expedition, of a Persian prince, **Cyrus the Younger**, and his 'Ten Thousand' Greek mercenaries passes through Celaenae en route for the East. After the prince's death near Baghdad it is **Xenophon**, an Athenian, who takes the lead – at least according to the *Anabasis*, his own eyewitness account of their heroic retreat to the Black Sea.

334 BC: **Alexander the Great**, King of Macedonia, passes through Celaenae en route for Gordium and an encounter with a legendary knot. He conquers all Asia, bringing to an end Persian rule in Anatolia.

312–188 BC: A Hellenistic dynasty, the Seleucids, rule the region. At the Peace of Apamea (188 BC) all western Anatolia is ceded to Pergamum, a client state of Rome, which progressively extends its administrative influence across the Hellenised region.

47: **St Paul** makes his first missionary journey, visiting Antioch in Pisidia, Iconium, Lystra and Derbe.

60: Earthquake flattens Hierapolis, Laodicea and Colossae.

c.100: Progressive silting of Meander Delta cities including Miletus, Priene and Myus.

c.200: Christian conversion at its height in Phrygia.

312: Legalisation of Christianity across the Roman world.

324: Adoption of the city on the Bosphorus – the newly named Constantinople – as the Eastern Roman Emperor's new capital announces the Byzantine Empire.

542: **Bishop John of Ephesus** persecutes pagan communities in the Meander Valley.

650–750: Raids by Muslim Saracens into Anatolia. Pergamum besieged in 717. At around the same time Turkish tribes begin their long migration west from the lands surrounding the Gobi Desert.

1045: Raids by Selçuk Turks and Turcomans reach the Lycus Valley.

1071: Defeat of the Byzantines by the Turks at Manzikert, eastern Anatolia.

1097: Knights of the First Crusade defeat the Turks at Dorylaeum. Establishment of Selçuk Turkish Sultanate with capital at Konya (Iconium).

1145: Turks raid west as far as the Aegean.

1146: Byzantine Emperor **Manuel Comnenus** skirmishes with Turcomans at the head of the Meander.

1148: Knights of the Second Crusade under **Louis VII** defeat the Turks by the Meander. They then suffer a major reverse in the mountains above Laodicea en route to the Mediterranean port of Adalia.

1176: Defeat of Byzantines by the Turks at Myriocephalon.

c.1200: Increased fear among settled Turks and Byzantines alike of unruly Turcoman raiders.

1282: Sack of Nysa and Tralles by Turkish clan chief **Menteşe**.

c.1300: Eclipse of Selçuk Turks and gradual rise from the competing Turkish clans of the Ottomans.

1453: Fall of Constantinople to the Turks. End of Byzantine Empire.

1529: Siege of Vienna. The pinnacle of Ottoman imperial power.

1683: Second siege of Vienna, marking the beginning of the Ottomans' decline.

1682: **George Wheler's** *Journey Into Greece*, among the first of many Western accounts of travels in Anatolia, is published.

c.1740: **Richard Pococke's** exploration of the Meander Valley and the surrounding region's ancient sites coincides with the rise of European neoclassicism. Another antiquary, **Richard Chandler**, follows in 1765.

1821: The Greek War of Independence focuses European prejudices against Turks. Over the next century the loss of further Ottoman territories in the Balkans, the Crimea and the Caucasus triggers a flood of Muslim refugees into Anatolia.

1826: **Reverend Francis Arundell** identifies the site of Celaenae-Apamea. Other scholars and antiquaries, among them **William Hamilton** and **Charles Fellows**, subsequently publish accounts of their travels in and around the Meander Valley.

c.1830: Outlaw zeybeks, popular rebels against Ottoman authority, rife in the Meander Valley. **Bald Mehmet** heads a local insurrection near Kuyucak.

1856: A British company begins to build Turkey's first railway line up the Meander Valley, connecting Smyrna with Aydın.

1911–12: Ottoman–Italian War in Libya.

1912–13: Balkan Wars between Ottomans and a coalition of Greeks, Bulgarians and Serbians.

1915–17: Caucasus Campaign against the Russians. Among the deserters is **Yörük Ali**, a peasant of the Meander Valley.

1915: Defence of the Gallipoli Peninsula against Allied invasion forces where **Colonel Mustafa Kemal** distinguishes himself.

1918: Surrender of the Ottomans to the Allies.

1919: Treaty negotiations at Sèvres, Paris, where the dismemberment of Anatolia among the victorious powers is proposed.

15 May 1919: 13,000 Greek forces land at Smyrna.

19 May 1919: Mustafa Kemal leaves Constantinople to lead the nationalist resistance in Anatolia.

27 May 1919: Greek forces occupy Aydın.

27 June–4 July 1919: Battle for Aydın where the Turkish zeybek bands are under the command of Yörük Ali.

1919–21: Greek forces advance east to threaten the Turkish nationalists' capital at Ankara. In August 1921 their advance is finally halted.

August 1922: The Turkish counter-offensive routs the Greeks, who fall back on Smyrna, which the Turks take in September.

1923: Turkey is reborn as a republic under the leadership of Mustafa Kemal, who will take the surname **Atatürk**. For the next fifteen years the country is radically Westernised.

1923–4: Anatolia's Greek Christians, more than a million, are forcibly exchanged with Greece's Muslims.

1938: Death of Atatürk.

1950: Election of **Adnan Menderes**' Democratic Party.

1960: Overthrow of Menderes, who is executed by command of a military tribunal in 1961. Further military interventions follow every decade or so.

2007: The Islamic party, *Ak*, wins a commanding majority in Turkey's national elections. In 2008 it is fined for attempting to undermine Atatürk's secular constitution but remains in power.

2008–9: Record rains cause floods along the Meander Valley.

Notes

The author's name and complete title of the work are given with the first citation of any source. In subsequent mentions titles are referenced by the author's surname; where the author is responsible for multiple titles, short forms are given for each title. Where not otherwise specified, page references are taken from the editions given in the bibliography: in the case of classical titles traditional references to books/chapters/verses/lines are also given. Preface page references are given in Roman numerals. FO (Foreign Office) files are held at the National Archives, Kew.

PROLOGUE

p. 2 **a particularly mazy stretch of the Nile**: 'the Nile here is winding like the Maeander'; Herodotus, *Histories*, 2.29 (vol 1, p. 307).

pp. 2–3 **'running in a direction excessively tortuous . . .'**: Strabo, *Geography*, 12.8.15 (vol. 2, p. 333).

p. 3 **a prodigious range of contexts**: see the various usages of the word given in the *Shorter Oxford English Dictionary*.

p. 3 **'soft Meander's wanton current'**: Ovid, *Metamorphoses*, 8.162 (Garth-Tonson translation).

CHAPTER 1

p. 11 **The climb from the coastlands . . .**: 'Nowhere else is the transition so abrupt'; Ronald Syme and Anthony Richard Birley, *Anatolica*, p. 17.

p. 11 **'the public frequented road . . .'**: Strabo, 14.2.29 (vol. 3, p. 43).

p. 12 **Pythius**: Herodotus, 7.27–29 (vol. 3, pp. 341–5).

p. 12 **Strabo called 'illustrious persons'**: Strabo, 14.1.7 (vol. 3, p. 5).

p. 13 **'pasture lands of Celaenae'**: Timotheus, *Lyra Graeca*, vol. 3, p. 319.

p. 14 **their combined thirst . . .**: Herodotus, 7.21 (vol. 3, p. 335).

p. 16 **immortalised Xerxes' invasion march . . .**: Herodotus, books 7–9 (vol. 3, pp. 303–557, and vol. 4).

p. 18 **'the common staple for merchandise . . .'**: Strabo, 12.8.15 (vol. 2, p. 333).

p. 18 **Alexander had considered so strongly positioned . . .**: Arrian, *Anabasis of Alexander*, vol. 1, p. 119.

CHAPTER 2

p. 26 **'many difficulties in relation to the account . . .'**: Richard Pococke, *A Description of the East and Some Other Countries*, vol. 2, part 2, p. 80.

CHAPTER 3

p. 29 **the local history book he had written**: *Marsyas'in Ilinden* by Mehmet Özalp.

p. 31 **'lurking in the secret places'**: Nonnos, *Dionysiaca*, 11.379.

p. 34 **'We now perceived four men . . .'**: Richard Chandler, *Travels in Asia Minor*, p. 110.

p. 35 **mistakenly associated with Memnon's Colossus . . .**: George Bean, *Turkey Beyond the Maeander*, p. 257.

p. 35 **'What spaces yet remain unappropriated'**: Rev. F. V. J. Arundell, *Discoveries in Asia Minor*, vol. 1, p. viii.

p. 35 **'The reader can now form . . .'**: Arundell, *Discoveries*, vol. 1, p. 203.

p. 36 **'a point of great importance . . .'**: Colonel William Martin Leake, *Journal of a Tour in Asia Minor*, p. 163.

p. 36 **Celaenae's abundant ancient detailing**: D. G. Hogarth, 'Notes upon a Visit to Celaenae-Apamea', p. 343, calls it 'the best described site in Phrygia, and among the most remarkable whether by reason of legend, history or natural position'.

p. 37 **'There cannot be a stronger proof . . .'**: Leake, p. 156.

p. 37 **'opportunity of an onward caravan'** and **'a high hill . . . and a village . . .'**: Pococke, p. 79.

p. 37 **'precisely with that of Celaenae . . .'**: Leake, p. 156.

pp. 37–8 **'the ruins could be no other . . .'**: Arundell, *Discoveries*, vol. 1, p. 184.

p. 38 **'little doubt that Apamea and Celaenae . . .'**: J. A. Cramer, *Description of Asia Minor*, vol. 2, p. 51.

p. 38 **'After examining the whole of the country . . .'**: William Hamilton, *Researches in Asia Minor, Pontus and Armenia*, vol. 1, p. 499.

p. 38 'modern barbarism and desolation': Leake, p. iii.

p. 38 'As the most interesting period . . .': Charles Fellows, *A Journal Written During an Excursion in Asia Minor*, p. iii.

CHAPTER 4

p. 44 'bright and varied' scenery, and 'continuation of Central Asia, vast, immobile, monotonous': William Ramsay, *The Historical Geography of Asia Minor*, pp. 23–4.

p. 45 mouthpieces of flutes or pipes: Strabo, 12.8.15 (vol. 2, p. 334).

p. 48 'As he screams, his skin . . .': Ovid, 6.387–391 (vol. 1, p. 315 of Miller translation).

p. 48 had a judge flayed . . .: Herodotus, 5.25 (vol. 3, p. 27).

p. 49 The hide remained on display . . .: Herodotus, 7.26 (vol. 3, p. 341).

p. 50 'large inscribed column thrown from its base': Hamilton, vol. 2, p. 364.

p. 56 here had stood 'the very market-place of Celaenae': Herodotus, 7.26 (vol. 3, p. 341).

p. 57 a shepherd was digging at Dereköy . . .: *Monumenta Asiae Minoris Antiqua* (MAMA), vol. 4, p. xii.

p. 58 'Cataract': Herodotus, 7.26 (vol. 3, p. 341).

p. 58 'the clearest river in all Phrygia': Ovid, 6.400 (vol. 1, p. 317 of Miller translation).

p. 58 'at the foot of a precipitous cliff . . .': D. G. Hogarth, 'Notes Upon a Visit to Celaenae-Apamea', p. 344.

p. 59 some 2,000 Jews, who had been relocated to Apamea . . .: for background see Stephen Mitchell, *Anatolia, Land, Men and Gods*, vol. 2, p. 32, and Abraham Schalit, 'The Letter of Antiochus III Regarding the Establishing of Jewish Military Colonies in Phrygia and Lydia', pp. 289–91.

p. 60 'in a Phrygian territory and village by themselves . . .': Herodotus, 5.98 (vol. 3, p. 119).

p. 61 picturesque communities of Cossacks and 'Old Believers': Ellsworth Huntingdon, 'The Karst Country of Southern Asia Minor', p. 102.

CHAPTER 5

p. 64 a prototype pontoon bridge . . .: Xenophon, *Anabasis*, 1.2.5 (p. 253).

p. 64 compared to the Moselle, or to the Forth . . .: Fellows, *Journal*, pp. 279 and 275.

p. 64 'with a certain train of pack-animals and attendants': D. G. Hogarth, 'Notes in Phrygia Paroreus and Lycaonia', p. 151.

CHAPTER 6

p. 77 **'incorrect in the highest degree'**: Hamilton, vol. 1, p. vi.

p. 78 **'imagine any other motive . . .'**: Leake, p. iv.

p. 86 **'Returning through the market place . . .'** and **'some with evident marks of displeasure . . .'**: Rev. F. V. J. Arundell, *A Visit to the Seven Churches of Asia*. p. 109.

CHAPTER 7

p. 89 **Beycesultan**: the excavation details are taken from Seton Lloyd and James Mellaart, *Beycesultan*.

p. 95 **Coups had been a prominent feature . . .**: Andrew Mango, *The Turks Today*, includes excellent material on Turkey's military interventions.

p. 98 **'poisonous drug'**: Hamilton, vol. 2, p. 113.

p. 100 **'a single stream which furnished palatable fish . . .'**: John A. Scott, 'The Taboo on Fish in the Worship of the Great Mother', p. 226.

p. 101 **'Rivers they chiefly reverence . . .'**: Herodotus, 1.138 (vol. 1, p. 179).

CHAPTER 8

p. 103 **'an assumption of the medical character'**: Leake, p. v.

p. 103 **'affording me an opportunity . . .'**: Arundell, *Discoveries*, vol. 1, p. 72.

p. 104 **'busy preparing channels and water-courses . . .'**: Hamilton, vol. 2, p. 119.

p. 109 **'were wont to carry neither shield nor spear . . .'**: Herodotus, 5.97 (vol. 3, p. 119).

pp. 110–1 **'enlist as many Peloponnesian soldiers . . .'**: Xenophon, 1.1.6 (p. 245).

p. 111 **'out of his land entirely'**: Xenophon, 1.2.1 (p. 249).

p. 112 **'the retreat of the Greeks under Xenophon'**: Polybius, *The Histories*, 1.1.6 (p. 19).

CHAPTER 9

p. 116 **Indian hounds**: Herodotus, 7.187 (vol. 3, p. 505).

p. 116 **the dogs of Magnesia** and **entire detachments of dogs**: E. S. Forster, 'Dogs in Ancient Warfare', p. 115.

p. 117 **'rather worrying'** and subsequent quotes: Arundell, *Seven Churches*, p. 77.

p. 117 **'in full exercise against the dogs'**: Arundell, *Discoveries*, vol. 1, p. 172.

pp. 118 'Nothing in Turkish travelling . . .', 'heavy, steel-pointed stick' and 'flock of goats or sheep appeared ahead': W. J. Childs, *Asia Minor On Foot*, pp. 164–7.

p. 118 *New Century: Yeni Asır*. Turkey's oldest newspaper, published in Izmir.

p. 121 'the orchard of Asia Minor': Fellows, *Journal*, p. 278.

p. 121 'a cornucopia in his arms . . .': Lord Kinross, *Europa Minor*, p. 98.

p. 122 'such crops of wheat . . .': John Uri Lloyd, 'Licorice', p. 1. From notes made while the author was journeying in Turkey in 1909.

p. 122 riverine tracts of land . . .: Strabo, 12.8.19 (vol. 2, p. 336).

p. 126 Lityerses: James Frazer, *The Golden Bough*, chapter 47.

p. 126 a less conditional notion of hospitality . . .: Herbert Muller, *The Loom of History*, p. 3.

p. 127 'when in came nine people . . .': Fellows, *Journal*, p. 136.

p. 127 'magnificent fire': Arundell, *Discoveries*, vol. 1, p. 173.

p. 130 'cream and honey . . .': Fellows, *Journal*, p. 158.

p. 130 'smoking Turks, full of curiosity . . .': Arundell, *Seven Churches*, p. 70.

CHAPTER 10

p. 136 'Greek' mills: for general background, see K. Donners, 'Water Mills in the Area of Sagalassos'.

p. 137 At Gordium, ancient capital of the eclipsed Phrygians: for more detail see Ernest A Fredricksmeyer, 'Alexander, Midas and the Oracle at Gordium'.

p. 139 Pythius: Herodotus, 7.27–29 (vol. 3, pp. 341–5).

p. 140 'that what is ours be under the Greeks . . .': Herodotus, 7.11 (vol. 3, p. 323).

p. 140 the Lydians, the original retailers . . .: see the footnote to Xenophon, p. 288 ('The Lydians were notorious as hucksters').

p. 140 rings in their ears: Xenophon, 3.1.31–32 (p. 29) and footnote: 'The Lydians were proverbially effeminate'.

p. 140 the mobile markets: Xenophon 1.5.6–7 (p. 289) and 3.2.21–22 (p. 447).

p. 140 prostitutes of their female children: Herodotus, 1.94 (vol. 1, p. 123).

CHAPTER 11

p. 145 'I was now entering upon the principal object . . .': Arundell, *Seven Churches*, p. 224.

p. 145 'a pathway not a foot wide . . .': Arundell, *Seven Churches*, p. 228.

p. 145 'first object . . . was to examine the course of the Meander . . .': Hamilton, vol. 2, p. 154.

p. 145 'became fully alive to the difficulties . . .': Hamilton, vol. 2, p. 159.

p. 145 were passable only by donkeys: W. K. C. Guthrie, 'Archaeological Travel in Anatolia', p. 136, adjudged the Çal region 'to this day remote enough from civilisation to be a stranger to wheeled traffic. Even the primitive solid-wheeled carts are lacking. All transport is by donkey, so that there are no roads.'

p. 148 river crossings had historic form . . .: Edward C. Echols' 'Crossing a Classical River' alerted me to many of the references in this section.

p. 149 [Thales'] solution was to dig a canal: Herodotus, 1.75 (vol. 1, pp. 93–5).

p. 149 sacrificed white chargers: Herodotus, 7.113 (vol. 3, p. 417).

p. 149 the Euphrates at Thapsacus: Xenophon, 1.4.18 (p. 285).

p. 149 a man from Rhodes: Xenophon, 3.5.8–11 (p. 487).

p. 149 the men filled their tent coverings with hay: Xenophon, 1.5.10 (p. 291).

p. 151 William Ramsay and David Hogarth: their visit is recounted in D. G. Hogarth, 'Apollo Lermenus', p. 376.

p. 151 'of the existence of ruins in or near Badinlar . . .' and 'a small temple situate on a conical eminence . . .': Hogarth, 'Apollo Lermenus', p. 376.

p. 152 inscribed stone slabs or steles: these inscriptions have inspired a considerable literature beyond the publications referenced below, including Stephen Mitchell, *Anatolia, Land, Men and Gods*, vol. 1, pp. 192–4, and Guthrie, pp. 136–8.

pp. 153–4 'mis-spelt, corrupted, distorted . . .': William Ramsay, 'Artemis-Leto and Apollo-Lairbenos', p. 216.

p. 154 'the extraordinary barbarism of their orthography . . .': Hogarth, 'Apollo Lermenus', p. 380.

p. 154 the hapless Apelles . . .: Kevin Miller, 'Apollo Lairbenos', p. 63.

p. 154 'disease, perhaps malarial . . .': Hogarth, 'Apollo Lermenus', p. 380.

p. 154 **'When illness struck an individual, especially fever'**: William Ramsay, 'Anatolica Quaedam', p. 282.

p. 155 **'sworn falsely, and being impure on that account'**: Ramsay, 'Artemis-Leto and Apollo-Lairbenos', p. 218.

p. 155 **Kleonymos, 'punished by the god . . .'**: Guthrie, p. 138.

p. 157 **'Does he know Peter?'**: Peter Thonemann, tutorial fellow at Wadham College and the acknowledged authority on the Meander Valley's classical history, had visited the site some years earlier.

p. 158 **to admire such a tree before bedecking it . . .**: Herodotus, 7.31 (vol. 3, p. 345).

p. 159 **the new creed that was sweeping Anatolia**: Eckhard J. Schnabel, 'Divine Tyranny and Public Humiliation' sees the steles as a specific attempt to check the advance of Christianity.

p. 159 **an offence not of ritual but of actual religion . . .**: Ramsay, 'Anatolica Quaedam', p. 282.

CHAPTER 12

p. 161 **a wet night in 1996**: the Susurluk incident is detailed in Stephen Kinzer, *Crescent & Star*, pp. 97–9.

CHAPTER 13

p. 175 **forcibly circumcised captured Gentiles, the authorities had responded . . .**: D. G. Dunn, *Beginning from Jerusalem*, p. 439.

p. 176 **securing top seats at the theatre**: Dunn, p. 558.

p. 176 **God-fearers**: the emergence of the God-fearers is comprehensively treated in Dunn.

p. 176 **Where Judaism barred its doors, in short, Christianity's stood open**: Dunn, p. 301.

p. 177 **'lo, we turn to the Gentiles'**: Acts 13, verse 46.

p. 177 **he mentioned the rivers**: See 2 Corinthians 11, verses 25–27.

p. 178 **Up came a bridge, a thing of two roughly equal halves**: the Ahmetli Bridge.

p. 185 **'We are also men of like passions'**: Acts 14, verse 15.

CHAPTER 14

p. 187 **the Roman governor of the Anatolian province of Bithynia**: Book 10, Letter 96 of Pliny the Younger's *Epistles*.

p. 187 **its contents were to be circulated among the Laodiceans**: Colossians 4, verse 16.

p. 188 **the respects of a fellow evangelist**: Colossians 4, verse 13.

p. 188 **'their dark or raven colour'**: Strabo, 12.8.16 (vol. 2, p. 334).

p. 188 **'the centre of native feeling . . .'**: William Ramsay, *Cities and Bishoprics of Phrygia*, vol. 1, part 1, p. 84.

p. 190 **'. . . worshipped the snake and had images of it'**: M. R. James, *The Apocryphal New Testament*, verse 113 (p. 448).

p. 190 **'about 7,000 men, save where the apostles were'**: James, verse 133 (p. 449).

p. 192 **a view 'so marvellous . . .'**: Chandler, p. 229.

p. 192 **'The warm waters here'**: Pococke, p. 76.

p. 192 **the shell of cuttlefish**: Fellows, *Journal*, p. 281.

p. 192 **'an immense frozen cascade . . .'**: Chandler, p. 229.

p. 192 **'Luna had once descended from the sky to Endymion . . .'**: Chandler, p. 231.

p. 193 **'clear or warm water . . .'**: Chandler, p. 231.

p. 193 **a fossil was fortuitously exposed**: see Mehmet Cihat Alçiçek et al., 'Brief Communication: First Homo Erectus from Turkey and Implications for Migrations into Temperate Asia'.

p. 194 **'nearly the whole of the country about the Meander . . .'**: Strabo, 12.8.17 (vol. 2, p. 335).

p. 195 **more headway here, in Phrygia . . .**: Mitchell, vol. 2, p. 63.

p. 195 **sin, an outward contamination**: E. von Dobschutz, 'Christianity and Hellenism', p. 248.

p. 195 **one second-century theologian**: Tertullian, quoted in John McManners, *Illustrated History of Christianity*, p. 43.

p. 197 **a purpose primarily political rather than purely artistic**: J. E. Wetherell, *The Land of Troy and Tarsus*, p. 34.

p. 198 **advising supplicants . . . against 'those who have forsaken the ways of their ancestors'**: Robin Lane Fox, *Pagans and Christians*, p. 258.

p. 199 **Apollo made one of his last recorded utterances**: Joseph Eddy Fontenrose, *Didyma; Apollo's Oracle, Cult and Companions*, p. 24 and Mitchell, vol. 2, p. 65.

p. 200 **'a considerable retinue' and 'had knowledge of hidden treasure . . .'**: Chandler, p. 241.

p. 200 **'apprehensive of immediate violence'**: Chandler, p. 242.

p. 200 **'beautiful body of a child'**: Fellows, *Journal*, p. 260.

p. 201 **'quarries of white marble . . .'**: Fellows, *Journal*, p. 281.

p. 201 **'a robed female statue of white marble . . .'**: Fellows, *Journal*, p. 260.

p. 201 'stonemason, who was chipping most unmercifully . . .': Arundell, *Seven Churches*, p. 157.

p. 201 'pedestals, capitals of columns or tombs': Fellows, *Journal*, p. 276.

p. 201 'in the advancement of civilisation the making of roads . . .': Guthrie, p. 130.

p. 201 newly built railway platforms: an example at 'Evjiler' is cited by J. G. C. Anderson, 'A Summer in Phrygia: II', p. 93.

p. 201 '. . . a little tomb-relief, a quaint representation of a native art . . .': Guthrie, p. 130.

p. 202 the martyrium, or sacred burial place of St Philip: Italian archaeologists engaged on the Hierapolis excavations claimed to have located St Philip's actual tomb in 2011.

CHAPTER 15

p. 204 'the letters of the Grecian alphabet': George Wheler, *A Journey Into Greece*, p. 268.

p. 205 'dry and easily reduced to powder . . .': Strabo, 12.8.17 (vol. 2, p. 335).

p. 206 their place names commonly concluded with 'anda': e.g. Oenonanda, Labranda, Aricanda.

p. 206 Virgil used the word to describe a cloak hem's decoration: *Aeneid*, 5.251.

p. 207 the pattern simply reflected . . .: the various origins of the meander pattern are explored in Lewis Foreman Day, *Pattern Design*, p. 57.

p. 211 'If any unholy or defiled pagan . . .': Frank R. Trombley, 'Paganism in the Greek World at the End of Antiquity', p. 328.

p. 212 'When God opened the minds . . .': Trombley, p. 333.

p. 212 a sorcerer persuaded some desperate residents: from Theophanes' *Chronographia*, quoted in Trombley, p. 334.

CHAPTER 16

p. 214 an impressive Roman bridge, all six stone arches . . .: Ramsay, *Cities and Bishoprics*, vol. 1, part 1, p. 162.

p. 215 'a triangular float, with a rope': Chandler, p. 162.

p. 215 'a sort of boat like a sledge . . .': Pococke, p. 57.

p. 217 'never held a foot of land . . .': William Ramsay, 'Geographical Conditions Determining History and Religion in Asia Minor', p. 261.

p. 221 'the whole plain in highest state of cultivation . . .': Arundell, *Seven Churches*, p. 63.

p. 221 'to titivate fog-dulled appetites': John Kolars and Henry J. Malin, 'Population and Accessibility', p. 241.

p. 221 'have been cultivated from the beginning of history': John Uri Lloyd, p. 1.

p. 222 'base and bastard Turks': the reported phrase of Pope Urban II.

p. 224 a sanctified template for their own enterprise: Christopher Tyerman, *God's War*, p. 291, calls the Second Crusade 'an adventure self-consciously undertaken in the shadow of past triumphs'.

p. 225 Word now reached the Crusader camp . . .: Odo of Deuil, *De Profectione Ludovici VII in Orientem*, p. 105.

p. 225 follow the coast road to Smyrna and Ephesus: Odo of Deuil, p. 105.

p. 225 Louis and his entourage spent several farcical days . . .: Odo of Deuil, p. 105.

p. 226 'nearly every day steep, stony mountains . . .': Odo of Deuil, p. 107.

p. 226 'massed on the other bank of the river . . .': Odo of Deuil, p. 111.

p. 226 'ordinarily was deep and wide . . .': Odo of Deuil, p. 109.

p. 227 'enemies of the cross of Christ': Niketas Choniates, *O City of Byzantium*, p. 40.

p. 227 'Massed in full battle array . . .': Choniates, p. 41.

p. 227 'cut to pieces in diverse ways . . .' and 'the mounds of bones are so many . . .': Choniates, p. 41.

p. 228 'I do know,' he wrote, 'that in such straits . . .' and 'at the ford a certain white-clad knight': Odo of Deuil, p. 113.

p. 228 feeding off the corpses of fallen horses: Odo of Deuil, p. 129.

p. 229 'a cloud of enemies . . .': Choniates, p. 35.

p. 229 the worst kind of tourist touts . . .: Odo of Deuil, p. 67.

p. 229 letting down baskets from the safety of high walls . . . and in some cases mixing the barley: Choniates, pp. 38–9.

p. 230 'by mingling with the Turks . . .': Choniates, p. 22.

p. 230 'apportioned fertile land for cultivation' and 'many who had not fallen into the Turks' hands . . .': Choniates, p. 273.

CHAPTER 17

p. 241 'made of interlaced rushes . . .': Tamara Talbot Rice, *The Seljuks in Asia Minor*, p. 95.

p. 241 'movement far off in the undergrowth' and 'many tents assembled there': John Kinnamos, *Deeds of John and Manuel Comnenus*, p. 53.

p. 243 **carpets 'without nap, and in broad stripes and figures'**: Pococke, p. 83.

p. 243 **Dorylaeum, where an estimated 2,000 tents . . .**: Kinnamos, quoted in Speros Vryonis, 'Nomadization and Islamization', p. 49.

p. 243 **100,000 Turcomans**: Salimbene, quoted in Vryonis, 'Nomadization and Islamization', p. 50.

p. 243 **Plain of the Turcomans**: Vryonis, 'Nomadization and Islamization', p. 50.

p. 243 **'numerous as locusts'**: Niketas Choniates, quoted in Speros Vryonis, *Decline of Medieval Hellenism*, p. 124.

p. 243 **'thus fear the Turkmens . . .'**: Ricoldus de Monte Crucis, quoted in Vryonis, 'Nomadization and Islamization', p. 55.

p. 245 **'arisen a certain amount of aversion . . .'**: from Nizam-al-Mulk, *The Book of Government or Rules for Kings* (trans. H. Darke, London, 1960, p. 105). Quoted in Vryonis, *Decline*, p. 211.

pp. 245–6 **'These Turcomen,' wrote Richard Pococke, 'when they attack people . . .'**: Pococke, p. 79.

p. 246 **'had very lately plundered some caravans'**: Chandler, p. 243.

p. 248 **Strabo had himself studied here . . .**: Strabo, 14.1.48 (vol. 3, p. 26).

p. 249 **'sea-water, sand, and an oar'**: Chandler, p. 147.

p. 249 **'one of the most considerable places by the Meander'**: Chandler, p. 210.

p. 249 **'it seemed impossible to dig sufficiently deep' wells**: Chandler, p. 210.

p. 250 **'so harsh that they rejoiced for those who had been slain'**: Vryonis, *Decline*, p. 251.

CHAPTER 18

p. 254 **muddy morasses that extended a full mile from the banks**: Pococke, p. 57.

p. 257 **by 1916 boys of just fifteen, and men as old as fifty-five**: Erik Jan Zürcher, 'Between Death and Desertion', p. 242.

p. 257 **an estimated half a million men**: Zürcher, p. 245.

p. 258 **the fighting talents that had repeatedly served the empire . . .**: Andrew G. Gould, 'The Derebeys of Cilicia', pp. 488 and 490.

p. 258 **'numerous pistols, dirks and yataghans', as 'the most ferocious-looking . . .'**: Hamilton, vol. 1, p. 527.

p. 259 **Bald Mehmet**: see Arundell, *Discoveries*, vol. 2, pp. 213–14.

p. 260 **'coat of manure'**: 'Report of Mr F. Wakefield', quoted in Sir R. M. Stephenson, *Railways in Turkey*, p. 34.

p. 265 **The bibles that America's nineteenth-century evangelists**: Arnold Toynbee, *The Western Question in Greece and Turkey*, p. 119.

p. 265 **passionate champions of a culture**: see FO371/5133, p. 49, in which James Morgan at the British High Commission in Smyrna describes Greece as the 'stepmother country' of the Ottoman Rums.

p. 266 **'finally put his hand on his heart . . .'**: Toynbee, p. 124.

p. 267 **'where our race largely predominates.'**: from 'Translation of a letter received from Bishop of Sochia', 7/6/1919; FO608/91, p. 294.

p. 267 **'The Aydın district,' according to another petition**: petition signed by George Scourso, Stelio Magnissali, Em. Anagnostopoulo, Athens, 15/4/1920; FO371/5133, p. 44.

p. 267 **Mr Papadopoulos, self-styled 'Delegate Plenipotentiary . . .'**: FO608/89, p. 187.

p. 267 **Turks had come to be in the majority . . .**: the respective populations for the Denizli region are given in FO608/89, p. 165.

CHAPTER 19

p. 269 **'Everybody wants Smyrna and the Meander Valley'**: Greek Minister Plenipotentiary at Rome, 27 December 1914, quoted in Erhan Cağrı, *Greek Occupation of Izmir and Adjoining Territories*, p. 3.

p. 269 **'the channel of communication between Europe and Asia . . .'**: Meredith Townsend, quoted in Stephenson, p. 13.

p. 269 **'the great entrepot of the internal trade . . .'**: Stephenson, p. 5.

p. 269 **not in passengers, however, but almost exclusively in goods**: Kolars and Malin, p. 241.

p. 270 **'the alluvial nature of the soil'**: Stephenson, p. 5.

p. 270 **'fertile to excess' and 'large bazaars filled to overflowing'**: 'Report of Mr F. Wakefield', extracted in Stephenson, p. 35.

p. 270 **'should have been in Marseilles or Liverpool . . .'**: 'Wakefield', in Stephenson, p. 37.

p. 270 **'caused, particularly in delicate products . . .'**: Stephenson, p. 5.

p. 270 **'six or seven inches'**: 'Wakefield', in Stephenson, p. 37.

p. 271 **'great centre of transit trade . . .'**: *Murray's Handbook to Turkey in Asia* (1873), p. 229.

p. 271 **'its finely placed church . . .'**: Toynbee, p. 151.

p. 271 **'silk-winderies'**: *Murray's Handbook to Turkey in Asia* (1873), p. 229.

p. 271 **the train that carried the season's first fig consignments**: Dido Sotiriou, *Farewell Anatolia*, p. 46.

p. 272 **With the line's every easterly extension**: Kolars and Malin, p. 239.

p. 272 **20,000 camels, 500 mules and their drivers . . .**: Stephenson, p. 6.

p. 272 **a matter of time before Greek armies followed the Greek settlers up the line**: Roderic H. Davison, *Reform in the Ottoman Empire 1856–76*, p. 78.

p. 280 **'trees, lofty domes and minarees . . . innumerable tame turtle-doves . . .'**: Chandler, p. 204.

p. 280 **'I have in England been at fairs and races . . .'**: Fellows, *Journal*, p. 277.

p. 282 **'fine yellow morocco'**: *Murray's . . . Turkey in Asia* (1873), p. 229.

CHAPTER 20

Eyewitness accounts of the events that occurred in and around Aydın in 1919 are mostly taken from the Foreign Office papers at the National Archives in Kew, notably in files FO608/86, 608/89 and 608/91, and in FO371/4220 and 371/5134. In an attempt at impartiality, I have prioritised the accounts of non-combatants, especially those whose findings appear at variance with the broad sympathies of their own governments or departments; conspicuous among these are the British reservists based at the time in the Meander Valley, who almost unanimously find fault with the Greek forces and their local supporters. This is not, however, to absolve the Turks of blame; they were responsible for their own share of atrocities.

p. 284 **'ruins flanked the railway for miles . . .'**: Toynbee, p. 274.

p. 284 **'The work was deliberately done'**: Toynbee, p. 152.

p. 285 **'cruel tyrants, bathed in the blood of their own Emperors'**: Thomas Smart Hughes, *Considerations*, p. 4, quoted in Virginia Penn, 'Philhellenism in England (1821–7)', p. 367.

p. 285 **No one but a congenital idiot could be pro-Turk**: Robert Vansittart, FO608/91, p. 139.

p. 285 **'strongly biased in favour of the Greeks . . .'**: Fellows, *Journal*, p. v.

p. 286 **'To their manners, habits and character . . .'**: Fellows, quoted in *Murray's . . . Turkey in Asia* (1854), p. 24.

p. 286 **'. . . prominent features of the modern Greek character . . .'**: Arundell, *Seven Churches*, p. 16.

p. 287 **the Tralles Stone, the marble . . .**: Freya Stark, *Ionia*, p. 273.

p. 287 **'continual processions with flags' and 'their level best to make themselves obnoxious . . .'**: 'THE TRUTH ABOUT AIDIN' by

'English eyewitness' Lt-Com. C. R. Hadkinson, RNVR. FO608/91, p. 827. For another Hadkinson report, dated 13/7/1919, see FO608/91, pp. 264–8.

p. 288 **'suddenly evacuating a town . . .'**: see the French-language *Inter-Allied Commission of Inquiry Report*, point 30 (FO/608/86, p. 528).

p. 288 **'was well defined in limits . . .'** and **'Turks of all classes . . .'**: letter from Admiral Calthorpe, High Commissioner at Constantinople, to Mr Balfour, 1 July 1919. FO608/89, p. 449.

p. 288 **'very picturesque *meidan* with coffee-houses'**: *Murray's . . . Turkey in Asia* (1873), p. 300.

p. 289 **'. . . at one time but a normal . . . state of brigandage'**: letter from Calthorpe to Earl Curzon, 27/7/1919. FO608/91, p. 278.

p. 290 **Hodder, the British control officer at Aydın**: Lt Hodder's experiences at Aydın are described in his own report, dated 8 July 1919 at Aydın, in FO608/91, pp. 138–42. See also the report of Lt-Col. Temple, RMA, dated 7 July 1919, Smyrna, FO608/91, pp. 102–5.

p. 291 **'burn and pillage the whole town'**: Hodder, p. 139.

p. 292 **'Aidin was in a state of terror'**: Hodder, p. 139.

p. 292 **'. . . a conflagration in the Turkish quarter'**: Hodder, p. 139.

p. 293 **'Hodder Efendi,'**: Hodder, p. 139.

p. 294 **shot without regard for age or sex**: *The Inter-Allied Commission of Enquiry Report* blames the bands of Yörük Ali for the slaughter in Aydın's Greek quarter.

p. 295 **an employee of the Ottoman Imperial Bank**: French-language report signed by 'Stolzenberg', elsewhere described as a Catholic bank manager who can be relied upon for his testimony. FO608/89, pp. 470–6.

p. 295 **'the most complete anarchy'** and **'simple accusations, ancient grudges . . .'**: Stolzenberg, p. 472.

p. 295 **'11 women and 8 children and 3 men . . .', 'a further lot of 13 women, 15 children and 22 men'**, and **'the remains of 8 children that had been burned in one house'**: Hodder, p. 141.

p. 295 **rank obscenities**: each side accused the other of appalling acts. Among the most extreme are: the accusations made against the Greeks by the Mayor of Denizli in a translated telegram, FO608/91, p. 312; and the comparable allegations levelled against the Turks in an unsigned report at FO371/4220, 'Enclosure no. 18, 13/7/1919'.

p. 296 **'a veritable stampede of Turks . . .'**: version of Hodder report. FO608/91, p. 121.

p. 296 **'I have done all in my power'**: Colonel Şefik, quoted in version of Hodder report. FO608/91, p. 121.

p. 297 **'fanatical hatred of the Greek . . .'**: letter from Hodder, 12 July 1919. FO608/91, p. 146.

p. 297 **Umurlu's Rum Greeks . . .**: report of Lt-Com. Hadkinson, 16 August 1919. FO608/91, p. 760.

p. 297 **fifty-three corpses**: telegram to Lloyd George, London, from 'Committee of Inhabitants of Aydin Nazli Saraykeuy Denizli Chones', 12 August 1920. FO371/5134, pp. 25–9.

p. 299 **'handfuls of singed grains'**: Annie I. Allen and Florence I. Billings, 'The Atrocities in Anatolia'.

CHAPTER 21

p. 307 **Salonika, where they were billeted . . .**: see 'Greek Refugees', *The Times*, 21 August 1924.

p. 308 **'They were packed like sardines'**: George Morgenthau, quoted in Bruce Clark, *Twice A Stranger*, p. 160.

p. 308 **'fanatical Nationalism . . .'** and **'as Asiatic conquerors dealt with the conquered . . .'**: 'Refugees from the Turk', *The Times*, 26 July 1923.

p. 309 **'. . . the Moslems had suffered only a few degrees . . .'**: 'Refugees from Asia Minor', *The Times*, 9 May 1924.

p. 309 **The wider historical truth**: the plight of Muslims in territories lost to the Ottoman Empire through the nineteenth and early twentieth centuries is comprehensively treated in Justin McCarthy, *Death and Exile*.

p. 311 **'monstrously wicked'**: 'Conventions Signed at Lausanne', *The Times*, 31 January 1923.

p. 313 **'Turk-heads'**: Ramsay, *Cities and Bishoprics*, vol. 1, part 1, p. 28. 'The term "Turk" is contemptuous; one Osmanli will express his scorn of another by addressing him as "Turk-Kafa", "Stupid-Head".'

p. 320 **200 warships riding at anchor**: Stark, p. 240.

p. 320 **'inland for three miles in rowing boats'**: Strabo, quoted in Stark, p. 240.

p. 320 **'had taken the sea from the navigator . . .'**: Chandler, paraphrasing Homerius, p. 175.

CHAPTER 22

p. 323 **'a grand resort of fanciful devotees . . .'**: Chandler, p. 166.

p. 327 **Chaste Tree**: also known as monk's pepper, Turkish *hayit*, known by the ancient Greeks and Romans for its power to subdue the sexual instinct.

CHAPTER 23

p. 332 'a profusion of pears and apricots': Lord Kinross, *Europa Minor*, p. 89.

p. 332 'twenty camels, each with a box . . .': Stark, p. 212.

p. 333 'Next year there will be no Yürüks . . .': Stark, p. 204.

p. 333 'new canalization . . .': Kinross, *Europa Minor*, p. 107.

p. 333 'Menderes regime for the Menderes Valley': Kinross, *Europa Minor*, p. 107.

p. 335 'the entire frame of everybody's existence': Geoffrey Lewis, 'The End of the First Republic', p. 384.

p. 336 polygamous marriage ceremonies . . . and An imam forbade people from having their teeth filled . . . and . . . his dying daughter to take medicine . . .: Lewis, pp. 384–5.

pp. 336–7 Landlords with burgeoning property portfolios . . . Mothers advised their daughters . . .: Kemal H. Karpat, 'The Military and Politics in Turkey', p. 1663.

p. 339 'the great maritime city of the archaic period . . .': George Bean, *Aegean Turkey*, p. 181.

p. 342 '. . . Athens and Augustine and Dante . . .': Stark, p. 231.

CHAPTER 24

p. 349 Chief among the promoted Lydian natives was one Pactyas . . .: Pactyas and the Cymean embassy to Didyma is treated by Herodotus, 1.154–161 (vol. 1, pp. 195–203).

p. 352 'at every step lodged in excavations . . .': Raoul Blanchard, 'The Exchange of Populations Between Greece and Turkey', p. 454.

p. 352 Nine hundred refugees were in one instance dispatched to new lives in Söke: Blanchard, p. 454.

p. 352 'torn account books lay scattered about among fragments . . .': this and subsequent descriptions of Yeronda from Saturnino Ximenez, *Asia Minor in Ruins*, pp. 245–6. Ximenez visited the town in 1923.

p. 353 'a good deal of the furniture . . .': Ximenez, p. 245.

BIBLIOGRAPHY

Alçiçek, Mehmet Cihat et al.: 'Brief Communication: First Homo Erectus from Turkey and Implications for Migrations into Temperate Asia', *American Journal of Physical Anthropology*, vol. 135, 2008, pp. 110–16.

Allen, Annie I. and Billings, Florence I.: 'The Atrocities in Anatolia'. By Two Members of the American Relief Mission. Undated pamphlet.

Anderson, J. G. C.: 'A Summer in Phrygia: II', *Journal of Hellenic Studies*, vol. 18, 1898, pp. 81–128 and 340–4.

Arrian: *Anabasis of Alexander*, vol. 1. Trans. E. Iliff Robson, London, 1948.

Arundell, Francis V. J.: *A Visit to the Seven Churches of Asia, with an excursion into Pisidia*, London, 1828.

Arundell, Francis V. J.: *Discoveries in Asia Minor*, 2 vols, London, 1834.

Bean, George: *Aegean Turkey*, London, 1989 ed.

Bean, George: *Turkey Beyond the Maeander*, London, 1971.

Berridge, Virginia and Edwards, Griffith: *Opium and the People*, London, 1981.

Blanchard, Raoul: 'The Exchange of Populations Between Greece and Turkey', *Geographical Review*, vol. 13, no. 3, July 1925, pp. 449–56.

Brennan, Shane: *In the Tracks of the Ten Thousand*, London, 2005.

Brown, James: 'The Military and Society: The Turkish Case', *Middle East Studies*, vol. 25, no. 3, July 1989, pp. 387–404.

Brown, Truesdell S.: 'Aristodicus of Cyme and the Branchidae', *American Journal of Philology*, vol. 99, no. 1, Spring 1978, pp. 64–78.

Buckler, W. H.: 'A Pagan Recantation', *The Classical Review*, vol. 47, no. 1, Febuary, 1933, pp. 7–8.

Buckler, Calder, Guthrie (eds): *Monumenta Asiae Minoris Antiqua*, vol. 4, Manchester, 1933.

Cağrı, Erhan: *Greek Occupation of Izmir and Adjoining Territories*, Papers no. 2/99. SAM (Centre for Strategic Research, Turkey's Foreign Office), Ankara, April 1999.

Cahen, Claude: 'The Turkish Invasion: The Seljukids', in Kenneth M. Setton (ed.), *A History of the Crusades*, vol. 1, Pennsylvania, 1955.

Chandler, Richard: *Travels in Asia Minor: or An Account of a Tour Made at the Expense of the Dilettanti*, London, 1776 (2nd ed.).

Childs, W. J.: *Asia Minor On Foot*, Edinburgh, 1917.

Choniates, Niketas (trans. Harry J. Magoulias): *O City of Byzantium: Annals of Niketas Choniates*, Detroit, 1984.

Clark, Bruce: *Twice a Stranger*, London, 2006.

Cramer, J. A.: *Description of Asia Minor*, vol. II, Oxford, 1832.

Davison, Roderic H.: *Reform in the Ottoman Empire 1856–76*, Princeton, 1963.

Day, Lewis Foreman: *Pattern Design*, London, 1903.

Dicks, D. R.: 'Thales', *Classical Quarterly*, vol. 9, no. 2, November 1959, pp. 294–309.

Dobschutz, E. von: 'Christianity and Hellenism', *Journal of Biblical Literature*, vol. 33, no. 4, December 1914, pp. 245–65.

Donners, K.: 'Water Mills in the Area of Sagalassos', *Anatolian Studies*, vol. 52, 2002, pp. 1–17.

Dunn, James D. G.: *Beginning from Jerusalem*, Grand Rapids, 2009.

Echols, Edward C.: 'Crossing a Classical River', *The Classical Journal*, vol. 48, no. 6, March 1953, pp. 215–24.

Edmonds, J. M. (trans.): *Lyra Graeca*, vol III, London, 1877.

Fellows, Charles: *A Journal Written During an Excursion in Asia Minor*, London, 1838.

Fellows, Charles: *Discoveries in Lycia*, London, 1840.

Fontenrose, Joseph Eddy: *Didyma; Apollo's Oracle, Cult and Companions*, Berkeley, 1988.

Forster, E. S.: 'Dogs in Ancient Warfare', *Greece and Rome*, vol. 10, no. 30, May 1941, pp. 114–17.

Frazer, James: *The Golden Bough; A Study in Magic and Religion*, London, 1890.

Fredricksmeyer, Ernest A.: 'Alexander, Midas and the Oracle at Gordium', *Classical Philology*, vol. 56, no. 3, July 1961, pp. 160–8.

Gould, Andrew G.: 'The Derebeys of Cilicia', *International Journal of Middle East Studies*, vol. 7, no. 4, October 1976, pp. 485–506.

Guthrie, William: 'Archaeological Travel in Anatolia', *Greece and Rome*, vol. 2, no. 6, May 1933, pp. 129–38.

Hamilton, William: *Researches in Asia Minor, Pontus and Armenia, with some account of their antiquities and geology*, 2 vols, London, 1842.

Herodotus: *Histories* (trans A. D. Godley), Cambridge, 1921.

Hogarth, D. G.: 'Notes upon a Visit to Celaenae-Apamea', *Journal of Hellenic Studies*, vol. 9, 1888, pp. 343–9.

Hogarth, D. G.: 'Notes in Phrygia Paroreus and Lycaonia', *Journal of Hellenic Studies*, vol. 11, 1890, pp. 151–66.

Hogarth, D. G.: 'Apollo Lermenus', *Journal of Hellenic Studies*, vol. 8, 1887, pp. 384–400.

Huntingdon, Ellsworth: 'The Karst Country of Southern Asia Minor', *Bulletin of the American Geographical Society*, vol. 43, no. 2, 1911, pp. 91–106.

James, M. R.: *The Apocryphal New Testament*, Oxford, 1924.

Jenkins, Gareth: *Between Fact and Fiction: Turkey's Ergenekon Investigation*, Central Asia Caucasus Institute Silk Road Studies Programme, Washington/Stockholm, 2009.

Jensen, Peter Kincaid: 'The Greco-Turkish War, 1920–22', *International Journal of Middle East Studies*, vol. 10, no. 4, November 1979, pp. 553–65.

Karpat, Kemal H.: 'The Military and Politics in Turkey, 1960–4', *The American Historical Review*, vol. 75, no. 6, October 1970, pp. 1654–83.

Kinnamos, John: *Deeds of John and Manuel Comnenus* (trans. Charles Brand), New York, 1976.

Kinross, Lord: *Europa Minor*, London, 1956.

Kinross, Lord: *Atatürk*, London, 1964.

Kinzer, Stephen: *Crescent & Star*, New York, 2008.

Kolars, John and Malin, Henry J.: 'Population and Accessibility: An Analysis of Turkish Railroads', *Geographical Review*, American Geographical Society, vol. 60, no. 2, April 1970, pp. 229–46.

Leake, Col. William Martin: *Journal of a Tour in Asia Minor*, London, 1824.

Lewis, Geoffrey: 'The End of the First Republic', *The World Today*, The Royal Institute of International Affairs, vol. 16, no. 9, September 1960, pp. 377–86.

Lloyd, John Uri: 'Licorice', *The Eclectic Medical Journal*, Cincinnati, 1929.

Lloyd, Seton: '25 Years', *Anatolian Studies*, vol. 24, 1974, pp. 197–220.

Lloyd, Seton and Mellaart, James: *Beycesultan*, vols 1 and 2, Ankara, 1962 and 1965.

Mango, Andrew: *The Turks Today*, London, 2004.

Mango, Andrew: 'The State of Turkey', *Middle Eastern Studies*, vol. 13, no. 2, May 1977, pp. 261–4.

McCarthy, Justin: *Death and Exile; The Ethnic Cleansing of Ottoman Muslims 1821–1922*, Princeton, 1995.

McManners, John (ed.): *Oxford Illustrated History of Christianity*, Oxford, 1990.

Miller, Kevin M.: 'Apollo Lairbenos', *Numen*, vol. 32, no. 1, 1985, pp. 46–70.

Mitchell, Stephen: *Anatolia, Land, Men and Gods*, 2 vols, Oxford, 1993.

Muller, Herbert J.: *The Loom of History*, New York, 1958.

Murray's Handbook to Turkey in Asia, London, 1854 and 1873.

Nonnos (trans. W. H. D. Rouse): *Dionysiaca*, vol. 1, Cambridge, Mass., 1940.

Odo of Deuil: *De Protectione Ludovici VII in Orientem* (trans. and ed. Virginia Berry), Columbia, 1948.

Ovid: *Metamorphoses*, Garth-Tonson, London, 1717 and F. J. Miller, London, 1916 translations.

Özalp, Mehmet: *Marsyas'in Ilinden*, Denizli, 1997.

Penn, Virginia: 'Philhellenism in England (1821–7)', *Slavonic and East European Review*, vol. 14, no. 41, January 1936, pp. 363–71.

Pliny the Younger: *Complete Letters of Pliny the Younger* (trans. and edited P. G. Walsh), Oxford, 2006.

Pococke, Richard: *A Description of the East and Some Other Countries*, vol. II, part II, London, 1745.

Polybius: *The Histories* (trans. W. R. Paton and revised by F. W. Walbank and Christian Habicht), Harvard, 2010.

Ramsay, William: *Cities and Bishoprics of Asia Minor*, vol. 1, part 1: The Lycos Valley and South Western Phrygia, Oxford, 1895–7.

Ramsay, William: *Cities and Bishoprics of Asia Minor*. vol. 1, part 2: West and West-Central Phrygia, Oxford, 1895–7.

Ramsay, William: *The Historical Geography of Asia Minor*, London, 1890.

Ramsay, William: 'Artemis-Leto and Apollo-Lairbenos', *Journal of Hellenic Studies*, vol. 10, 1889, pp. 216–30.

Ramsay, William: 'Geographical Conditions Determining History and Religion in Asia Minor', *Geographical Journal*, vol. 20, no. 3, September 1902, pp. 257–75.

Ramsay, William: 'Anatolica Quaedam, part II', *Journal of Hellenic Studies*, vol. 50, 1930, pp. 263–87.

Ramsay, William: 'Metropolitanus Campus', *Journal of Hellenic Studies*, vol. 4, 1883, pp. 53–72.

Schalit, Abraham, 'The Letter of Antiochus III Regarding the Establishing of Jewish Military Colonies in Phrygia and Lydia', *Jewish Quarterly Review*, vol. 50, no. 4, April 1960, pp. 289–318.

Schnabel, Eckhard J.: 'Divine Tyranny and Public Humiliation', *Novum Testamentum*, vol. 45, April 2003, pp. 160–88.

Scott, John A.: 'The Taboo on Fish in the Worship of the Great Mother', *The Classical Journal*, vol. 17, no. 4, January 1922, p. 226.

Shaw, Stanford: *From Empire to Republic: The Turkish War of National Liberation, 1918–23*, 5 vols, Ankara, 2000.

Sotiriou, Dido: *Farewell Anatolia* (trans. Fred A. Reed), Athens, 1991.

Stark, Freya: *Ionia*, London, 1954.

Stephenson, Sir R. M.: *Railways in Turkey: Remarks upon the Practicability and Advantage of Railway Communication in European and Asiatic Turkey*, London, 1859. On-line FCO paper, National Archives, Kew.

Strabo: *Geography* (trans. Hamilton and Falconer), 3 vols, London, 1857.

Syme, Ronald and Birley, Anthony Richard: *Anatolica: Studies in Strabo*, Oxford, 1995.

Talbot Rice, Tamara: *The Seljuks in Asia Minor*, London, 1961.

Thonemann, Peter: *The Maeander Valley: A Historical Geography from Antiquity to Byzantium*, Cambridge, 2011.

Toynbee, Arnold: *The Western Question in Greece and Turkey*, London, 1922.

Trombley, Frank R.: 'Paganism in the Greek World at the End of Antiquity; The case of Rural Anatolia and Greece', *Harvard Theological Review*, vol. 78, no. 3/4, July–October 1985, pp. 327–52.

Tyerman, Christopher: *God's War*, London, 2006.

Vryonis, Speros, Jr: *Decline of Medieval Hellenism*, Berkeley, Calif., 1971.

Vryonis, Speros, Jr: 'Nomadization and Islamization in Asia Minor', *Dumbarton Oaks Papers*, vol. 29, 1975.

Weber, G.: *Dinair (Gueikler) Celenes Apamee Cibotos*, Besançon, 1892.

Wetherell, J. E. *The Land of Troy and Tarsus*, London, 1931.

Wheler, George: *A Journey Into Greece*, London, 1682.

Xenophon: *Anabasis* (trans. Carleton L. Brownson), London, 1921.

Ximenez, Saturnino: *Asia Minor in Ruins* (trans. Arthur Chambers), London, 1926.

Zürcher, Erik Jan: 'Between Death and Desertion. The Experience of the Ottoman Soldier in World War 1' *Turcica*, vol. 28, 1996, pp. 235–58.

ACKNOWLEDGEMENTS

I am grateful to many kind and bright people for the help they provided in the making of this book. Many of them shared valuable insights with me, answered queries, offered suggestions or directed me to particular sources; others variously encouraged and advised, fed and housed me. To all of them, especially those I have inadvertently omitted, my warm thanks. Any crass assumptions, conclusions or mistakes are entirely mine.

Among those I must specially mention are Peter Thonemann, who generously briefed me on his own extensive forays in the Meander Valley as I first mapped out my travel plans for the region, and who also gave me access to early drafts of key chapters from his excellent study, *The Maeander Valley*. Michael Metcalfe, another authority on the region's classical history, was an excellent source of invaluable information. It was Peter Sommer, Turkophile tour operator and traveller of the first rank, who originally put me in touch with Thonemann, Metcalfe and many others. I am also indebted to Sevan Nisanyan, who hosted me at Şirince and whose voluminous mind became my default resource on most things Turkish. The late Nick Morris, the best of friends, was a generous lender of volumes on Byzantine history and my go-to man for, among other things, the identification of freshwater fish species.

Thanks are also due to Jane Akatay, Sedat Aktay, Mehmet Cihat Alçicek, Serpil Awdry, Grahame and Linda Baker Smith, Phil Buckley and Ufuk Güven at Bougainville Travels in Kaş,

Bruce Clark, Kate Clow, Patricia Daunt, Ayça Duffrene, Kim Erkan, Seçil Fuller, Katya Galitzine, Brian Giraud, Sinan Guler, Nick Laing, John Laughland and Bea Bonchis, Andrew Lee at Exclusive Escapes, Philip Marsden, Giles Milton, Matthew Nicholls, John Julius Norwich, Maggie O'Sullivan, Iffet Özgönul, John Penney, David Quinton, Barnaby Rogerson, John Scott at the admirable *Cornucopia* magazine, Sarah Spankie, Richard Stoneman, Rob Tavernor and Christine Walker.

Others went out of their way to help in the course of my journey. In this respect I owe a special debt to Mehmet Özalp and his family for their friendship and support in Dinar. The Korkmaz family near Kavak, the Hayta family in Gelinören, and Mehmet Halil Akşit in Bahadınlar all confirmed the very best traditions of rural Turkish hospitality. Mehmet Özçakır went out of his way to introduce me to the history and culture of Aydın. Thanks to Ömhur Kaynak for his friendship in the course of several visits to Didim. Thanks, too, to Duygu Doğan, also of Didim, for her generous help and translation skills. I would also like to thank Ahmet Sezgin of Akköy; Muammer, Nilüfer and Mehmet Çakır at Kaya Pansiyon in Kapıkırı; Mehmet Demir of Çakırbeyli; Ali Demirel; Osman Eptilik; Mahmut and Ahmet Gönul at the Oracle Pansiyon in Didim; Hasan Gümüş at Çivril's town council; Başak Kamacı, director of the Meandros Festival; Turgay Karagöz of the Devran Otel, Dinar; Ali Kip of Buharkent; Veysel Karalar; Mithat Serçin; Aydın Ulupınar of Sultanhisar; Coşkun and Binnaz Uyanık of Güllübahçe; and Cevdet Üzüm.

Thanks to Irfan Önal and Tolga Tuyluoğlu, Joanna Marsh and Jill Guest at the Turkish Ministry of Tourism and Culture, and to the staff of Turkish Airlines for their generous support. Thanks to Knoydart kayak specialists in Cumbria for advising me on my trusty Pakboat Puffin – which proved perfectly suited to the job.

I have been wonderfully served by my agents, David Miller at Rogers Coleridge & White, London, and Jill Grinberg at Jill Grinberg Literary Management, Brooklyn, New York. Poppy Hampson and Silvia Crompton at Chatto were the best of editors; their patience, rigour and passion have done so much to shape this book. Thanks, too, to Kathy Belden and Rachel Mannheimer at Bloomsbury USA. Jane Randfield's maps are a joy; particular thanks to her for her patience, brilliance and good humour, and similarly to Rob Shaw at Northbank Design, Bath, for setting the maps' place names.

Thanks to the staff of the various libraries where I researched *Meander*: the London Library, especially their online J-STOR resource; the British Library, London; and the National Archives, Kew, London.

All the images are my own, except for the one on p. 215, which I reproduce with thanks to Cevdet Üzüm.

Thanks and love, finally, to Ash, Anna and Lizzie for putting up with my regular absences and bouts of absent-mindedness over the last few years. I suppose I could have done it without you, but it wouldn't have been half the fun.

INDEX